D0849022

THE AESTHETICS OF SERVICE IN EARLY MODERN ENGLAND

THE AESTHETICS OF SERVICE IN EARLY MODERN ENGLAND

≈

Elizabeth Rivlin

NORTHWESTERN UNIVERSITY PRESS

EVANSTON, ILLINOIS

Northwestern University Press
www.nupress.northwestern.edu

Printed in the United States of America

10 9 8 7 6 5 4 3 2 1

Library of Congress Cataloging-in-Publication Data

Rivlin, Elizabeth J., 1971–
    The aesthetics of service in Early Modern England / Elizabeth Rivlin.
      p. cm.
    Includes bibliographical references and index.
    ISBN 978-0-8101-2781-4 (cloth : alk. paper)
    1. English literature—Early modern, 1500–1700—History and criticism. 2.
Master and servant in literature. 3. Household employees in literature. I. Title.
PR428.M375R58 2012
820.9'352624—dc23

                                                        2011028658

∞ The paper used in this publication meets the minimum requirements of the
American National Standard for Information Sciences—Permanence of Paper for
Printed Library Materials, ANSI Z39.48-1992.

CONTENTS

Acknowledgments   vii

Introduction
The Aesthetics of Service   3

Chapter One
Shakespeare's Apprenticeship: Performing Service in
    The Comedy of Errors and *The Two Gentlemen of Verona*   27

Chapter Two
Prose Fiction and the Mobile Servant: Nashe's
    The Unfortunate Traveller   53

Chapter Three
"Play the Shoemaker": Craft and Commerce in Deloney's
    The Gentle Craft and Dekker's *The Shoemaker's Holiday*   73

Chapter Four
"Iterate the Work": *The Alchemist* and Ben Jonson's
    Labors of Service   107

Chapter Five
Tragicomic Service: *The Winter's Tale* and *The Tempest*   135

Notes   165

Bibliography   195

Index   209

ACKNOWLEDGMENTS

Hillary Clinton said that it takes a village to raise a child. The same could be said of writing a book. For me, the experiences of raising children and writing a book have been interwoven. I have many people to thank who made it possible for me to do both.

This project began at the University of Wisconsin–Madison, under the warm and wonderful supervision of Susanne Wofford. Her scholarly brilliance always gave me insights about my work, and her unflagging encouragement propelled me beyond the dissertation phase. She and Jacques Lezra also showed me that it was possible to combine academic and family life. I owe many thanks to my rigorous, always supportive teachers at Wisconsin: Heather Dubrow, Jacques Lezra, David Loewenstein, Eric Rothstein, Johann Sommerville, Jane Tylus, Andrew Weiner, and Neil Whitehead. I enjoyed the company of dear friends and learned a great deal from them, including Gretchen Bartlett, Alex Block, Thomas Crofts, Matt Hussey, Kristin Matthews, Elizabeth C. Miller, Jack Opel, Matthew Stratton, John Tiedemann, and Jesse Wolfe. Special thanks go to Henry Turner and Rebecca Walkowitz for their wise counsel and their friendship through the years. As an undergraduate, I was lucky to have Donald W. Foster and Miranda Johnson-Haddad as mentors.

I have benefited from colleagues and friends at Clemson University whose smart suggestions about the manuscript kept me moving forward: Susanna Ashton, Stephanie Barczewski, Cameron Bushnell, David Coombs, Joanna Grisinger, Joe Mai, Kim Manganelli, Angela Naimou, Aga Skrodska-Bates, and Rhondda Thomas. Brian McGrath asked questions that only he could and that made the book better. Thanks to Catherine Paul, Jonathan Beecher Field, Will Stockton, and my other colleagues who make the English department at Clemson such a good professional home. For their support of flexible work and leave policies, I want to thank the chairs of the English department during my time at Clemson: Mark Charney, Chip Egan, Lee Morrissey, and Barton Palmer. The faculty senate passed a provision allowing new parents to stop their tenure clocks, and I am grateful for its progressive action. I received course release grants and research grants from Clemson University and the College of Architecture, Arts, and Humanities to travel to collections at the Bodleian Library, the Pepys Library, and the British Library. The

English department's Idol South Award allowed me to do research at the Folger Shakespeare Library.

I owe thanks to people whose work has been important to me and who have shown an interest in my work, often expressed with great kindness and enthusiasm. They include Simon Barker, Christy Desmet, Arthur Kinney, Natasha Korda, Mary Ellen Lamb, Courtney Lehmann, Joan Pong Linton, Jeff Masten, Sharon O'Dair, David Schalkwyk, Jyotsna Singh, and Wendy Wall. Many thanks to Michelle Dowd and Stephen Guy-Bray, the readers for Northwestern University Press, whose suggestions helped me tighten and focus the book considerably. Henry Carrigan has been a more patient and sympathetic editor than I could have hoped for. Thanks to Heather Antti at Northwestern University Press for her expert supervision of the editing process and to James Funk for his editorial assistance with the bibliography. Any errors are of course my own. Portions of chapter 1 appeared in *English Literary History* and *Critical Survey.* Portions of chapter 3 appeared in *English Literary Renaissance,* and portions of chapter 4 appeared in *Working Subjects in Early Modern Drama,* edited by Michelle Dowd and Natasha Korda, published by Ashgate Press. I thank the publishers for permission to reprint this material.

Every day I am thankful for the people who have helped care for my children and have given me the extensive time that writing a book requires. The Clemson Child Development Center has been essential to our family over the past five years. I thank our babysitters, who hold down the fort in good times and bad and who have enriched our lives immeasurably: Whitney Ford, Samantha Hoehner, Jessica Vierela Roberts, Rachel Sparks, and Bekah Austin. My sincere love and thanks go to family and friends, including the LeMahieus, who put up with our eccentric schedules and are always glad to see us. I depend on long-lasting and long-distance friendships, especially that of Sarah Hopkins. My sister, Madeline, is an unfailing source of love and strength. My mother travels to our home every two months to cook, shop, and otherwise dote on us. Although my father isn't here to read this book, his great influence endures, as does his faith in me. My deepest thanks go to Michael LeMahieu, who has read every word of this book, most of them multiple times. He is my spouse, biggest champion, and indispensable partner in parenting. It's safe to say that this book would not have been written without him. Finally, this book is for Alice and Theo, with all my love.

The Aesthetics of Service in Early Modern England

INTRODUCTION

⁓

The Aesthetics of Service

Servants and masters in early modern literature always seem to be changing places. In *The Taming of the Shrew,* Lucentio and Tranio hatch a plan
so that Lucentio can woo his beloved, Bianca, on the sly. In response to
his master's order to impersonate him, Tranio says: "I am content to be
Lucentio/Because so well I love Lucentio" (1.1.210–11). His reply encapsulates a paradox of early modern service as it is often portrayed in the
period's literature: the servant is enjoined to obey his master out of love,
but that obedience actually amounts to imitating his master, a move that
opens the possibility, as *Taming* and many other texts explore, of becoming him or her. Such moments of servant-master imitation lend an insight
that is central to this book: service is fundamentally a representational
practice, in which acting *for* one's master shades, often imperceptibly,
into acting *as* one's master.[1] Out of these imitative performances emerges
what I call aesthetic service.

This book argues that the representational possibilities of aesthetic
service gave early modern dramas and prose fictions a model for material
intervention and textual invention. In both representing and replacing
their masters, servants found new subject positions and authors found
new forms of literature. Tropes of service took on these valences as neofeudal, patriarchal forms of service began to yield to emerging capitalist
forms. Counterintuitively, service became the basis for a subjectivity that
was self-determining and even, in contrast to older ideas of the servant
subject, self-possessing. It is also true that servant subjects were vulnerable to dispossession, a possibility augmented by the same capitalist
system that promised self-possession. Because aesthetic service partook
of the deep uncertainties of a transitional period, it became a vital
method of subject formation.

Examining works by Shakespeare, Jonson, Thomas Dekker, Thomas
Deloney, and Thomas Nashe, I suggest that they represent their own excit-
ing and unstable projects in the mixture of excitement and instability that

they project onto service. Dramatic and textual production were understood as material forms of service, while service was seen as an aesthetic act. Given these intersections, early modern authors imagined new possibilities for literary and theatrical forms that were often undervalued and marginalized. The self-images that their texts conjure are, like the servants they portray, simultaneously imitative and transformative. If servants have the ability to change their masters through the act of imitating them, as many of my readings suggest, then drama and fiction invest themselves with the power to affect and alter their audiences and readers. Aesthetic considerations, in other words, are embroiled with, even inseparable from, the social, economic, and subjective effects of drama and prose fiction.

My argument operates on the premise that early modern aesthetics were not in opposition to material form but, as Joseph Roach puts it, represented "the vitality and sensuous presence of material forms."[2] In many of the works I analyze, servants are analogous to players, playwrights, authors, or even texts. But what I intend in using "aesthetic" to modify service is not limited to an allegorical relationship with the material. In my use, aesthetics refer to performances of service that operate in the realm of sensory perception and that open themselves to judgments on the basis of their perceived beauty and skill. These may be unfamiliar criteria to apply to service, and yet they convey its idealized shapes and affective dynamics, as well as its corporeal embodiment, its material practices, and its integration into everyday social life. The aesthetic properties of service were redoubled in literature, which used service to reflect on the relation between aesthetic practices and material relationships. Service was specially equipped to motivate drama and prose fiction's self-perception.

The manifestation of aesthetic service which I discuss most frequently is "performance," a word that I use in the sense of Roach's claim that to perform is "to bring forth, to make manifest, and to transmit," as well as "though often more secretly, to reinvent."[3] Roach defines performance as an essentially mimetic activity that seeks both to stand in for and to replace that which it represents.[4] The doubled dynamic of representation and invention, reproduction and production, instrumentality and agency that Roach describes applies to performances of service in early modern dramas and fictions. Tranio is mandated to offer a performance of his master that will help realize his master's command. And yet his impersonation of Lucentio fundamentally destabilizes Lucentio's position, creating the conditions for unforeseen substitutions and inventions. That process is bidirectional, resulting in cases in which the master imitates his servant or appropriates his role. Thus, Lucentio exchanges clothing with Tranio and adopts the role of a tutor: "let me be a slave t'achieve that maid" (1.1.213), initiating a new process of surrogation and transformation. Performing service creates possibilities, then, for reinventing the real.

That service is performative is an assertion that can be made broadly across historical periods. But in the transitional era of the late sixteenth and early seventeenth centuries, the performances that constituted service became increasingly and self-consciously histrionic, plentiful, and unrestrained. This new emphasis predates the role that Terry Eagleton has argued the aesthetic played in the rise of the modern bourgeois subject and state. In Eagleton's account, from the eighteenth century on, the aesthetic functions as a subordinate—we might even say a servant—to reason in order to manage a realm of human sense, affect, and perception that is newly located in the individual: "What is at stake here is nothing less than the production of an entirely new kind of human subject—one which, like the work of art itself, discovers the law in the depths of its own free identity, rather than in some oppressive external power."[5] The evolution Eagleton assigns to the Enlightenment was already under way in early modern England, and so, I would argue, was the function of the aesthetic in beginning to articulate a self-possessed subject. Although it may seem contradictory to pair service with autonomous subjectivity, this is precisely the coupling that authors imagined at a time when new, often provisional configurations of service and subjectivity were emerging. Yet the aesthetic is unpredictable and polysemous, and the same performances of service that constitute new subject positions can also imply their undoing.[6] The texts I analyze exhibit this propensity to work in several directions at once: to generate performances that inaugurate not only new dispositions and conjunctions but also new dispossessions and disjunctions.

To understand how early modern texts exploited the aesthetic qualities of service, we need to grasp, first, the ready analogy between poetry and service that early modern poetic theory provides, and second, the limitations of this analogy for drama and prose fiction. The analogy begins with Sidney's contention in *The Defence of Poesy* (1580–85) that the creation of poetry is a mimetic act. Sidney defines mimesis as joining the aesthetic imperative to provide pleasure with the moral inculcation of virtue. This project involves the merging of imitative and creative faculties: "Poesy therefore is an art of imitation, for so Aristotle termeth it in the word *mimesis*—that is to say, a representing, counterfeiting, or figuring forth—to speak metaphorically, a speaking picture—with this end, to teach and delight."[7] Sidney identifies mimesis with an Aristotelian tradition: in the *Poetics*, Aristotle traces the "general origin of poetry" to the human instinct to imitate, coupled with a universal "delight in works of imitation."[8] For Aristotle, as later for Sidney, mimesis as poetic practice derives from a natural human disposition expressed through social relations as well as through aesthetic taste. Sidney's definition is also Platonic in its elevating of earthly forms through imaging the divine: "Representing" and "counterfeiting" are both integral to imitating "the divine consideration of what may be and should be."[9] Together with "figuring forth," these techniques create "a speaking picture," that is, a simulacrum of the material world, but one that improves upon its imperfections. Rather than producing an exact copy or reproduction of reality, poets render reality in the image of the divine, creating a "golden world" in place of the everyday "brazen" one. Sidney links the poet's mimetic power to the injunction to "teach and delight" readers or audiences, and in this way to "move" them toward self-improvement.[10] Thus, poets are not limited to a strict reproduction of reality and in fact are exhorted to produce transformed, superior images.

In Aristotle's conception, so influential for early modern authors, what follows from the mimetic faculty is a vision of the poet's work as *poiēsis:* making or craftsmanship. The poet "must be more the poet of his plots than of his verses, inasmuch as he is a poet by virtue of the imitative element in his work, and it is actions that he imitates."[11] The poet's representation of actions manifests in his construction of plots. As Henry Turner has shown, in classical and early modern usage "plot" connoted artisanal, geometric, and practical modes of production.[12] The poet transforms the raw substance of action through the technology of the plot, or to put it in Roach's terms, the plot performs action, substituting for and displacing it. Sidney adapts Aristotle's *poiēsis* to his aspirational definition of the poet: "Indeed that name of making is fit for him, considering that where all other arts retain themselves within their subject, and receive, as it were, their being from it, the poet only bringeth his own stuff, and doth not learn a conceit out of a matter, but maketh matter for a conceit."[13] Turner points out that Sidney means by "matter" not only a subject for rhetorical argument but also the substance on which artisanal transformation does its work. For Sidney, the poet is an artisan who manipulates the material world, molding the "clayey lodgings" of human existence or working brass into gold. The yield of the poetic image reinforces the sense that the poet performs matter in the act of aesthetic creation.[14] Sidney lays the groundwork for classifying the poet as an artisanal servant laboring in recognizable fashion with "stuff." True, he is a servant endowed with a preternatural ability to create surrogates and make one thing into another; then again, servants are often depicted as possessing just such miraculous mimetic skills, as for instance in Jonson's *The Alchemist,* which I discuss in chapter 4, or Shakespeare's *The Winter's Tale* and *The Tempest,* the subjects of chapter 5.

In aligning service with mimetic poetic practice, however, early modern authors confronted a set of social interdictions against the improper use of mimesis and its close cousin, *imitatio,* an essential tenet of the humanist program for education. Roger Ascham's *The Schoolmaster* (1570) is characteristic in both prescribing *imitatio* and restricting it from misuse by unelite or undiscriminating subjects. Although *imitatio* is one of the "six ways appointed by the best learned men for the learning of tongues and increase of eloquence," it is also "fitter for the master than the scholar, for men than for children, for the universities rather than for grammar schools."[15] The dangers that attend imitation make it imperative that he who imitates is already experienced in a wide range of literary models, has extensive practice in translation, which is the primary mode of instruction for beginning students, and possesses a degree of interpretive judgment that allows him to meet the challenges of *imitatio* successfully. These specifications mandate a prior education that belies *imitatio*'s pedagogical function.

Given Ascham's stringent criteria, it is not surprising that servants appear in *The Schoolmaster* as figures associated with the wrongful use of imitation. Ascham testifies to the troubling imitation of servants by children and young men: "I know many servingmen of good order and well staid, and again I hear say there be some servingmen do but ill service to their young masters. Yea, read Terence and Plautus advisedly over and ye shall find in those two wise writers, almost in every comedy, no unthrifty young man that is not brought thereunto by the subtle enticement of some lewd servant."[16] A few pages later, he recounts having met a young boy who spoke "ugly oaths": "This child, using much the company of servingmen and giving good ear to their talk, did easily learn which he shall hardly forget all days of his life hereafter."[17] In these instances, the servants do not imitate but, perhaps even more dangerous from Ascham's perspective, are the objects of their young masters' imitations. Moreover, there is no distinction between imitating servants in life and in literature; in both spheres, the influences to which the young gentleman is exposed are determinative. Imitation emerges as all too susceptible to abuse when it comes into contact with the servant's contaminating influence.[18] The contagion spreads in multiple ways: from servants to their impressionable masters; from the representation of servant characters to poetic form and from thence to vulnerable readers who imitate "bad" examples in the poetry.[19]

At stake in *The Schoolmaster*, as in Sidney's *Defence* and George Puttenham's *The Arte of English Poesie* (1589), is anxiety about how certain imitations might violate the principle of decorum, which Ascham defines as the fit between matter and form, the latter variously described as "style," "words," and "utterance."[20] Because both matter and form are hierarchically organized, a mismatch between them signals an unauthorized mixing of ranks and an affront to the divine hierarchy that dictates earthly ones.[21] Puttenham offers an especially acute version of the conventional counsel to the poet about adapting style to subject: "that is, if his matter be high and lofty, that the style be so too; if mean, the style also to be mean; if base, the style humble and base accordingly."[22] Identifying the referent of "mean" matter, he gives examples based on "humble" service occupations: "the doings of the common artificer, serving man, yeoman, groom, husbandman, day-laborer, sailor, shepherd, swineherd."[23] Servants should be represented, if at all, in the meanest forms in order to correspond with their hierarchical place. Decorum relies, then, on form and matter imitating each other along a horizontal plane; while Sidney in particular endorses a transformative poetic mimesis, the vision does not extend to transgressing vertical distinctions within or between form and matter. Sidney's famous phrase, "mingling Kings and Clownes," implies just such an inappropriate melding of dramatic matters.[24] While the poet is a servant and poetry his self-generated matter, nonetheless, the form that matter takes is subject to a strict taxonomy that suppresses the role of the servant.

Thus, even as theories of mimesis and *imitatio* made it possible for fiction and drama to imagine the impact of aesthetic service, it also set boundaries that texts circumvented and resisted.[25] It comes as no surprise that Puttenham's advice was not very carefully followed by early modern authors who were writing for expansive—and expanding—readerships and audiences that included the courtier, who is Puttenham's frequent subject, as well as his "common artificer" and "serving man." It was commonplace for writers to put servant characters in the middle of courtly and even royal plots, as is true for example of Shakespeare's positioning of Autolycus in *The Winter's Tale*. Just as ordinary were cases in which aristocrats and kings are treated in the same low style as their servants, as in Thomas Nashe's *The Unfortunate Traveller* (chapter 2) and Thomas Dekker's *The Shoemaker's Holiday* (chapter 3). In all of my chapters, I explore ways in which the representations of service violate conventions of decorum and in doing so allow the matter—as it refers to both subject and materiality—of service to create new forms of expression.[26]

In highlighting the mimetic properties of service, early modern dramas and prose fictions insistently drew attention to the capacity of literary form to intervene in scenes of social and political power. Postmodern theories of mimesis helpfully foreground this capability. Gunter Gebauer and Christoph Wulf, for instance, call mimesis a "metaliterary *anthropological* concept": anthropological because it is about the identifications, often fraught and combative, between people; metaliterary because it is about the positioning of literature in terms of such identifications.[27] Precisely because mimesis connects people to one another, Gebauer and Wulf claim, it negotiates the power of representation. In *Mimesis and Alterity*, Michael Taussig amplifies the idea that mimesis reveals the contested, intimate nature of representations. Using the methods of colonial ethnography, he argues that mimetic representations gain primacy over the originals that they represent, "the image affecting what it is an image of, wherein the representation shares in or takes power from the represented."[28] Taussig suggests that by the logic of mimesis, key moments of contact between unequal parties can fundamentally alter the relations of power and identity: the colonizer/master becomes the object of the colonized's/slave's representation and is remade in the image of an image, while in turn the colonized/slave is remade in the colonizer's/master's changing image. This process continues indefinitely, as the slave and master perform and transform each other. The unsettling of hierarchical power that Taussig identifies was also at work in the metropolitan center of early modern England, where service manipulated the societal instabilities it was supposed to protect against. Following Gebauer, Wulf, and Taussig, I view early modern service as a practice that draws energy from a particular ordering of persons in a society but that also has the ability to put those relations in flux and generate new orderings.

Until the late 1990s, the complications that Taussig introduces into discussions of abjection and disempowerment had no place in critical discussions of service. In fact, it would be fair to say that service itself had almost no place in criticism. When in *The Tempest* Prospero says of Caliban, "This thing of darkness I/Acknowledge mine" (5.1.278–79), he summarizes, at least on some readings, a conventionally degrading view of the servant, and one that twentieth-century critical discourse was mostly content to replicate.[29] Servants were written out of criticism as efficiently as they were expected to serve their masters, hovering on the periphery of the narrative. Only when they transgressed were they noticed and held to account, and then only briefly. Writing in 1938 on *The Two Gentlemen of Verona*, a play discussed in my first chapter, H. B. Charlton claims that Proteus's servant, Launce, "has no real right within the play, except that gentlemen must have servants, and Elizabethan audiences must have clowns. But coming in thus by a back-door, he earns an unexpected importance in the play."[30] The servant is assumed to be the gentleman's ahistorical appendage; insofar as he is given any independent or historicized role, it is that of the clown who entertains audiences in a break from the play's "real" action. Even as Charlton acknowledges Launce's surprising significance, he imagines the servant entering the plot by a "back-door," as if literally through the servants' entrance. Charlton's reading is a poignant example of the narrow function servants once served in literary criticism. It also perhaps channels critics' desires to be identified with the "gentlemen" rather than the "servants."

As interest in power, social class, and subjectivity spread in the late twentieth century into various fields of inquiry, scholars began finally to notice that literary servants can define a text's engagement with these subjects. Service is now recognized as one of the most pervasive and threatened social bonds of the early modern period. Whereas institutions of service had traditionally been rooted in the aristocratic household and the durable relation of retainer to lord, in an increasingly capitalist economy service was taking more contractual and occasional forms. Mark Thornton Burnett's was the first study to open this transitional moment to scrutiny, and it remains essential for the wide range of archival and dramatic texts that it canvasses, as well as for its thesis that servants were represented in drama as disruptive to social and political hierarchies. On independent tracks, Richard Strier and Michael Neill began to inquire into the servant's disposition, defined in terms of ethics and affect, to historically based analyses of service. Each of these critics identified a theme of agonistic struggle between servant and master. Neill, in particular, reads moments of servants' opposition, resistance, and vilification as symptomatic of a "crisis" in the institution of service, during a period when a structure based on affective bonds was yielding to a competitive, impersonal capitalist system in which everything and everyone could be displaced and replaced.[31]

Defining early modern service through its relation to ethics and affect has become even more prevalent in the flurry of work published in the first decade of the twenty-first century, as has been the tendency to moderate, even at times to counter, the Marxist-inflected materialism of Neill and Burnett. Whether the primary relational term is dependency (Weil), love (Schalkwyk), morality (Anderson), or "volitional primacy" (Evett), each critic proposes that service and servant-master relations are a way to define early modern subjectivity, as it is mediated between the social networks in which servants participated and a sense of interiority that might variously be phrased as a spiritual calling, moral conscience, libratory impulse, or autonomous will.[32] These readings depart from a focus on class struggle between servants and masters, and they point less to oppression and confrontation and more to complex, variegated modes of working out the personal and social dynamics of service.[33]

This study reframes through aesthetics the questions that other critics have asked about the relationship between service and subjectivity, social class, and material structures. In the rich profusion of recent research, the obvious fact that we receive service in and as texts has gotten lost. Few questions have been asked about how the changing material conditions of service in early modern England interacted with the equally far-reaching changes in dramatic and literary form, despite the facts that playwrights and authors were themselves servants and that service and servant characters feature prominently in a great deal of the period's drama and prose fiction. By focusing on service as taking shape in a variety of performances, I show that service's aesthetics constitute a set of material interventions. By paying attention to the representational forms that service takes in literature, I also pay attention to the representations that were rearranging individual and collective forms of identity.

I depart from the catastrophic narrative about service told by early modern commentators and some critics today to tell a different story, one based on the stories that dramas and prose fictions chose to tell about service and about themselves. The catastrophic narrative has it that the deterioration of neofeudal and patriarchal paradigms of service precipitated a crisis in social structure and subjectivity. Indeed, most scholars concur that institutions of service underwent profound and permanent changes in the period. The paternalistic model of service, still the standard in the late sixteenth century, had its roots in neofeudal households, in which service was based on the relation of retainer to lord, and in which compensation came in the form of room, board, livery, and protection. But with the accelerating movement toward money as the dominant means of exchange, many forms of service adapted to contractual models based on wages, including those paid on a daily or sporadic basis.[34] The integration of capital with service conspired with a rapidly increasing population, land enclosure, grain shortages, rising prices, and the devaluing of wages to produce unemployment and a high rate of poverty in the last part of the sixteenth century, particularly in the 1590s.[35] As competition for service work grew, arguably the effects of downward mobility for servants spread: gentlemen and yeomen entered apprenticeships in greater numbers and displaced husbandmen and yeomen "into the ranks of wage labour."[36]

The story that I emphasize accounts for the fracturing of traditional ideologies of service but features literature stepping into the breach with an inquisitive, experimental, and self-justifying set of strategies. The fact that neofeudal structures of service were increasingly vulnerable is turned into a plot in Nashe's *The Unfortunate Traveller* in which a page persuasively impersonates an earl. The fact that youths of gentle birth were apprentices translates in Deloney's *The Gentle Craft* into a narrative about aristocrats who are ennobled by serving as apprentices and another about a humbly born apprentice who achieves a stunning upward mobility. The fact that capitalist forms of exchange were becoming more dominant raises the possibility in Jonson's *The Alchemist* (chapter 4) that even the most abject of servants might earn a profit. Not all of these stories end well for servants, and most of the texts I discuss are well aware of the negative consequences, as well as the positive ones, that attend changing practices of service. Nevertheless, the story line is marked not by retreat or denial in the face of fear but by an investment in service creating new subjective and social forms.

For authors, service offered the chance to tell a story about changing literary forms, too. Although critics have addressed some formal features of service, they have not discussed the impact of literary form on service, or service on literary form.[37] In addition, critics have concentrated almost exclusively on drama, and Shakespeare in particular.[38] This book takes a broader approach to representations of service, juxtaposing Shakespeare with several of his contemporaries working in drama and prose fiction: Ben Jonson, Thomas Dekker, Thomas Deloney, and Thomas Nashe. By reading service comparatively across authors and literary forms, I demonstrate that form both determines and participates in the stories about service literary texts tell, as well as the stories they tell about themselves.[39] In service, early modern authors lit upon both theme and method.

In arguing that service helps authors narrate the potential of literary forms, I follow the precedent of Bruce Robbins's study of servants in the British novel tradition. Robbins shows that servant characters represent not only the dynamics of class power but also the intervention of novelistic representation in history. Reflecting on the particular "hermeneutic authority" assigned to servants in the novel, he states that "those who polish the mirror held up to nature, and are thus briefly reflected in it, determine in part what it will and will not reflect."[40] The mimetic image of the mirror articulates the seeming paradox of subordination and agency that emerges from the servant's—and the author's—position. The pairing between servant and author is one I make repeatedly as I argue that writers used their servant characters to imagine new authorial roles.

At the same time, as Kristina Straub's more recent study has shown, Robbins's construction of an "othered" servant class that seems a synonym for the proletariat can get us only so far toward understanding how new servant subjectivities lent literature powerful new self-images.[41] Straub conceives of eighteenth-century literature on servants as participating in a "rhetorical ordering of the family" and "the process by which modern theories of identity—particularly class, gender, and sexuality—could come into being."[42] I share her sense that servant figures are not consistently "othered" in earlier representations and, to the contrary, redefine the boundaries of the subject. This claim is, if anything, even more resonant in the late sixteenth and early seventeenth centuries than in later centuries. Where Robbins's servants constitute an underclass and Straub's reside within the family, early modern servants were everywhere. Because of service's ubiquity and its structural coherence across social boundaries, my definition of service is not limited to domestic work but includes a wide range of occupations and labor.[43] The encompassing nature of service, combined with its versatility, allowed early modern authors and their texts to occupy a gamut of subject positions that reflected their conditions of marginality and ambition.

The story of service's decay and its disastrous consequences was told fervently in early modern England in what I call the didactic literature on service—religious sermons and tracts, service manuals, and household conduct books. These works share with dramas and prose fictions an attention to the aesthetics of service, although they see aesthetics from a markedly dissimilar perspective. They also share with fictional literature an understanding that uncertainties over the servant's subjective and social position underlie the new emphasis on aesthetics. The narrative that the didactic literature shapes around the major economic and social shifts in the institutions and practices of service focuses on how the reciprocal, enduring bond between servant and master—and by consequence, the servant's security—was deteriorating alongside the property-based household economy which it had supported.[44] Such texts present the instabilities of early modern service as an urgent epistemological problem that derives from the servant's improper aesthetics. In an effort, reminiscent of the discourse of *imitatio,* to police the effects of social imitation, these texts prescribe an ideal of reproduction that ostensibly guarantees hierarchical separation and ensures the dependency of servant on master. But the same texts repeatedly point to the failure of the ideal by showing that the servant's imitation can lead to his usurpation of his master's place and thus to a destabilization or even inversion of hierarchy. The epistemological issue the didactic literature raises is how masters can distinguish between a servant who fully inhabits his socially subordinate role and a servant who disguises an insubordinate will behind a duplicitous, convincing performance of service. The discourse reveals a self-contradictory quality, for it both dictates the necessity for the servant to imitate his master and points to the dangers of this mimesis.

An apprehension about what writers referred to as "eye-service" pervades the literature. The term derives from Paul's mandates on servants, as stated in 1 Corinthians and especially Ephesians, where there is a particular concern with *how* the servant manifests his obedience. Ephesians advises servants: "Seruants, be obedient vnto them that are *your* masters, according to the flesh, with feare and trembling in singlenes of your hearts as vnto Christ,/Not with seruice to the eye, as men pleasers, but as the seruants of Christ, doing the wil of God from the heart,/With good wil seruing the Lord, and not men."[45] The singleness of heart with which servants should approach their masters implies a wholeness and purity of intention toward Christ, and by extension toward the master as Christ's representative; it rules out multiple layers of motivation. It finds its antithesis in eye-service, which suggests an action that is based on superficial perception, aiming to please in the eyes of the master rather than in the eyes of God. Eye-service reveals a split between the internal and the external, divine and earthly service, dichotomies that signify the servant's potential to have a double relation of representation to his master. Early modern commentators turned to Paul to provide the scriptural rationale for servants' subordination, but they also gleaned from these passages a doctrine that the security of patriarchal service rested on the internal dispositions of servants, who when they appeared to work hardest to please their masters might be masking their profound disregard.

The didactic literature implies the existence of a servant subjectivity even as it strenuously resists the implications of this subjectivity. Thomas Becon's popular mid-sixteenth-century *New Catechism,* for example, tries to subordinate the servant's subjectivity to his master's by urging both to follow the principle of *imitatio christi*, the imitation of Christ, as filtered through social hierarchy: "Let masters and mistresses therefore shine in their houses as great lights, full of godliness and virtue, that their servants, seeing their good works, may take an occasion to practise the like."[46] If masters make themselves worthy of imitation and servants dutifully imitate their masters, both will be ennobled and servants will come to absorb the virtue that they "practise" in their masters' image. Becon stresses the intimacy of the servant-master bond, but it is an intimacy shot through with an awareness of inequality.[47] In the didactic literature generally, servant and master share a "soul" and yet the servant is a dependent appendage—often visualized in corporeal terms—to his master. Thomas Fosset's *The Servants Dutie* (1613) declares that the servant should have "no will of his owne, nor power over him selfe, but wholly to resign himselfe to the will of his Master, and this is to obey."[48] Thus, the servant can claim no right of ownership over his actions nor even over his body. He is more his master than he is himself.

But like fictional texts, didactic texts recognize that for servants, acting as extensions of their masters often entails acting *for* them, a license that exposes their potential to substitute for, and even supplant, their masters. Precisely because a hierarchically respectful service can look identical to a transgressive one, policing the boundary between them requires knowledge of the servant's interior disposition. And yet it is this interiority that remains inaccessible to the master. Hence the obsessive concern with eye-service. One of the best-known conduct books, *Of Domesticall Duties* (1622), by the Puritan minister William Gouge, is typical in labeling the phenomenon "hypocriticall service, when servants have a heart, and a heart, making shew of one heart outwardly, and have another, even a cleane contrary heart within them."[49] Richard Brathwait's *The English Gentleman* (1630) makes the distinction in terms of priority of interest. That servant who practices "service only to the eye," Brathwait says, aims "only at his owne private profit," whereas the true servant thinks first of his "Masters benefit."[50] These authors use eye-service as a symptom of the frustrated desire to differentiate between earthly, external, fraudulent motivations for service and divine promptings that make the servant's inner self transparent to his master. The problem they encounter is that it is difficult, if not impossible, to read the difference between fraudulent eye-service and service occasioned by a pure singleness of heart. In fact, the more skilled the servant is in acting his part, the more anxiety is aroused that he is merely feigning.

As these examples suggest, eye-service and the anxieties it raises about the servant's subjectivity are actually the condition of possibility for an aesthetics of service in which appearance and perception are paramount. We could also say that the didactic literature evinces a deep distrust of aesthetic service, even as it suggests that aesthetic service is necessary and even in some ways desirable in order for the servant to fulfill his duties. This contradiction articulates a moment of serious uncertainty in the history of service, when its practices began to be seen as both a platform for advancement and an increasingly insecure livelihood. Many didactic texts openly disapprove of servants from well-to-do but common backgrounds. One targets "the riche Farmours sonne" who enters service to avoid military duty. Such servingmen "may be properly called Suck-linges, or otherwise Caterpillers . . . For they use a kinde of diligence, but to serve their owne turnes."[51] Another maligns the "Yeomans Sonne," who aspires to trade up from "the Plough to the Parlor," and "breedeth as many inconveniences in the Commonwealth, as want of exercises begetteth diseases in a corpulent body."[52] If servants are represented as using imitation to launch themselves upward, they are also shown to be at risk of descending to lower, even animalistic, realms. Alongside servants who abuse their mandate to imitate are masters who fail to provide the proper example for their servants to emulate. If "nothing maketh good servants so much as the goodnesse of the Master," the converse is also true: bad masters make their servants bad, too. The results of a failure in the reciprocal ideal of service, according to Fosset and others, is that "servants many times and in many places are so badly used that some of them forsake all service, give themselves to idlenesse, become vagabonds, rogues and theeves."[53] To be out of service could mean a loss of material sustenance and social identity, a catastrophic pairing.[54] In the didactic literature, uncontrollably imitative service is both symptom and source of what its authors see as grave dislocations. According to the narratives featured in the didactic literature, aesthetics emerge from the fragility of subject positions and threaten their total dissolution.

The plays and prose fictions in this study similarly identify aesthetic service as arising from and furthering epistemological and societal confusion. But rather than construe service as fomenting a crisis in subjectivity, they envisage the formation of new subjectivities. The performative qualities that are glossed as eye-service in the didactic literature become translated into facilities—including adaptability, skill in impersonation, and explicitly artistic abilities—that these texts depict as instrumental to succeeding in service in a changing economy. For while traditional arrangements of service were fraying, new arrangements were arising to meet the needs of a burgeoning commercial economy. The displacement of a "master" narrative of service by multiple, often more provisional and improvisatory narratives gives context to the possible replacement of the master by the servant. It was not the case that service was disappearing; on the contrary, it was proliferating, both in terms of the number of possible approaches to service and in terms of the aesthetic images produced.

Because many emerging service roles did not adhere to a traditional formula, they have not been adequately understood *as* service. Nevertheless, service was the category in which contemporaries placed many kinds of work in an increasingly capitalist economy. We might frame many of the developments, especially in urban economies, in terms of what Peter Clark and Paul Slack labeled a "service sector," defined by the increased circulation of liquid capital and the consumption of commodities.[55] As Joan Thirsk explains, the promotion of domestic production—an effort that originated with the Crown—resulted in new forms of employment at all social levels, more money being exchanged, and a rapid growth in markets, particularly for "luxury" items.[56] Where a consumer orientation appears, service will follow. Using the criterion that services are provided for clients or customers in exchange for a fee, Clark and Slack include such occupational identities as the lawyer, apothecary, physician, and bookbinder. But their definition applies to many other kinds of labor, both those easily named (like shoemaking) and those that elude classification (like odd jobs on demand), which contributed to the expanding part of the economy built on capital and commerce.[57] The domestic servant who changed masters on a yearly basis, the apprentice, the purveyor of imported cloths, the underemployed laborer, the rogue, the entrepreneurial courtier, the player and the playwright: all of these roles were redefining the parameters of service.[58]

The shift toward a service economy entailed a new concept of the servant's subjectivity. While in paternalistic models of service what mattered most—and what was most elusive to the master—was the servant's internal disposition toward his master, in a capitalist context, what mattered more was how one enacted or performed one's service role. This change did not necessarily entail a loss of affect or the "personal" but what we might see as a consolidation of the affective in the *action* of service rather than in the person of the servant.[59] In a commercialized urban economy, servants and masters were not necessarily bound permanently and incontrovertibly; accordingly, the need for a stable identification between servant and master diminished. Another consequence was that the master could morph into a client or customer. Whereas the servant's lack of self-determination was a tenet of patriarchal service, the servant working in a service sector had, at least in theory, the opportunity to determine the conditions of his labor, to set a price for it, and to enter into a contract or other service relation voluntarily. Rather than stipulating a single paradigm for service, the new economy demanded, and accommodated, varied performances of service to keep goods, money, and people in profitable circulation. When we look at the ways in which service arrangements arose to meet the needs of a changing economy, we see that its aesthetics might not be viewed in all quarters as a sign of catastrophe but could instead signify aspiration: to perform service could mean to make a profit and to advance one's social position. Seen from the vantage point of nascent capitalism, aesthetic service could spawn as well a newly robust subjectivity rooted in role-playing, imitation, and the "crafting" of images. This is not to say that most or even many servants suddenly became upwardly mobile; the evidence suggests what most commentators have already emphasized, that downward mobility was perhaps the greater possibility. As I explore in later chapters, servants' dispossession haunts many early modern dramas and prose fictions. What I am saying, rather, is that a new set of desires and values surrounded service practices.

Several of the most accomplished practitioners of aesthetic service that I discuss in this book are women characters. This is no accident, for women were at the vanguard of aesthetic service. Women and servants were often treated as comparative cases in service and household manuals. *A Health to the Gentlemanly Profession of Servingmen,* for example, delineates the servant-master bond by reference to marital and filial bonds: "For in these dayes what greater loue could almost be found, then betwixt the Maister and the Seruant: it was in maner equall with the Husbandes to the Wyfe, and the Childes to the Parent."[60] If servants are as intimate with their masters as wives are with their husbands (who are also the masters), then women are also in some ways already in the servant's position; those women who were servants redoubled the effects of gender and social subordination. Female servants also tended to occupy more marginal and less well-defined service positions in comparison to their male counterparts, meaning that they were especially likely to be identified with aesthetic service. In theory, the relative openness and urbanity of a service economy presented opportunities for women to generate markets for their services. Such work often did not fit the categories of household or courtly service. In Natasha Korda's formulation, women participated in an "immense web of unlicensed commercial activity" that included work for the theater and other sectors of "a 'shadow' economy of unregulated crafts and trades" in which women might act as "secondhand clothing dealers, pawnbrokers, peddlers, hawkers, etc."[61] At the same time, women's employment tended to cluster at the very bottom of the economic ladder, putting many women servants in precarious positions. In the case of some, aesthetics were closely tied to vulnerability.

My treatment of *The Alchemist* in chapter 4 allows me to consider one contradictory figure of women's service in a commercial economy: the prostitute. Prostitutes engaged in a service that was almost certainly oppressive and not profitable (for them), that was in demand by consumers and also illicit, that made their bodies a prime commodity and yet was often represented as a means for women to exercise agency.[62]

Dol's impersonation of a noblewoman illustrates the traffic between the marriage market and the market for sex, but although she sells her wares in both markets, her lack of capital denies her marriage and mobility. At the other end of the social spectrum, Shakespeare's Julia in *The Two Gentlemen of Verona* (chapter 1) and Paulina in *The Winter's Tale* (chapter 5) approach courtly service by mixing high and low identities and discourses of service. Their socially diverse performances offer an analogue to Dol's, and indeed, the courtly women sometimes come dangerously close to her failure. By virtue of their identification with commerce and commodities, as well as their position of gendered subordination, women servants in early modern literature crystallize the risks and potential attached to aesthetic service in a changing economy.[63]

The service identities that authors imagined for Dol Common and Paulina, as well as for male servants, provided new identities for dramas and prose fictions. Like other service occupations, print authorship and playwriting were undergoing redefinition. On the one hand, writers in both print and the theater worked under the auspices of monied, often aristocratic, patrons. On the other hand, they increasingly oriented that work toward the reading or playgoing public: the commercial market for printed books was expanding exponentially, and playing companies were structured as shareholding enterprises on a capitalist model. In a very material sense, then, the restructuring of service led to the restructuring of literature.

Both book production and the public theater in the late sixteenth century were moving toward full participation in the service sector. From the middle of the century, theater companies had relied on patronage: in return for the right to travel and perform without sanction by the authorities, members of the playing companies were servants of their noble and royal patrons, formally entitled to wear their livery and indebted to their interests.[64] Though there was no such codified system in place for prose fiction, most works in print addressed themselves to potential or actual patrons.[65] The first edition of *The Unfortunate Traveller*, for example, was dedicated to the Earl of Southampton, and the two early editions of *The Alchemist* to Lady Mary Wroth. Patronage relied on an exchange of the master's subsidy, protection, and social prestige not only for his servants' labors but also for their performances, whether corporeal or textual, of obedience, deference, and loyalty.[66] Social hierarchy and affective reciprocity were fundamental to patronage, as they were to other forms of service.

Patronage remained important, but it began to coexist toward the end of the sixteenth century with commercial and capitalist paradigms of service. The cumulative evidence points to writers occupying several service roles at once, serving aristocratic patrons while participating in guild communities and selling their texts in the commercial marketplace. The most significant change in the theater was that playing companies began to be structured as shareholding enterprises. By the early seventeenth century, shareholders in the King's Men, for example, were in the position of largely controlling their own investments, risk, and profits.[67] In the same span of time, opportunities for writers to earn money outside of a patronage model expanded, through playwriting, pamphleteering, and book sales more generally. Printed books entered the commercial marketplace through a web of service and guild relations, from the printer to the bookbinder to the Stationer to the bookseller, not to mention their various apprentices and journeymen.[68] Likewise, the livery companies and their apprenticeship system served as an important model for socioeconomic relations within the playing companies.[69] The multiplying forms of service competed with one another on occasion but more frequently cooperated in ad hoc fashion.

The economic conditions of the marketplace increasingly supported an understanding of service as a relation between producer and consumer, and authors were quick to register what that shift meant for traditional appeals to patronage.[70] In an unsympathetic portrait of the player, John Cocke wrote that "howsoever hee pretends to have a royal master or mistress, his wages and dependence prove him to be the servant of the people." The statement is meant to confirm the "common" nature of the player, which Cocke links to the player's professional vocation: "For his best action is but an imitation of truth, and an imitation is not the thing itself."[71] But playwrights embraced what for Cocke was a pejorative description as they revamped the rhetoric of patronage to fit playgoers. In the prologue to The Alchemist, Jonson asks for the "grace" of "judging spectators," and The Tempest closes with Prospero asking the audience to "release me from my bands" (9), echoing the language of bonds that featured so prominently across discourses of service.[72] In these moments of direct address to playgoers, the playwright or his characters offer them a service: the play. In so doing, the playwright gives voice to an entity, represented by the audience, that is simultaneously nameless and personalized, general and individuated, socially mixed and elevated to a position of mastery. In this context, plays imitate and transform their masters, just as servants in the audience might, too. As Cocke seems to fear, the "imitation of truth" merges with "the thing itself." The service relationships represented in dramas shape the dynamic between playwright and spectators in the space of the early modern theater.

Prose fiction was similarly both inventing and serving an idea of the public through its engagements with service. Increased rates of literacy and publication, together with the impersonality of the print medium meant, as David Margolies has argued, that the readership's anonymity was becoming a factor with which authors had to reckon.[73] As servants reconceived of their masters as clients, prose fictions employed the same method to claim authorial control. Several authors aligned themselves with shoemakers, who, as I explore in discussions of Deloney's and Dekker's texts (chapter 3), were associated with innovations to service. "I am of the shoemaker's mind," says John Lyly in the dedication "To the Gentleman Readers" that accompanies his dedication to Sir William West in *Euphues, the Anatomy of Wit* (1578), while Thomas Lodge promises readers in the dedication to *Rosalynde* (1590) that "I will go no further than the latchet, and then all is well," a punning reference to shoelaces and the occupational decorum classically prescribed for shoemaking and other trades. These texts declare the humility of their services and solicit would-be book buyers as masters; they also construct varying images of mastery that they urge consumers to emulate—and shy away from. Lyly announces that "I submit myself to the judgement of the wise and little esteem the censure of fools," inviting readers to wonder to which category they belong.[74]

The story of the representation of service is also the story of the concurrent rise of drama and prose fiction. Too often, early modern studies enforce an artificial separation between drama and prose, but my analysis suggests that they were developing in close, mutually influential contact. Although the former has long been associated with an era of extraordinary prolific creativity in English letters, the latter has lagged far behind in recognition. Only recently has prose fiction come in for a modest share of attention.[75] This study aims to add to the gradually growing body of scholarship on early modern prose fiction while making a case for the importance of taking prose fiction out of isolation and putting it beside drama. Douglas Bruster argues that the fluid exchanges that occurred between authors, characters, texts, readers, and audiences in both drama and print produced a public sphere.[76] Performances of service articulated such exchanges and provided the connections between texts and the social world that allowed a public sphere to develop. In representing themselves through service, drama and prose fiction collaborated to generate a concept of the public.[77]

A confusion of places characterizes the public sphere. Indeed, as shown in my opening example from *The Taming of the Shrew,* early modern servants and masters did not, and often could not, know their

places. This book explores the implications of their displacements, substitutions, identifications, and exchanges. I track such representations in
roughly chronological fashion but without asserting a strict linear trajectory, for the book focuses on the cross-fertilization of older and newer
paradigms of service during the roughly two decades that mark the end
of the sixteenth century and the beginning of the seventeenth. Service
did not adhere to a single place, any more than servants and masters
did. Thus, while the chapters trace the emergence of urban, commercial,
and capitalist practices of service, they also return to the courtly, which,
even as it is altered by exchange with other forms, remains a significant
influence. Nor, of course, was service represented in a single literary
form but rather in heterogeneous forms that engrossed and transformed
a myriad of genres, discourses, and traditions. Therefore, the chapters
tack between drama and prose, with chapter 3 comparing them most
thoroughly.

Chapter 1 considers two plays—*The Comedy of Errors* (1591–94)
and *The Two Gentlemen of Verona* (1592–93)—from the period that
has been called Shakespeare's apprenticeship. Instead of embodying
a moment in which Shakespeare was not yet "himself," the apprentice
crystallized Shakespeare's vision of emerging dramatic possibilities. In
both plays, I argue, servants exploit the doubleness of representation in
ways that give them agency and undermine the guarantees of mastery
and elite identity. In *Comedy of Errors,* the twin slaves, the Dromios,
are treated as material texts authored by their twin masters, but they
prove to have a share of authorship by disrupting, altering, and entering on their accord the economic and social bonds that tie them to the
Antipholuses. The play suggests that when servants are called upon
to participate in commercial transactions, service cannot be a passive
or static form of representation but actively intervenes in the scene of
mastery. I apply this reading to the circumstances surrounding a 1594
performance of *Comedy of Errors* at the Inns of Court. In this case, it
was the audience that took the place of the play's servants, staging a
disruption of mastery and dramatic decorum. The second half of the
chapter turns to *Two Gentlemen of Verona,* where Shakespeare extends
his exploration of the potential for service to create servant subjectivities through misrepresentation. The servants Launce, Speed, and Lucetta
almost steal the show with their distorting and generative imitations of
their respective masters and mistress. The play ultimately shifts the servant's mimetic energy onto the gentlewoman Julia, in disguise as a male
page. I argue that Julia's layered performance revises the position of the
elite courtly subject and assigns an agency to the servant subject that is,

however, tempered by a recognition that such agency is most effectively manipulated by a gentlewoman playing a servant's role. In synthesizing in one character an apprentice boy actor, a page boy, and a courtly mistress, Shakespeare generates a bold, yet nuanced, image of his own authorship and of drama's socially transformative abilities.

Misrepresentation remains a theme in chapter 2, which turns to prose fiction. Informed by the print medium, prose fictions showed an enduring preoccupation with textual reproduction and instability, a fascination that figured in dynamically unstable roles for servants and in a project of formal self-definition.[78] Thomas Nashe's *The Unfortunate Traveller* (1593–94) identifies itself with a page of the court, whose chaotic itinerary includes, at one extreme, changing places with his master, the Earl of Surrey, and, at the other, being sold into slavery. As a writer who was not easily categorized, Nashe exploits the lack of established generic boundaries for prose fiction so that the narrative, like its main character, ranges widely and indiscreetly among literary forms. The text relies on an iterative cycle of imitation, reproduction, and creation to define and defend emergent concepts of authorship and textuality that found aesthetic validation in economic success. This chapter proposes that in *The Unfortunate Traveller,* prose fiction gains through service a new formal self-awareness.

An urban economy edging toward capitalism is also essential to narratives about shoemakers and aristocrats who imitate each other, blithely rather than transgressively, in the texts in chapter 3: Thomas Dekker's *The Shoemaker's Holiday* (1599) and its source, Thomas Deloney's *The Gentle Craft* (1597–98). For Deloney, like Nashe, prose fiction represents its ability to flourish in a mixed economy through the representation of service; but Deloney goes further than either Nashe or Shakespeare in envisaging service as breeding social advancement and new alignments of class and subjectivity. Accommodating Deloney's narrative to the stage, *The Shoemaker's Holiday* stages service as theater and theater as service: service consists of skilled performances that promote individual profit and social cohesion, while the theater is a public space where transformative relations are both materialized (in the conditions of service involved in working in the theater) and imagined (in the plays presented).

Even as the texts treated in chapter 3 spin out fantasies about imitative service, they are also attuned to the unsettling effects of capital on servants. Deloney and Dekker imply the servant's self-possession, and with it the idea that service can be the foundation for an independent and self-willed subjectivity. And yet, Deloney and Dekker also portray servants, like the journeyman Ralph in *The Shoemaker's Holiday*, who become materially dispossessed as they fail to perform service aesthetically. The idea that service can confer subjectivity collides with the insecurities of pursuing a livelihood in an economy increasingly detached from the patriarchal bonds of service. Ben Jonson's *The Alchemist* (1610–11), written a decade later, pursues the darker implications of aesthetic service. Chapter 4, on *The Alchemist*, examines a limit case for the transforming potential of performances of service. Jonson treats service as an illicit and disreputable profession; there exist only ill-defined boundaries between the marginal or displaced servant and the rogue. In the play, profit is won by fraudulently enacting the servant-master relationship: aesthetics seem to have entirely supplanted the labors of service. But social mobility does not result from the frenetic performances of Jonson's servant-rogues; instead, because they lack capital, they find themselves on the margins of the economy in which they had sought to prosper. The parallels between their shareholding venture and the shareholding enterprise of the King's Men highlight the constraints on playwrights and other workers in the theater. However, by joining imitation and service, Jonson identifies a powerful definition for his emerging concept of authorship, which was both proprietary and dependent, self-possessed and dispossessed. Reading tropes of service and imitation in his *Discoveries*, as well as in several of his lyric poems, I show that service was a preoccupation to which Jonson returned across his corpus and which helped him frame the strength and vicissitudes of his authorial subjectivity.

If *The Alchemist* tests the extremes of aesthetic service, we might expect that *The Winter's Tale* (1610–11) and *The Tempest* (1610–11), two courtly plays often read as conservative, would retrench against Jonson's urban fraud. But writing in the genre of tragicomedy, which admits of multiple, diverse constituents, Shakespeare shares Jonson's interest in the contamination between categories of service and revisits from a new dramatic vantage point his own early comedies. I argue in chapter 5 that Shakespeare's tragicomic form models itself on the iterative, yet transformative power of service. Servants in *The Winter's Tale* create elaborate performances, opening a theatrical space between their royal masters' often disastrous commands and their fulfillment, a space in which solutions appear and tragedy is converted into comedy. I draw on courtly and rogue manuals to show that although the courtiers, Camillo and Paulina, and the rogue, Autolycus, come from disparate textual genres and extreme ends of the social hierarchy of service, it is their cooperative dramatic work, hybrid and uneven, that gives Shakespeare's tragicomedy its shape.

New combinations of service infuse *The Tempest*, too, although in this tragicomedy they emerge from seemingly even more intractable oppositions. Shakespeare places Caliban and Ariel in relation to discourses of servitude and slavery that, as in *Comedy of Errors*, hark back to classical traditions but that also introduce the category of the racialized slave. Caliban, who, as Jonathan Goldberg has argued, is written off as incapable of humanist *imitatio* and thus of attaining full subjectivity, in fact does use his highly developed mimetic abilities to develop a tenable subject position.[79] *The Tempest* stands poised at an equivocal moment, when England was tentatively entering a global market that would make service into both a commercial proposition and an extreme form of cross-cultural oppression. In this sense, *The Tempest* extends into a new era the logic that the other texts in this study began to pursue, exploring what happens—for the servant, the text, the author, the audience—when service engages with the early stages of capitalism. The results, Shakespeare suggests at the end of his career, are ambivalent: the servant's self-determination is just the other side of the coin of his enslavement. And yet, even in the worst-case scenario, performances of service continue, and with them the possibility of new creations.

In some ways, the story of early modern service that this book tells is that of replacements—the servant replaces his master, a capitalist version of service replaces a neofeudal one, the author as an entrepreneurial agent replaces the author as noble servant, an aesthetic that invented new formal combinations and new social interventions replaces one that valued formal decorum and social hierarchy. And yet, the emphasis in this book is more often on multiplicity and fluidity, not linear replacements. On the stage and on the page, the courtier, who emblematizes all that the "old" service stood for, participated in exchanges with the aspiring apprentice, who stands for the "new." Their fellow character was the rogue, who embodies the contradictions of a moment caught between "old" and "new." What I suggest was most endangered in this period of coexistence was the absoluteness and singularity of a concept of mastery that rested on an unchanging social order and that was in this way detached from history. In the early modern period, drama and prose fictions reimagined service as participating in history and thus imagined themselves as reshaping history, too.

CHAPTER ONE

~

Shakespeare's Apprenticeship

Performing Service in *The Comedy of Errors* and *The Two Gentlemen of Verona*

While it once was conventional to designate Shakespeare's early plays as belonging to his "apprenticeship," that period of his career when "he still has much to learn about the mechanics of his craft,"[1] most critics have stopped derogating these works as immature and have begun to analyze them more seriously on their own terms. At this point, we might do well to reclaim the positive valences of what a nineteenth-century French scholar called "les années d'apprentissage" or a late-twentieth-century scholar his "prentice work."[2] The past few years have brought new recognition of how embedded the theater was in the guild system; young players and others who trained for careers in the theater did not entertain simply a metaphoric relation to apprenticeship but often served actual apprenticeships. This chapter is framed by the supposition that through his associations with theatrical apprenticeship in the first stages of his career, Shakespeare was particularly attuned to the servant's position. This framing reveals how the early comedies *The Comedy of Errors* (1591–94) and *The Two Gentlemen of Verona* (1592–93) develop an aesthetics of service in the theater.

These two plays establish how servants acting for masters might become servants acting as masters. The chapter explores several implications of this representational instability. First, the servant's position is defined as both aesthetic and influential. *Comedy of Errors* and *Two Gentlemen* portray servants as textual inscriptions that begin to author themselves and their masters, as players who skillfully misperform their masters' commands, and as exemplars whom their masters imitate. These plays investigate the potential for service to spur social mobility, but they do so without dramatizing mobility for servants themselves. Instead, the agency servants display leads to a second point about social identities:

27

when servants misrepresent their masters, mastery loses a stable foundation, and the patriarchal hierarchy that supports mastery likewise weakens. The texts reveal more about the insecurities of elite identity at two key sites for their formation—the court and the city—than they do about empirical servant identities.

In moving from *Comedy of Errors* to *Two Gentlemen*, I trace a deepening investment of elite identity in the subject positions that service makes available. In *Comedy of Errors*, the twin Dromios have a flat, textualized quality, an effect only enhanced by the fact that they are identical "copies," down to their shared name. Yet the Dromios defy their status as static material texts by rewriting and (mis)performing their masters' texts. *Two Gentlemen* features servants who similarly offer disruptive imitations of their masters. The play explores servant agency most intensely in the plot of Julia, a courtly woman who impersonates a page boy and thereby reconstructs herself as a layered composite of servant and mistress. In her disguise, Julia offers the play's most successful assertion both of mastery and service. Shakespeare suggests that aesthetic service violates hierarchical class and gender distinctions and redefines mastery in more provisional, less absolute terms.

The final point of the chapter is that in showing how servants' representations move between the copy and the original, reproduction and production, imitation and transformation, Shakespeare sketches a blueprint for drama. The model of aesthetic service that emerges from *Comedy of Errors* and *Two Gentlemen* aligns drama with Sidney's theory of poetic mimesis, which envisages poetry as deriving its creative power from its imitative faculties. Yet this same model also lends drama a mixed identity, aligning it with low or marginal influences associated with service and with the socially mixed, even disreputable, sixteenth-century public theater. The plays announce drama's ability, analogous to the servant's, to imitate and alter theatrical audiences, a mimetic process that puts an apprentice in the theater in the position of a master and, through that very identification, renders fragile the position of a gentleman playgoer. Sidney suggests that plays, like other forms of poetry, deploy the transformative component of mimesis to generate a superior, ordered version of the social world; by contrast, *Comedy of Errors* and *Two Gentlemen* suggest that the theater uses that transformative component to confuse further the categories of an already unidealized social world. These plays, still critically underregarded, make a radical statement about drama: its connections with the submission and abjectness of service are not a limitation but a source of aesthetic invention and resourcefulness that dismantles entrenched social and subjective identifications and produces new ones. These actions and interactions occur not only in the fictional worlds of the plays but also in the space of the theater. The aesthetic that Shakespeare develops in the early comedies implicates spectators as collaborators and participants.

Shakespeare, the Servant

My argument that Shakespeare's early comedies use service to shape dramatic form is sympathetic to a strand of critical argument about Shakespeare's "apprenticeship" that in other ways poses significant problems. This criticism, prevalent into the late twentieth century, apologized for supposedly immature, underdeveloped, or defective qualities in the early plays by ascribing them to a Shakespeare who was not yet truly Shakespeare.[3] But it is possible to construct a less pejorative version of the playwright's apprenticeship, as Robert Y. Turner does, for example: "As I see the continuum in Shakespeare's apprentice plays, they recapitulate phylogenetically the main historical movement in drama of the sixteenth century from the generalized didactic morality play to the relatively literal drama as a distinctive art form."[4] Turner understands Shakespeare's early plays as forging a path from drama's subordinate functions toward its realization as an autonomous aesthetic form: "Mimetic drama is drama which realizes the distinctive properties of its medium, drama *qua* drama rather than drama *qua* oration or drama *qua* sermon."[5] It is by no means my contention that in the early comedies we discover a triumphal narrative of drama, nor that Shakespeare single-handedly "invented" "drama *qua* drama" in the early 1590s. Indeed, one of this book's purposes is to study Shakespeare in context with other playwrights and fiction writers who, in my estimation, severally and jointly were generating new aesthetic possibilities for literary form. Nevertheless, I share Turner's sense that the early plays perform aesthetic formation at a moment in the early 1590s when the London theater industry was growing exponentially and Shakespeare was participating in a system of service that excited dramatic self-reflection.

Although we have almost no firm evidence about Shakespeare's early years in London in the late 1580s and early '90s, much less the details of any apprenticeship he may have undertaken, we can say confidently that he was implicated in the structures of apprenticeship and service that dominated training in theatrical work. The knowledge that he was at some point a player makes it quite possible that he was bound as an apprentice, like other boy players, during the 1580s, when he would have been in his late teens or early twenties.[6] Less is known about apprenticeships or other means of training for aspiring playwrights, except that it was not uncommon to be apprenticed as a player and then turn to other theatrical occupations.[7] Many scholars believe that Shakespeare began his foray into playwriting by revising the work of others or collaborating with them; the latter scenario may apply to one of the earliest plays in the Shakespeare canon, *1 Henry VI*, which was possibly cowritten with Thomas Nashe.[8] In addition, scholars have argued that Shakespeare belonged for a period to the Queen's Men, which enjoyed a burst of success in the late 1580s. Katherine Duncan-Jones conjectures that on top of acting and revising plays, he might have "fulfilled the offices of book-keeper and stage-keeper" for the Queen's Men.[9] The first formal record of Shakespeare's affiliation with a theater company dates from 1594, when he was listed as a core member of the newly formed Chamberlain's Men, an elevated position which suggests that he had earlier worked in less prominent capacities for other companies.[10] Therefore, while there is a paucity of concrete evidence, we know enough to say that Shakespeare was thoroughly ensconced in a workplace where, in common with most other early modern workplaces, service was a fundamental structuring principle and identity, especially for young people being initiated into a trade.

To imagine Shakespeare as an apprentice, a covenant servant (a shorter term of service also in common use in the theater), or as some less formalized type of servant is to recognize that he had a special opportunity in his early plays, in which servants are so dramatically prominent, to explore the relationship between service and the theater. *Two Gentlemen* in particular was traditionally lambasted for allowing its servants to get out of hand: thirteen of the twenty scenes in the First Folio edition of the play feature speaking parts for servant characters, not including the scenes in which Julia appears disguised as a male servant boy.[11] It is precisely the servants' failure of decorum that has often led commentators to describe Shakespeare's first comedies as "apprentice" works. I reinterpret the apprentice as a figure for Shakespeare's sensitivity to the ways in which in representing their masters, servants intervene in texts, thereby turning them into new and unexpected texts and performances.

Literate Characters in *The Comedy of Errors*

"Thou art Dromio, thou art my man, thou art thyself" (3.2.75–76), says Antipholus of Syracuse (S.), for once addressing his own servant, not the identical twin he repeatedly mistakes for him. Almost every time that he or his twin brother, Antipholus of Ephesus (E.), issues an order to his own servant, it is misperformed or unperformed, for it is invariably the other Dromio who returns, without the gold with which he has been entrusted (in act 1) or, perversely, *with* a bag of gold (in act 4) about which his master knows nothing. Taken as a unit, the Dromios are a faulty conduit for their masters' commands. Where in the main source for the play, Plautus's *Menaechmi,* there are twin masters but only one slave, Shakespeare doubles the role, borrowing the idea of the slave confronted by a doppelgänger from another of Plautus's comedies, *Amphitruo.*[12] The doubling of servants allows Shakespeare to embody the doubleness of representation: for each Antipholus, there is the Dromio who goes off to reproduce and fulfill his master's will, and there is the Dromio who returns having performed a completely different action, often one that contravenes his master's will. In their function as transmitters, the Dromios derive from Plautus's *servus currens,* the "running" slave. But true to the play's title, they prove to be errant messengers: letters are misdirected or misconstrued, and their writers' intentions go unfulfilled. In failing to deliver things for their masters or to deliver on their commands, servants become authors in their own right.

The role of the errant messenger is only one of the Dromios' textual functions, but it illustrates a pattern in their relation to textuality: although they appear to be merely the material on which their masters' literacy is inscribed or through which it is communicated, the Dromios in fact intervene in literate domains and alter the texts of their masters. Their investment in literacy changes our understanding of the "bonds" that connect all of the plays' characters but especially servants and masters. Bonds have contradictory meanings in the play, signifying both hierarchical relationships and commercial exchange. In manipulating bonds, then, Shakespeare's servants figure the transition from a patriarchal model of service in which servants are the register of their masters to a nascent capitalist model in which servants are literate agents.

Although literacy rates were rising in the period, literacy remained an important signifier of social rank. Its ability to signify social identity hinged on its externality and visibility.[13] As Douglas Lanier has shown, early modern definitions of "character" couple the sense of individual persona with that of "a distinctive external mark, conceived most often as a kind of inscription, that identifies its bearer's nature, wittingly or not."[14] This notion that writing concretizes the individual subjectivity by placing its legible imprint upon the world plays a key role in *Comedy of Errors,* where the jointly constituted properties of literacy and inscription seem to adhere to the Antipholuses. But the play's emphasis on the performative characters of the Dromios—the fact that they join and alter discourses of literacy rather than simply serving as the material upon which the character of mastery is inscribed—lessens the transparency of the relation between literacy and mastery. *Comedy of Errors* calls into question the master's self-inscription of his character on his servant and concurrently ascribes power to the servant who acts out, and thereby transforms, inscriptions of mastery.

As texts for their masters, the Dromios' bodies literally receive the imprints of their masters and, in the case of Dromio of E., his mistress. Punning on "score," a synonym for "engrave," Dromio anticipates for Antipholus the mark Adriana's punishment will leave on him: "If I return I shall be post indeed,/For she will scour your fault upon my pate" (1.2.64–65). Here, Dromio visualizes himself as the proxy for his master, absorbing Adriana's anger in Antipholus's place. A moment later, he extends the metaphor to suggest that he is a table or book upon which his master's and mistress's emotions are written and made visible to each other: "I have some marks of yours upon my pate,/Some of my mistress' marks upon my shoulders,/But not a thousand marks between you both" (1.2.82–84). The beatings that Dromio wears on his head and shoulders testify to his subservience and seem initially to reinforce his lack of participation in conjoined acts of literacy and identity formation, as well as his lack of monetary gain ("not a thousand marks"). Dromio is the material literally marked by the will of his social superiors, an instrument for their self-identification.

Shakespeare complicates the objectified materiality of the servants by having them perform unpredictably. Thus, the play continually reminds spectators that when they watch the Dromios perform, they are not reading a text, though the Antipholuses often seem oblivious of this fact. By functioning as theatrical characters, the Dromios literalize the way in which representing a master necessarily merges with a transforming performance of the master. Shakespeare reinforces this point by linking the Dromio twins both to material inscription and to theatrical "playing." In act 3, having been beaten by the other Antipholus, Dromio of E. accuses the wrong Antipholus of being the author of his beating. Both he and Antipholus believe that the servant's body is a legible register of the master's violence, which is why in this scene Antipholus is so perplexed by the evidence of a hand that seems to be his but is not. Dromio insists:

> Say what you will, sir, but I know what I know—
> That you beat me at the mart I have your hand to show.
> If the skin were parchment, and the blows you gave were ink,
> Your own handwriting would tell you what I think. (3.1.11–14)

In this passage, the proof of the master's hand, his "handwriting," on the servant's body is misleading. The authorial origins of that material trace remain oblique; the trace gains its power to signify through the surface on which it is written, recasting servant as mimetic material into servant as mimetic agent. Antipholus's "handwriting" is a false gauge of identity. Moreover, the replacement of "you" by "I" in the final line means that it is Dromio's thoughts that are at issue. The master's authorship and authority do not substitute for the servant's internal thoughts but are instead supplanted by them: the master yields to the servant. Servants are supposed to form the material for character, but they are not supposed to perform as characters. Here, however, Dromio shows that the material and the performance have collapsed into one. The material text alters in performances of service, even or especially when servants change places not only with their masters, but with one another, too. That masters, too, prove easily substitutable only underlines the deceptive security of the master's persona and its claims to originary authority.

Entering into Bonds

The Comedy of Errors inherits from Plautus the pervasive rhetoric of bonds. Variations of "bond," "band," and "bound" appear throughout the play.[15] In addition to its more easily recognized meanings, "bond" in a slightly archaic usage could mean "base vassal, serf; one in bondage to a superior; also a slave." The closely related "bondman" for one or other of the Dromios is used three times.[16] Shakespeare used "bondman" extremely rarely. Besides its three appearances in *Comedy of Errors,* it turns up six times in *Julius Caesar* and once in *Antony and Cleopatra.* From this short list, it seems that the word had Roman connotations for Shakespeare, and clearly he does evoke the context of classical slavery in portraying the Dromios. His use of bonds is also indebted to another discourse of constraint, the biblical, Pauline rhetoric of bonds employed by service manuals and treatises to illustrate the mutual obligations of servant and master, alongside filial and marital relations. But where Paul's rendering of the bond dictates hierarchical love and submission, bonds in *Comedy of Errors* are associated with literate, legal, and commercial discourses that give servants a surprising degree of control.

Bonds are a problem for the Antipholuses. The Pauline injunction for husbands and wives, parents and children, and masters and servants to be joined in indissoluble bonds afflicts the Antipholuses because, on the one hand, they have been, or become, disjoined from parents, brothers, and wives, while on the other hand, these same bonds chafe at them like the shackles of a bondman.[17] By contrast, the masters' bonds with their servants offer a constancy unrivaled by ostensibly more intimate relationships. No matter the degree of estrangement from, or stifling closeness to, wife, parents, and brother, each Antipholus remains bound to a Dromio. From this perspective, the last line of Antipholus of S.'s soliloquy in act 1—"Here comes the almanac of my true date," a throw-away reference to Dromio—gains special poignancy.[18] So long as he has Dromio, Antipholus still possesses the "almanac" that testifies to his birthday and, by extension, to his identity. The proximate verses on marital and servant-master bonds from Ephesians, cited in the introduction to this book, achieve a heightened significance in *Comedy of Errors,* where servants, more than wives, guarantee the identity of the mastering subject.

The bond also has legal and commercial meanings in the play that undercut its implications of durability and stasis. Much of the plot hinges, in fact, on failed attempts to discharge bonds in the form of a deed, by which one person commits himself to pay a specified amount of money to another. The Dromios convey and discharge their masters' bonds, and in some moments they embody them. They also misperform and fail to discharge these bonds. The substitutability of one master for another and one servant for another makes the transaction of bonds an error-prone process and one, by that very logic, that allows servants to intervene in the circulation of commerce. A. W. B. Simpson discusses the criteria for bonds in the early modern period: "The essentials were the use of parchment or paper, sealing by the obligor, and delivery as a deed, normally witnessed and attested. ... Loss of the seal, or any material erasure or alteration of the bond rendered the bond invalid."[19] Each time that servants or masters change places, it constitutes such an "erasure or alteration," and the validity of the bond is endangered. First, Antipholus of E. does not pay the debt he owes to Angelo the goldsmith (who, in turn, needs the money in order to "discharge my bond" to a merchant [4.1.13]) because his twin has mistakenly accepted the gold chain upon which payment is due. Then Dromio of E. is unable to discharge his master's bond because his master had unknowingly ordered the other Dromio to fetch the money from Adriana. The exchange of one bond, or bondman, for another, thus prevents the redemption of the legal bond. Having failed to pay off Antipholus of E.'s debt, Dromio of E. is physically bound alongside his master. He takes the occasion to pun: "Master, I am here entered in bond for you" (4.4.120). "To enter bonds" meant "to give a bond, pledge oneself."[20] Dromio's joke has him claiming that he can act as his master's legal substitute. It slyly positions the servant as literate and capable of initiating a bond on his own account.[21] The moment encapsulates the paradox of the Dromios' position, bound to the Antipholuses as almanacs of the mastering self and entering into bonds in their places. The discourse of the bond reinforces the instabilities of the servant as mimetic representation of his master, for the servant is the bond for his master's identity at the same time that he actively generates, denies, transmits, and destabilizes that bond.

When we reflect on the commercial significance of the bond, it is evident that a sea change is under way in the economics of early modern service. That is, the Dromios participate in the perpetual deferral and dilation of bonds, which is an aspect of the "commercialized interconnectedness" and "network of indebtedness" that Curtis Perry has identified as hallmarks of the play's fictive economy.[22] In place of the golden chain that was conventionally believed to connect divine and human hierarchies, we get Antipholus's gold chain as a commodity put into circulation and as the occasion for a bond that is not executed in a timely manner. Whereas in the first paradigm the servant is a low link in a chain, connected to but subordinated to others, in the second the servant is one of many actors who participates in commercial exchange, his agency enhanced by his license to act for his master and in his master's place. According to Paul's Epistles, the bond between servant and master ensures the servant's earthly submission; according to Shakespeare in *Comedy of Errors,* the bond gives servants literate and economic opportunities that weaken the biblically warranted servant-master bond. Of course, the rhetoric of bonds also raises the obverse point: the Dromios remain "bonds" in the most objective sense, for they are slaves without any right to economic profit or social mobility. Although they perform literacy, commerce, and character, on some level they remain the material text—and in a nascent capitalist system, a commodified text—that their masters exchange. The polarizing possibilities with which capitalism presents the servant-slave return in my discussion of Caliban in chapter 5.

Audience Aesthetics in the *Gesta Grayorum*

An early performance record of *The Comedy of Errors* intriguingly suggests how the thematic misrepresentations of service might translate into the interaction between play and audiences in a theatrical space. One of the first performances of *Comedy of Errors* took place in December

1594, the same year that Shakespeare enters the documentary record as a member of the Lord Chamberlain's Men. The occasion was the Christmas revels traditionally held at Gray's Inn, one of the four Inns of Court (along with the Inner Temple, the Middle Temple, and Lincoln's Inn) that served as both law schools and finishing schools. The revels were mandatory student exercises which extended intermittently over the course of the long holiday season and consisted of satiric performances variously skewering the court, prominent figures, statesmanship, foreign diplomacy, and advice treatises. Unusually, the 1594 revels survived in the form of a retrospective text, the *Gesta Grayorum* (1688), which details the festivities in general but pays special attention to the opening events of the season, when a melee that featured Shakespeare's play broke out.[23]

The Inns of Court seems at first a curious setting for audience disorder. The purpose of the Christmas revels at Gray's Inn was not to overturn or even to question existing social structures but rather to celebrate the inns' "insider" status, their close relationship with the purveyors of political, economic, and social influence.[24] It would be a mistake, however, to view the inns as an oasis from the rapidly changing urban economy that surrounded them.[25] Young aristocrats and gentlemen with ties to the court made up a substantial portion of the student body, to be sure. But during the sixteenth century, members of the growing commercial and civic elite, including merchants, tradesmen, and yeomen, sent their sons to the Inns of Court to study and play alongside the sons of gentry and nobility. The Inns of Court were implicated, then, in a form of the same question that underwrites the Dromios' unstable performances in *Comedy of Errors:* how does a changing economy affect definitions of elite status?[26] The inns functioned as a theater of, and for, an aspiring elite, and so a performance—or, more precisely, a misperformance—of *Comedy of Errors* highlights the inns' own struggles to delineate mastery and elite identities, struggles that the play itself seems to activate.

According to the *Gesta Grayorum*'s narration, expectations for the second evening of the revels ran high: "The next grand Night was intended to be upon Innocents-Day at Night; at which time there was a great Presence of Lords, Ladies, and worshipful Personages, that did expect some notable Performance at that time" (29). A delegation from the Inner Temple was received with great pomp and circumstance by the elected Prince of Purpoole and his court. The presence of the Inner Templarians raised the stakes for the planned entertainment, which seems not to have originally included *Comedy of Errors*, at least not as the centerpiece. The plan began to unravel, however, almost before it could get under way:

> There arose such a disordered Tumult and Crowd upon the Stage, that there was no Opportunity to effect that which was intended. There came so great a number of worshipful Personages upon the Stage, that might not be displaced; and Gentlewomen, whose Sex did privilege them from Violence, that when the Prince and his Officers had in vain, a good while, expected and endeavoured a Reformation, at length there was no hope of Redress for that present. The Lord Ambassador and his Train thought that they were not so kindly entertained, as was before expected, and thereupon would not stay any longer at that time, but, in a sort, discontented and displeased. It was thought good not to offer any thing of Account, saving Dancing and Revelling with Gentlewomen; and after such Sports, a Comedy of Errors (like to Plautus his *Menechmus*) was played by the Players. (31–32)[27]

The retrospective labeling of this series of incidents as "the Night of Errors" stresses the role of the play itself, which seemingly enters as a last-minute replacement for more ambitious entertainments and then is conveniently transformed into an emblem for, perhaps even a cause of, the evening's confusions and displacements.[28]

Two days later, the revelers staged a mock trial of a "sorcerer" held responsible for the unrest and for "foist[ing] a Company of base and common Fellows, to make up our Disorders with a Play of Errors and Confusions" (33).[29] Not only does the rhetoric here point to the similarity between the disruptions in the audience and those within the world of the play, but it also disparages the social status of the players, emphasizing the alleged discrepancy between them and the audience. The classification of players as servants was conventionally understood, and the text plays up their associations with marginality and abjectness, as if to suggest that somehow the players had conspired with the "sorcerer" to interrupt and infect an elite audience. In the *Gesta Grayorum*, Shakespeare's play becomes a humorous scapegoat, displacing the disorder within the inns' own ranks onto the play and its performers.

The unruly conditions surrounding this performance of *Comedy of Errors* testify to the ways in which Shakespeare's early comedies rework humanist *imitatio*—which was, as discussed in the introduction, closely related to Sidney's concept of poetic mimesis—into considerably messier forms of imitation that early modern drama could claim. While its performance at Gray's Inn may to some critics be proof that *The Comedy of Errors* was "situated firmly within the humanist reception of classical drama," I see its reception as compromising the reproductive functions of *imitatio*.[30] Eve Sanders writes that "the theater translated . . . a scribal text written for an elite like a poem circulated in a courtly coterie, into a performance medium accessible to literate and illiterate, writers and readers, men and women, alike."[31] Whereas young gentlemen were expected to read approved texts as a means of reinforcing elite identities, playgoers were admonished not to become "infected" by emulating unauthorized, sometimes scandalous play texts. In the mixed environment of the London theaters, audiences could see unsanctioned images of themselves in the interaction of servants and masters onstage.

The version of the revels in which a self-enclosed, socially privileged group produces drama to affirm existing hierarchies remains only a fantasy, continually interrupted from within. The Inns of Court were an institution that promoted and perpetuated the aims of humanist and courtly education, and the fact that students of nongentle origin but rising economic power were filling the ranks of the inns' students in the late sixteenth century bespeaks the permeability of elite identity to more socially and economically diverse influences. In the process, *imitatio* yields to a disorderly mimesis in which gentlemen, would-be gentlemen, and gentlewomen (perhaps including female aspirants, too) mingle without distinction. The main attraction as depicted in the account of the "Night of Errors" is actually not the play, nor the entertainment "which was intended," but the audience's takeover of the stage and its usurpation of the scripted entertainment. The audience stages its own theater of disruptive representation and unstable mastery. It was Shakespeare's play that made this particular encounter between aesthetics and social life possible.

Playing the Servant in *The Two Gentlemen of Verona*

With its mistakes and confusions of identity, *The Comedy of Errors* prompts a theater of audience discord into being. By contrast, *The Two Gentlemen of Verona* features a courtly romance plot that would seem to adhere to prescriptions for social and dramatic decorum. If the *Gesta Grayorum* disrupts the reproduction of elite identities from the inside out, the court is a closed circuit of service in which highborn courtiers imitate and reproduce one another. But as readers of *Two Gentlemen* know, this stereotype of courtly service has little traction in the play. The mastery of the eponymous gentlemen comes in for just as much scrutiny as is afforded the Antipholuses in *Comedy of Errors*. In fact, *Two Gentlemen* advances the critique of mastery by portraying servants of humble status as more aesthetically skilled than their courtly masters. At the same time, in the figure of Julia, the play puts mastery back together in a radically altered form, one that poses an alternative to bankrupt methods of courtly male subject formation. Shakespeare invests Julia's performance of service with an aesthetic self-consciousness that challenges the more conservative precepts of early modern poetic theory.

Service in *Two Gentlemen* highlights conflicting ideas of elite subjectivity. The first idea, put into practice by the play's courtiers, suggests that imitations duplicate and naturalize homogenous subject positions. This viewpoint has been echoed in Jeffrey Masten's important analysis of the play, which argues that the play's male homoerotic friendship in the play regulates and conserves power structures, thereby defending the borders of gentility.[32] The notion that male friendship and homoerotic bonds participate in a self-reproducing circle of imitation supports a relatively static vision of early modern social forms. The second idea, based on servants' performances, suggests that imitations can create new subject positions. In contrast to the circumscribed, fixed concept of the subject posed by the first model, the second model of subjectivity proves heterogeneous and mutable, capable of accommodating the shifting influence of multiple social positions.

Two Gentlemen redefines the elite subject through Julia's cross-dressing as a page boy in the final two acts. Although the play recognizes the pervasiveness of socially aspirant desires, Shakespeare displays little interest in the upward mobility of either domestic servants or courtiers. Rather, in Julia it traces a narrative of the elite subject who finds effectiveness in subservience. In this heroine who "change[s] . . . shapes" (5.4.107), Shakespeare represents a subject shaped not only by gender difference but also by the asymmetrical social dynamic of mistress and servant. The implications of locating the servant's agency in an elite subject are twofold, for even as this move implies that members of the elite classes are best positioned to appropriate the servant's productive performances, it also demonstrates that such performances undercut hierarchies by presenting elite identities as aesthetically produced and sustained. In other words, elite subjects are no less performative and contingent than the service roles that they assume.

From its opening scene, *Two Gentlemen* features collaborative performances of agency between servants and masters that stress the servant's constitutive imitations and undermine the master's authority. Thus, in act 1, scene 1, Proteus tries to prove to Speed, Valentine's servant, that Valentine is the shepherd and Speed the sheep. But Speed's response, "Why then, my horns are his horns" (1.1.78), points to the inseparability of his own and his master's interests and effectively demotes Valentine to the status of sheep or, worse, a cuckold. What belongs to the servant belongs equally to the master, and while that principle confers ownership on the master, it also suggests that "low" qualities spread from servants to their masters.

Julia's scenes with her waiting woman, Lucetta, turn textual production—and by extension, subjective and cultural productions—into collaborative efforts. Charles Hallett was right to say that "Shakespeare gives the maid the best lines."[33] Before their first scene together, Lucetta has intercepted Proteus's letter to Julia: "I being in the way / Did in your name receive it" (1.2.39–40). Her ostensible meaning is that she has received the letter for Julia in her absence, but Julia's reaction makes it clear that she believes that Lucetta has intervened improperly. Lucetta's propensity to act not only for her mistress but as her is manifested in the scene's stichomythia, the alternation of verse lines between two characters, which involves frequent plays on "I" and "you." When Julia asks, "What think'st thou of the fair Sir Eglamour?" Lucetta answers, "As of a knight well spoken, neat, and fine, / But were I you, he never should be mine" (1.2.9–11). Her phrasing offers an alternative to Iago's better-known line in *Othello*: "Were I the Moor I would not be Iago" (1.1.57), which opposes the master's identity to the servant's. Whereas Iago betrays fear that Othello will subsume and consume him, Lucetta uses the conditional as an opportunity to rehearse an appropriate response for her mistress.

Shakespeare portrays Lucetta as a pedagogue for her mistress, albeit one who proceeds through rhetorical indirection. Lucetta responds to Julia's accusation—"Dare you presume to harbour wanton lines? / To whisper, and conspire against my youth?" (1.2.42–43)—by initiating an extended musical metaphor that the two exchange through dialogue. Lucetta claims that she would not impersonate her mistress as Proteus's lover—"I cannot reach so high" (1.2.87)—a sentiment Julia reinforces by chastising Lucetta for her sauciness and her "unruly bass" (1.2.97), a pun on her base rank. But Lucetta also asserts that Julia needs "a mean to fill your song" (1.2.95). "Mean" is extraordinarily dense, implying, as the note in *The Norton Shakespeare* says, that Julia needs a male voice with which to harmonize but also that it is Lucetta herself, as a person of "mean" status, who completes the song.[34] Even more provocatively, the line indicates that their conversation has produced its own kind of mean, an intermediary discourse that servant and mistress create together. The discrepancies that mark their "song" evoke the asymmetries of theatrical performance, in which the identifications between common players, elite roles, and socially mixed audiences create heterogeneous forms. Their dialogue is imbued with an awareness of how the theatricality of the servant-master relationship crosses social boundaries.

The second scene featuring Lucetta is reminiscent of *Comedy of Errors* in blurring the distinction between servant as she who is written on and servant as she who writes. With Proteus having decamped to Milan, Julia implores her servant's help in plotting a reunion:

> Counsel, Lucetta. Gentle girl, assist me,
> And e'en in kind love I do conjure thee,
> Who art the table wherein all my thoughts
> Are visibly charactered and engraved,
> To lesson me, and tell me some good mean
> How with my honour I may undertake
> A journey to my loving Proteus. (2.7.1–7)

Here, Lucetta becomes material on which is "engraved" the "character[ed]" of Julia's thoughts.[35] In its verb form, used in this passage, "character" could mean to represent or portray, which reminds us that servants by necessity perform that which they may seem at first only to register.[36] Accordingly, Lucetta is asked to "lesson" Julia, and in this sense to assume a pedagogical function. In the first acts, Julia looks to Lucetta to access and interpret those wider spheres from which she is insulated because of her rank and gender. The "table" of Lucetta's mind writes the letter of Julia's thoughts. The passage suggests that even as the servant offers a mimetic, textual record of her mistress's will, she also participates in authoring that text. We can add this passage to a repertoire of scenes in the play in which Launce and Speed, too, either interpret letters for their respective masters or, in the case of the "love letter" cataloging the "conditions" of Launce's milkmaid, in which the two servants jointly interpret a text (3.1.361; 3.1.269).

These scenes suggest that elite subjects, like their servants, are texts that are performed and transformed through mutual contact. Jonathan Goldberg has argued that servants in *Two Gentlemen* act as letters that purportedly transcribe the master's intention but in fact alter and re-reconstruct it.[37] In enacting these multiple roles, the secretary becomes what Richard Rambuss has termed a "simulacrum" of his master and, though Rambuss does not say so explicitly, a simulacrum that produces a new version of the master he duplicates and transcribes. Goldberg maintains that the text's alterity, as both manipulated and embodied by the servant, determines the master's character. By this logic, Lucetta provides the textual material through which Julia is enabled to reconstitute her self. Yet on my reading, the alterity of the servant reveals itself to be illusory, for in the latter acts of the play Julia absorbs Lucetta's lessons in the power of imitative service and puts them to practice in her own stint as servant. The servant becomes integrated into performances of self.

Julia's performances at once echo and complicate Frank Whigham's assertion that in Elizabethan England "movement across the gap between ruling and subject classes was becoming increasingly possible, and elite identity had begun to be a function of actions rather than of birth—to be achieved rather than ascribed."[38] Like Whigham's opportunistic subjects, Julia achieves her aims through service; unlike them, she moves down the social ladder to do so. Whigham's survey of courtesy literature does not account for masqued downward mobility, although in this play it allows Julia to intervene more effectively in her own affairs. The servant's role offers an alternative method of subject formation to that pursued by either Whigham's or Shakespeare's ambitious courtiers, one that allows Julia as servant to copy and remake the text that she and Lucetta had collaboratively produced.

Two Gentlemen sets Julia's unorthodox narrative of mobility against the more conventional material and aesthetic expectations attached to courtly service.[39] One of the major assumptions supporting courtly service in the play is that the budding courtier will "be in eye of every exercise/Worthy his youth and nobleness of birth" (1.3.32–33). In other words, courtly service figures as a series of performances that reveal native worth. These performances are expected to reproduce qualities inherent to courtiers and are intended to affirm the fixity and stability of preexisting social privilege. In practice, however, the iterative function of courtly service exposes its own pitfalls, particularly in the arena of courtly love, which absorbs much of the attention of *Two Gentlemen*'s courtiers. The performances associated with courtly love drive the rivalries that unfold between Valentine and Proteus, among others. Courtly love offers another version of servant-master relationships, in that the lovers fashion themselves as servants to their courtly mistress. As suggested by the metamorphic and mimetic connotations of Proteus's name, however, these servants frequently change their affections, rendering the mistress an exchangeable commodity in an insular economy of affections.[40] The mistress of courtly love both exemplifies and exaggerates the fragility that the play assigns all masters. Silvia, who is the object of court rivalries in Milan, enters with the imperative "Servant!" on her lips; but although her suitors assume obsequious stances, her lack of actual authority over them becomes quickly apparent, culminating in her near rape by Proteus. The courtiers direct their mimetic energies not toward the Duke of Milan, who occupies the nominal position of master, but toward rivalry with their peers. Masten and Lorna Hutson have each suggested that in this kind of scenario, the mistress acts as a vehicle for a reproductive process that occurs between and for men.[41] The lover's subordination to his courtly mistress is the thinnest of veils for his domination of her.

The play undercuts such declarations of authority and control, for the nature of the game forces the courtiers into a single mold. Competition and emulation empty out the courtly subject and prove the flip side of Julia's increasingly dense subjectivity. This self-destructive mechanism is evident in a dialogue between Valentine and Thurio that shows the limits of discourses of courtiership. Like Lucetta and Julia, Valentine and Thurio verbally spar, but where mistress and servant suggest a sense of subjective interchange, the courtiers' dialogue reveals the irony of each character's desire to set himself apart within a system that enforces conformity. Thurio's retort to Valentine, "Sir, if you spend word for word with me, I shall make your wit bankrupt" (2.4.36–37), has the unintended effect of revealing the bankruptcy of his own wit. As René Girard argued, rivalry derives not from difference but from the similitude of desire, a similitude that threatens to eradicate distinct identities.[42] The more that the courtiers strive to outdo one another in the conventions of courtly service, the less distinct from one another they become.

In the virtuosic comic scenes that feature Launce, Shakespeare draws a sharp contrast between the ineffectual imitations of the courtiers and the productive imitations of their servants. Launce's extended soliloquies have traditionally met with a conflicted reception. While they are read as accomplished set pieces in an otherwise lackluster play, their very success is read as a failure, for they breach dramatic decorum by overtaking the courtly romance they parody. The "master" plot is incorrectly subordinated to the plot of the servants. Audiences tend to be drawn to these scenes, though without being indebted to the criteria that have so often led critics to condemn their effect on the play as a whole. John Madden's film *Shakespeare in Love* (1998) cleverly imagines Launce's popularity in the theater by depicting Will Kempe performing the role, with his dog Crab, for a thoroughly entertained Whitehall audience, including Queen Elizabeth, who comments, "Well played, Master Crab, I commend you." Afterward, the film's Henslowe observes, "Love and a bit with a dog, that's what they like," a reflection both of Launce and Crab's popular appeal and of the aesthetic denigration that has often accompanied it.[43] Critics long held that the servants' clowning and commentary should function as comedic parallels to their masters' serious dilemmas.[44] Parallelism implies narratives and issues that run alongside one another but do not meet or influence one another, but Launce does more than that: in his interactions with his unresponsive dog/"servant" Crab, he forces scrutiny of the substance—or more accurately, the insubstantiality—of Proteus's mastery. Launce's soliloquies exemplify the ways in which performances of service in *Two Gentlemen* trespass across the boundaries that separate the subject positions of servant and master and, in the process, initiate a generic mixture of "high" and "low" that has long made readers feel that something is out of order. This discomfort, I want to stress, is a crucial effect of these scenes, as Launce refuses to remain at the periphery of the action and instead literally takes over the stage.

In act 2, scene 3, Launce, aided by Crab, reenacts Proteus's overwrought departure from Julia by acting out for the audience his own leave-taking from his family. Launce breezes through the casting of parts in his family melodrama until he comes to one of the central dramatic figures, "this cruel-hearted cur" Crab, whom he accuses of having "no more pity in him than a dog" (2.3.8, 2.3.9). Launce thus analogizes a dog to a dog. But who, then, will play the dog?: "I am the dog. No, the dog is himself, and I am the dog. O, the dog is me, and I am myself" (2.3.18–20). Launce recognizes neither tautology nor contradiction in establishing an equivalence between himself and his alleged servant. On another level, the humor comes from the dog's passive resistance to being anything other than *dog*. Crab refuses to imitate, a defiance that becomes strikingly apparent in Launce's final, frustrated comment: "Now the dog all this while sheds not a tear nor speaks a word. But see how I lay the dust with my tears" (2.3.26–27). The dog is a stable fixture of nonrepresentation: within both the fiction and its representation, Crab does nothing and issues no response.[45] In this way, the dog points to the absurdity of masters' desires for servants to be purely instrumental in function; if a servant is stripped of all human agency, all that remains is Crab.

Launce, on the other hand, finds himself deeply affected by the staged drama and responds mimetically—and tearfully—to his own plight. He foreshadows Julia/Sebastian's narration of a performance that makes its audiences weep from feelings of sympathetic identification, a moment to which I will return shortly. Launce and Julia are similar in that each responds to himself or herself as if to another, an externality fostered by the doubled stance of servant and master. But it is also true that the hyperbolic, metatheatrical quality to Launce's maneuvering between subject positions makes an unsettling background to Julia's performance of downward mobility. Launce's parody insinuates that social roles and relationships are inseparable from their aesthetic manifestations; the only nonparticipant in the social world is Crab, who cannot act. By extension, the aesthetic basis for social roles and relationships makes it difficult to police elite identity, which Launce's comic improvisations have unmoored from its mode of self-authorization.

In staging his unseemly submission to his dog, Launce's second monologue gestures toward the effects on Proteus of his own insouciant role-playing: "When a man's servant shall play the cur with him, look you, it goes hard" (4.4.1.2). Launce has played the role of the cur with his master, outwitting and upstaging him, and now he finds himself mirroring his master's folly. It turns out, actually, that he has done Proteus one better, having taken a literal whipping for his dog's transgressions. (Crab micturates in Silvia's dining chamber.) "How many masters would do this for a servant?" wonders Launce finally (4.4.25). Despite, or maybe because of, his resistance to playing the part of the faithful servant, Crab seems to gain an infectious power over Launce, impelling Launce to follow Crab's dogged "dogginess." Launce's debasement in imitating his dog concretizes the process of debasement to which Proteus submits himself in the quest for dominance at court. Earlier, Launce has observed that his master "is a kind of a knave" (3.1.261), an epithet that in its connotations of a lowborn villain might more predictably apply to a domestic servant than to a courtier.[46]

It is appropriate, then, that as Proteus and the disguised Julia enter, bringing an end to Launce's clowning in this scene, Proteus is preoccupied with servants and service. Always alert to the advantages that service might bring, Proteus now seeks a servant—a reliable second self—to execute his desires in his name. Julia, disguised as the page boy Sebastian, fits the bill. This part of the scene also marks Launce's dismissal, enforced until he can recover Proteus's missing dog, for whom Crab has proven a poor substitute. Julia, as Sebastian, essentially replaces Launce. Like Cordelia and Lear's fool in *King Lear,* Julia and Launce never interact, although they do briefly share the stage.[47] Julia is in the unique position of playing both sides of the servant-master equation, not as Launce does through parodic role-playing but by shifting her role from that of mistress in the earlier scenes with Lucetta, conveniently absent after act 2, to that of Proteus's servant and finally back to mistress in the final scene. She alone has the opportunity to play the role of the clever, creative domestic servant from the vantage point of elite privilege. Julia incorporates in her single, but also multiple, character the mimetic tension that animates relations between servants and their masters. As a result, acts 4 and 5 press hard on questions about the interrelationship of subjectivity and social position.

Proteus chooses to retain Sebastian's services because Sebastian appears at once to be a gentleman and a socially submissive youth. This coupling is important, as Proteus requires a servant whose breeding is "good" enough to be trusted as his proxy in wooing Silvia but one who is also wholly subservient to his will. Thus, Proteus announces that he has retained Sebastian "chiefly for thy face and thy behaviour,/Which, if my augury deceive me not,/Witness good bringing up, fortune, and truth" (4.4.59–61). But he fails to notice that there is a potential contradiction between the reproductive and proxy functions of the servant. He orders Sebastian to deliver Julia's ring to Silvia, assuming the servant's mandate to act as a transparent replication of his master while ignoring the power of representation that accompanies this role. His failure to recognize Julia in a male servant's clothes merely literalizes the broader problem facing masters who trust their servants to transcribe their wills.

Proteus misreads the role his servant plays. Julia says that Proteus's betrayal has made her into a "shadow" (4.2.120); this self-characterization seems to fit her for the role of obedient servant, a shadow of her new master. Her very presence in Milan, however, bespeaks her decision to turn her shadowy position to advantage: "Alas, poor Proteus, thou hast entertained/A fox to be the shepherd of thy lambs" (4.4.84–85), she says in an echo of Speed and Valentine's wordplay on sheep and shepherds, servants and masters. She reveals her intention to substitute her own agency for Proteus's under cover of carrying out his wishes:

> I am my master's true-confirmèd love,
> But cannot be true servant to my master
> Unless I prove false traitor to myself.
> Yet will I woo for him, but yet so coldly
> As, heaven it knows, I would not have him speed. (4.4.96–100)

Unlike Silvia and her suitors, Julia resists folding courtly love into a discourse of service; her love for Proteus opposes itself to the figure of the "true servant." She sees the conventional expectations attached to servitude as entailing a treachery to the self, in that the servant is obliged to make the master's desires his own. Julia's idea of service instead entails placing her own will and desires before those of Proteus, while simultaneously exploiting the entanglement of wills between servant and master. The passage shows Julia to be alert to the potential space that the servant's position as a reproductive text creates for her to act on her own desires and to reshape Proteus's. Like servant figures in the didactic literature of service discussed in the introduction, she practices eye-service to secure Proteus's trust, concealing a double heart within.

The redevelopment of Julia's identity in act 4 is defined not so much by the imposition of servant upon mistress as by a continued interplay between these parts, both of which are treated as theatrical performances rather than essential identities. As Proteus's emissary, she pays a visit to Silvia, who greets her with curiosity about Proteus's former lover, Julia. Julia thus is in the strange position of discoursing about herself in the third person, detached from both her original subject position and the one she acts out here. Sebastian tells Silvia that he once played "the woman's part" in a Pentecost pageant: "And I was trimmed in Madam Julia's gown,/Which servèd me as fit, by all men's judgements,/As if the garment had been made for me" (4.4.152, 4.4.153–55). At this moment, Shakespeare's audiences would have watched a boy actor playing a gentle female character disguised as a servant boy who conjures up a vision of himself as a gentlewoman. Stephen Orgel makes the point that economic, social, and erotic analogies linked male apprentices to women, so that in performing the woman's part, the boy actor crystallized both homosexual and heterosexual modes of desire.[48] In evoking a performance that overlays the male servant and the female gentlewoman, Julia manipulates a recognition of their cultural equivalence, deploying the power of a transgender image over male spectators ("by all men's judgements") and inviting a renewal of that erotic gaze. But Julia also makes herself an implicit spectator of Sebastian's performance, suggesting both an internalization and a mutuality of gaze: Julia watched Sebastian, and Sebastian watched Julia watching him, while all along the audience knows that Julia has fabricated the memory and, in this sense, that she watches both imagined personae. As her "true" self, the mistress, she imitates the role of the servant, while as servant she envisions wearing the garment of her mistress. In effect, "herself" has become an evolving product of multiple performances and gazes.

To the erotics of this compound identity I would add that this composite figure of apprentice actor, page boy, and gentlewoman generates control from a submissive, imitative position. It is worth noting, along these lines, that the specific spectators in this scene, both imagined and actual, are women. Orgel has argued that "for a female audience . . . to see the youth in skirts might be . . . to see him not as a possessor or master, but as companionable and pliable and one of them."[49] But here, the servant boy also models for elite women the successful use of the mimetic faculty or, to put it another way, a site where a frustrated desire for productive action can be activated. In contrast to Silvia, Julia recognizes that more influence resides in the role of servant than in the constricting part of a mistress of courtly love. When we recall that *Two Gentlemen* has often been designated an "apprentice" work, it is provocative that the scene invests the apprentice body with considerable aesthetic agency and subjective complexity.[50]

The scene played between Julia/Sebastian and Silvia distills both the power of the early modern theater to forge identities based on aesthetic service and the power the theater might draw from modeling itself on service. Sebastian describes his participation in the Pentecost pageant in a way that underscores the collaboration between servant and mistress and represents Proteus's interests in a fashion he had not intended:

> And at that time I made her weep agood,
> For I did play a lamentable part.
> Madam, 'twas Ariadne, passioning
> For Theseus' perjury and unjust flight;
> Which I so lively acted with my tears
> That my poor mistress, movèd therewithal,
> Wept bitterly; and would I might be dead
> If I in thought felt not her very sorrow. (4.4.157–64)

Sebastian so convincingly emotes that Julia is moved to imitate his tears; he, in turn, reacts to his mistress's response. As if all this was not sufficiently dense, the play within a play also moves Silvia, who mimetically enacts the same process as the imagined Julia: "Alas, poor lady, desolate and left./I weep myself to think upon thy words" (4.4.166–67). The benefits of this staging for Julia are tangible. She usurps Proteus's authority and further alienates Silvia from Proteus. She incorporates female lamentation without being dominated by it. By virtue of the overlapping position of servants and women, the servant's performance can articulate and translate the desires of the gentlewoman into action. The moment stages the theater bringing within its compass servant and woman and allowing them to speak for and to each other.

If act 4, scene 4 marks a radical conjoining of service, performance, and subjectivity in Julia/Sebastian's character, *Two Gentlemen's* last act seemingly restores Julia to her former position. Domestic servants are noticeably absent from the comic resolution hastily precipitated by Proteus's attempted rape of Silvia and Valentine's proposed sacrifice of Silvia to Proteus.[51] In the process, Julia's downward mobility is swiftly corrected, and she nominally returns to her status as a gentlewoman of the court and the beloved of Proteus. Accordingly, Masten has proposed that the ending reinforces "the homogeneity of the gentlemanly subject," inscribed through a network of homosocial relations.[52] Masten makes readers aware of how *Two Gentlemen* privileges and normalizes an explicitly male, erotic, and collaborative principle of social reproduction that tends to subsume heterosexual unions and render women invisible. But while the play supports the argument that social imitation was a linchpin of subject formation, an emphasis on reproduction underplays the role of transformative imitations that are productive across class and gender lines. I have argued, in fact, that Shakespeare presents male courtiership as portending a disintegration of the structures of power and mastery it is meant to support. I have also pointed to places in the play where servants' imitations and performances undercut the naturalized claims of the elite subject to authority and dominance. The strongest assertion of mastery in *Two Gentlemen* is carried out by a woman in the role of a servant boy. The male courtiers may well be celebrating the perpetuation of a tightly circumscribed courtly culture, but Julia's presence in the last scene, still in the "habit" (5.4.102) of the page boy, exposes the flimsiness of such claims and reminds us of a compelling alternative, one that provides an intriguing model for Shakespeare the young playwright.

"Rude Groomes"

In 1592, before Shakespeare joined the Chamberlain's Men and during the years when most scholars believe he wrote *Comedy of Errors* and *Two Gentlemen,* he drew fire in a text, *Greene's Groats-worth of Wit,* published posthumously under Robert Greene's name. An accusation directed against Shakespeare is famously put forward in the following lines:

> Yes trust them not: for there is an vpstart Crow, beautified with our feathers, that with his *Tygers hart wrapt in a Players hyde,* supposes he is as well able to bombast out a blanke verse as the best of you: and beeing an absolute *Iohannes fac totum,* is in his owne conceit the onely Shake-scene in a countrey.[53]

The passage has often been explained in part by pairing it with the lines that follow shortly thereafter: "yet whilest you may, seeke you better Maisters; for it is pittie men of such rare wits, should be subiect to the pleasure of such rude groomes."[54] The tenor of the complaint against

Shakespeare is that he is just a player who has taken upon himself the unwarranted presumption to act the playwright's part and usurp his mastery. As Stephen Greenblatt remarks, "he is merely a second-rate drudge, a 'rude groom,' who thinks he is an accomplished poet when he is only an 'ape' imitating the inventions of others."[55] "Groom" was a word denoting a menial male servant, with connotations in its earliest uses of a boy on the verge of adulthood, a "man-child."[56] Duncan-Jones points out, following Chambers and others, that the Queen's Men, with which Shakespeare might have been affiliated, were specifically designated "grooms of the chamber" to the queen.[57] The *Groats-worth of Wit* identifies the player as a low-ranking servant, incapable of making a contribution to the poetic arts, performing in the "feathers" that costume characters written for him by "real" dramatists.[58] The suggestion that Shakespeare is a servant who does not know his place uncannily foreshadows, perhaps even prescribes, the later dismissal of Shakespeare's plays from this period as works of "apprenticeship."

Implicit in the attack on Shakespeare is a sense that the proper divisions between players and poets, and between theatrical apprentices and their masters, have been breached. It is tempting to wonder if the writer of the passage was reacting to a deliberately conceived transgression on the part of Shakespeare, not only in his brazen assumption of authorship but also in his aesthetic choices. If this is so, it is intriguing that the passage pays a distorted homage to Shakespeare's *3 Henry VI,* converting "O tiger's heart wrapped in a woman's hide!" (1.4.138) to "*Tygers hart wrapt in a Players hyde.*" In an effort to turn Shakespeare's line against him, the author of *Groats-worth of Wit* finds himself imitating Shakespeare. There is no better witness to the success of Shakespeare's modeling of his early plays after the servant than this moment, when the *Groats-worth* finds itself imitating the work of the imitative servant.

In closing, I want to comment on the phrase that refers to Shakespeare as *Johannes fac totum,* a phrase glossed by the *OED* as "a Jack of all trades, a would-be universal genius." In somewhat later use, "factotum," taken on its own, could mean "a servant who has the entire management of his master's affairs."[59] With its implications of a servant who by attempting to prove the "jack of all trades" is "the master of none," and its prefiguring of a servant who takes on everything—that is, more than he should—for his master, *Johannes fac totum* is an insult that by my reckoning, Shakespeare was proud to own. The epithet means to condemn Shakespeare for failing to respect taxonomy in life and drama, perhaps for failing above all to observe the proprieties of apprenticeship. But what it tells *us* is that Shakespeare used his lack of mastery to create a theater that was not beholden to poetic or social taxonomies. It is provocative, then, that one of the candidates for authorship of *Greene's Groats-worth of Wit* is Thomas Nashe, whose prose fiction *The Unfortunate Traveller,* the subject of the following chapter, centers on a servant equally heedless of taxonomies—a servant named, of all things, Jack.

CHAPTER TWO

~

Prose Fiction and the Mobile Servant

Nashe's *The Unfortunate Traveller*

If it was Thomas Nashe who attacked Shakespeare as an "upstart crow," a possibility mentioned at the end of the previous chapter, the gibe is the kind of self-lacerating impulse that Nashe seems not to have been able to resist.[1] The invective against Shakespeare suggests that he unforgivably muddled social, occupational, and generic distinctions. The same might be said of *The Unfortunate Traveller*'s (1593–94) protagonist, a servant named Jack Wilton who impersonates his noble master and slips in and out of service identities with opportunistic flair and an utter lack of respect for social proprieties. And the same might also be said of Nashe's text, which, I argue in this chapter, patterns itself on Jack's imitative, creative, and unabashedly self-serving approach to service. Finally, the same might be said of Nashe himself: although he had the university pedigree that Shakespeare lacked, he was equally, if not more, resistant to poetic classifications. Despite whatever tensions there may have been between their respective social and professional affiliations, Nashe and Shakespeare were both developing in the 1590s a new sense of aesthetic and authorial possibilities closely tied to representations of service.

In *The Unfortunate Traveller*, service is a representational practice that plays on the inscrutability—and yet crucial importance—of the servant's interior while demonstrating the efficacy of the servant's externalized performances. The exchange of personae between Jack Wilton and his master, the Earl of Surrey, in a key section of the narrative illustrates the impermanence and instability of patriarchal social identities. The introduction to *The Aesthetics of Service* discusses how early modern didactic literature tried to shore up servant-master hierarchies by condemning servants for "eye-service," performances of service that concealed the servant's dissenting will. Nashe's prose fiction contests the social and subjective implications of eye-service; in his text, a rebellious, active servant subjectivity is not a worrisome possibility but an operative assumption based on the servant's aesthetic dexterity. The idea that aesthetic service constitutes a subjectivity that cannot be harnessed reliably to patriarchal duty is exactly the fear that the didactic literature expresses, but for Nashe it signals a productive unsettling in which new modes of social and textual production can step forward and assert themselves in the guise of the insouciant servant.

In this chapter, I argue that Nashe develops just such a mode, based on aesthetic service, for the emerging form of prose fiction. Form in *The Unfortunate Traveller* often manifests as its lack, as the text ranges widely across textual and service genres alike. The adaptability and versatility of Jack's performances express the capabilities that Nashe locates in prose fiction, which he described as "a cleane different vaine from other my former courses of writing" (201).[2] This "vaine" allows Nashe to mediate between a patronage-based authorship that he identifies with patriarchal, often rigidly hierarchical structures of service and an authorship increasingly identified with capitalist rearrangements of service and the fluid circulations they imply. According to the changing imperatives of the urban economy which Nashe inhabited and about which he wrote, authors were beginning to write more openly for the marketplace and to acknowledge the economic power of book buyers. In one sense, Jack and the earl's exchange represents the transaction between the author and his "masters," whether these are understood as patrons, consumers, or both. In another sense, the exchange of servant and master signifies the shift in paradigms of authorship. As Arthur Marotti claims, the changing socioeconomic relations of print helped redefine "authorial authority" and "the ownership of texts."[3] The author replaces the patron as the putative owner of the text. But rather than assert himself as a master through possession and authority, Nashe articulates his authorship through service, defining the master as a nascent public readership which is anonymous, mutating, heterogeneous, and sufficiently capacious to include the aristocratic patron. Nashe embraces this new model of authorial and textual service, which relies not on the servant's disposition but on an exchange of money for services rendered and an accompanying dispersal of mastery. Under these conditions, the author is no longer a servant obligated to reflect and reproduce his patron's will but instead a servant who makes a profit by exchanging performances of authority with his masters. *The Unfortunate Traveller* enacts formally the exchanges that were transforming material relations.

Jack Wilton's aesthetic service generates new relations between author, text, and readers. Yet there are few stabilizing assurances for any of these parties, and the text denies any underwriting moral authority for service, whether divine or poetic. Unlike Thomas Deloney's *The Gentle Craft,* to which I turn in the next chapter, *The Unfortunate Traveller* does not express a mythology of service that promotes upward social mobility and burgeoning class interests. Instead, Nashe makes a strong material- ist claim via the unruliness of service for the instability of patriarchal structures. While the productivity of aesthetic service is tangible in the "pages," both social and textual, of the fiction, its yield for servants is indefinite. The most certain effect is the interrogation of an absolute, morally derived principle of mastery. By extension, Nashe leaves little doubt that any authority that fictions gain by identifying with service is provisional and contingent. Servants obey no moral imperatives because there are no moral imperatives in service to obey. The lack of such guarantees only makes prose fiction uncommonly fitted to the task of reflecting and contributing to economic and social flux.

During the same few years that *Two Gentlemen* and *Comedy of Errors* were distinguishing themselves from poetic theory, Nashe's development of prose fiction signaled another departure from it. Like Shakespeare, Nashe conveys the sense that Sidney's version of mimetic poetry does not adequately account for the transformative agency of service, which creates unprecedented social and aesthetic mixtures. In the final section of the chapter, I will argue that Nashe used *The Unfortunate Traveller* to satirize elite courtly poetry: its practitioners, its methods, and its aims. Turning away from Sidney's "golden world," Nashe denies the poet's mandate to generate a more perfect universe than the imperfect, oppor- tunistic one that his characters inhabit. Instead, he constructs service as an alternative aesthetic which puts into play a series of circulatory exchanges and substitutions that have no end point.

Patronage and the Reading Public

For Nashe, books and service had a number of equivalent features. At the outset of his unfortunate travels, Jack Wilton describes himself as having been "a certain kind of an appendix or page" at the English court. "Appendix" refers equally to text and servant: both are dependent supplements, one to the text's main content and the other to the mas- ter. "Page" similarly works to suggest an analogy between the book and Jack Wilton's occupation as a low-ranking servant of the court.[4] One conclusion we could draw, following from "appendix," is that service is an addendum, since the servant derives his value from his dependent and submissive relation to his master. An alternate reading, following from "page," is that aesthetic value lies in the material of the text, which is also the servant.[5] The dual dedications in the first edition of *The Unfortunate Traveller* set the stage for the text's treatment of appendixes and pages as supplements, in the Derridean sense, that create that which they are supposed only to append or accessorize.[6]

Both dedicatory appeals, the first addressed to the Earl of Southampton and the second to the pages of the court, use images of service to represent the relation of the text to potential patrons and readers. As we might predict, the text's self-representations undergo a dramatic change in the movement from the first addressee to the second, but they also display a common purpose. In the dedication to the earl, Nashe strikes a self-deprecating, flattering tone to solicit aristocratic patronage, spinning an extended metaphor that features a pun on "leaves" of a book and of a tree. Here, the pages are decidedly dependent upon the master "branch":

> This handfull of leaues I offer to your view, to the leaues on trees I compare, which as they cannot grow of themselues except they haue some branches or boughes to cleaue too, & with whose iuice and sap they be evermore recreated & nourisht; so except these vnpolisht leaues of mine haue some braunch of Nobilitie whereon to depend and cleaue, and with the vigorous nutriment of whose authorized commendation they may be continually fosterd and refresht, neuer wil they grow to the worlds good liking, but forthwith fade and die on the first houre of their birth. Your Lordship is the large spreading branch of renown, from whence these my idle leaues seek to deriue their whole nourishing: it resteth you either scornfully shake them off, as worm-eaten & worthles, or in pity preserue them and cherish them, for some little summer frute you hope to finde amongst them. (202)

As Nashe neatly puts it, the author requires the patron's "authorized commendation" to have his work yield fruit and avoid a "worthles" fate; aesthetic worth—and, it is implied, economic success—hinges wholly on the authority and authorization of the nobleman. The book "deriue[s]" its "nutriment" from the earl's elevated position, which, as throughout the dedication, conflates his social and poetic standing. Nashe anticipates here the hierarchical courtly service that Jack Wilton offers his master. Knowing that Jack Wilton hardly proves a faithful servant ironizes the dedication's obsequious homage. But even on a first reading, the exaggerated quality of Nashe's conceit stands out. It is not enough for him to praise the earl's judgment and fame, but he must refer to it as "the large spreading branch of renown"; likewise, it is not enough for him to call his book a set of "vnpolisht leaves," but they must also be "idle" and potentially "worm-eaten." Even his "reuerent duetifull thoughts (euen from their infancie) have been retayners to your glorie" (201), a phrase that summons an inelegant image of the author as a wailing baby clamoring for his parent's attention. The author gives his patron access to the inner recesses of his mind, those regions of affect and cognition that servants were believed so often to withhold from their masters. But while the effect should be satisfying, the rhetoric is hyperbolically hollow.

In competition with the appeal for patronage is an economic language of commodities, sales, and markets. In fact, Nashe opens the dedication by likening the obtaining of patronage to acquiring a commercial endorsement, or alternately paying a tax, that will make his book a legitimate player in the marketplace:

> I know not what blinde custome methodicall antiquity hath thrust vpon vs, to dedicate such books as we publish to one great man or other; In which respect, laest anie man should challenge these my papers as vncustomd and so extend upon them as forfeite to contempt, to the seale of your excellent censure loe here I present them to bee seene and allowed. (201)

This scarcely sounds a ringing approval of the customary construction of authorial service, for Nashe needs merely the earl's "seale," a legalistic stamp, for the book to be licensed in the marketplace, where it can profit on the size of its readership. He goes on to profess his indifference to the value the earl assigns his "papers": "Prize them as high or as low as you list: if you set anie price on them, I hold my labor well satisfide" (201). The main requirement is that the earl fix a price. Later, he returns to the fear that his book will be "taxed," now for "presumption," if it lacks his patron's approval. The master's power here is authorized by economics, not theology, and despite or even because of Nashe's elaborate defense of the patron's prerogative, it seems to participate in the vagaries of the marketplace from which it should ostensibly shield the author.[7]

"The Induction to the Dapper Monsieur Pages of the Court" makes explicit the materialism and commodification of the text that have a more subtle presence in the dedication to the Earl of Southampton. Dedication and induction both contain a reference to the text as wastepaper, which was a common fate for chapbooks and other cheap reading material.[8] In the dedication, Nashe seems to want to preserve his book from this fate, contingent on Southampton's favor: "Vnrepriueably perisheth that booke whatsoeuer to wast paper, which on the diamond rocke of your iudgement disasterly chanceth to be shipwrackt" (201). By contrast, in the induction, Nashe accepts that his readers will use the book pragmatically: he "bequeath[s]" it "for wast paper among you" (207), as if to indicate that the earl's disfavor is not only inevitable but perhaps also inconsequential. Now the material status of the book's pages *is* their meaning. "To any vse about meat & drinke put them to and spare not, for they cannot doe theyr countrie better seruice," says Nashe, interweaving poetic, domestic, and national service. The dietary function of the pages follows a listing of other functions, including rolling tobacco and wrapping "velvet pantofles." What Nashe offers his readers is a bare exchange: the pages pay the price of the book, and in return they get a material object that they are at liberty to use in almost any way they please.

And yet, the control granted the pages of the court over the pages of Nashe's book is more provisional than might at first appear. While giving readers the impression that they can dispose of the book's leaves as they wish, the induction also imposes a growing list of injunctions and restrictions. It tells the pages of the court to "keepe them preciously as a *privie* token of his [the author's] good will toward you" and forbids the use of the book's pages by grocers to wrap mace in, since the author dislikes it: "a strong hot costly spice it is, which aboue all things he hates." In purchasing the book, readers are obligated to defend it, with "ponyardes," from criticism; when they induct new pages into their ranks, "you shall sweare them on nothing but this Chronicle of the king of Pages hence forward" (208). The grandiose tone culminates with the order for readers to "put off theyr hats" and "make a low legge" every time they pass a "Stationers stall ... in regard their grand printed Capitano is there entomd." By this point, the book has become its own guarantor of worth. In the model of authorship reflected in the dedication to the Earl of Southampton, authority adheres to the patron, although Nashe undercuts its effectiveness by insinuating that the book is an agent in the marketplace. In the model of authorship promulgated in the induction, authority is dispersed between buyers, author, and book, allowing none of these parties to claim complete ownership over the text.

The front matter moves toward the position that the real "master" for prose fiction may be its consumers, a transition that repeats itself in Jack Wilton's narrative trajectory toward more commercial and commodified forms of service. The servant offers his product—which is also himself—to the purchaser in exchange for money. It is simultaneously an anonymous, generalized transaction and an intimate, personal one. All consumers need the same amount of money to claim their mastery, but having completed the economic transaction, each consumer is entitled to play the master. Nashe thus teases the reader with the prospect that the author's services confer absolute mastery. But this mastery, far from bestowing permanent or holistic power, is still dependent in many ways on the servant, who has taken upon himself new agency, too. The induction strengthens the servant-author's position and mines a vein of insecure promises first tapped in the dedication to the earl.

Perhaps most telling is that Nashe does not settle on a single approach or readership, although certainly the omission of the dedication from the second edition suggests that a winnowing of focus took place.[9] Nashe did not have much luck securing long-term patronage for his works,[10] and judging by its excision, the dedication of *The Unfortunate Traveller* to the Earl of Southampton met with a characteristically cold reception.[11] G. R. Hibbard says that this was Nashe's last real attempt at a dedication, for "at this point in his career he seems to have decided that the system of patronage was of no help to him."[12] The dedication to the earl, and its juxtaposition with the induction to the pages, evinces Nashe's ambivalence toward patronage and his search for alternatives. As framed by the front matter, Jack Wilton's narrative allegorizes the process whereby authorship and textual form were being redefined according to changing economic and social opportunities.

Trading Places

Like the story told by the front matter, Jack Wilton's story does not eliminate a patriarchal structure of service altogether but instead puts it into play with other modes of service. In terms of the didactic literature of service, Jack is a nightmare; and yet, in one way or another, a servant he remains, suggesting the subjective and textual viability Nashe finds in service. An overview of the plot shows that although Jack runs the risk of the "bad" servants warned against in didactic literature, he continually—if at times narrowly—avoids the prescribed fall of such servants into penury, beggary, and utter ruin. Jack metamorphoses from a servant of the court to a soldier in the continental wars before becoming an attendant to the Earl of Surrey on his travels through Europe and for a time taking on his identity. After the earl returns to England, Jack is temporarily out of service; but even the condition of the traveler is construed as a kind of service by the banished English earl whom Jack encounters in Rome: "Wee had rather live as slaves in another land, croutch and cap, and be servile to everie jelous Italians and proud Spaniards humor, where we may neither speak, looke, nor doo anie thing, but what pleaseth them, than live as freemen and Lords in our owne Countrey" (297). Comparing travel to the Israelites' torturous exile, the earl suggests that residing in a foreign country is "to live in the land of bondage" (298). This discourse of slavery directly anticipates Jack's fall through a trapdoor and, in an inversion of scripture, into bondage by a Jew. By Roman law, Jack becomes first one Jew's, and then another's, bondman. He is "rescued" from this enslavement by the pope's concubine, Juliana, who enforces upon him a sexual slavery that proves even more demanding. But by the end of the story, Jack escapes, marries his "curtizan," Diamante, and returns to the king's camp in France, where, we might assume, he will take up yet another service position.

Although the plot flirts with both upward and downward mobility for Jack, Nashe's fictional form relies on a sequential chain of episodes that resist the logic of moral and economic accumulation upon which Deloney's 1590s fictions, for example, proceed. The text thus plays against the patriarchal ideal of the servant who labors diligently for his master and is duly rewarded. In fact, the device that Nashe uses to get his protagonist back from England to the continent, early in the narrative, is a joke that reverses the worthlessness of the "idle" servant. An epidemic of sweating sickness has befallen the nation, leading Jack to comment: "Manie Masters desire to haue such seruants as would worke till they sweate againe, but in those dayes hee that sweate neuer wrought againe" (228). The sweating sickness translates the lackadaisical servant into the servant who survives, an emblem for the strategy that both Jack and the narrative pursue throughout.

In his adventures, Jack denies any moral grounding for service that transcends economic exchange. As an important aspect of this denial, *The Unfortunate Traveller* exposes the hypocrisy of theological justifications for patriarchal service, nowhere more clearly than in the episode that features the rebellion and martyrdom of the Anabaptists. This section refers to the 1534–35 massacre of members of the radical Protestant sect, who had attempted to found a theocracy in Münster that rejected secular and religious structures of authority and embraced an apocalyptic vision. After a long siege, the bishop of Münster and his forces ultimately took back the city and killed its leaders.[13] Though he appears an unlikely spokesperson for obedience, it is Jack, in the position of Nashe's narrator, who lambastes the demands the Anabaptists place on God in the name of service. The sect's members are described with historical accuracy as "all base handicrafts, as coblers and curriers and tinkers"; their humble origins stress the audacity of their presumptions toward God and their failure to adhere to the divine hierarchy (232). To make these points, Jack turns to scripture, combining verses from Acts and the Gospel according to John: "*Saue your selues from this froward genera-tion. Verily, verily, the seruant is not greater than his master*" (235).[14] The verses warn people against earthly corruption and remind them that they are God's servants. The Anabaptists do not heed these lessons:

> They did not serue God simplie, but that he should serue their turnes; and after that tenure are many content to serue as bondmen to saue the danger of hanging: but hee that serues God aright, whose vpright conscience hath for his mot, *Amor est mihi causa sequendi*, I serue because I loue, he saies, *Ego te potius, Domine, quam tua dona sequar*, Ile rather follow thee, O Lord, for thine own sake, than for anie couetous respect of that thou canst doe for me. (239)

The passage makes a sharp distinction between false and true service. False servants make themselves "bondmen" of the Lord only in the inter-est of self-preservation, as opposed to true servants, who serve from the pure motives of selfless love and obedience. Evoking the sanctified bond of servant and master in Paul's letter to the Ephesians, Jack as the voice of Nashe seemingly reiterates the divine basis for service that underwrote the didactic literature on service. But what the Anabaptists actually dis-play is the failure of theology to offer a structuring principle for earthly service. The Anabaptists resemble Jack in their humble origins, their insubordination, their "desires of reuenge and innouation" (239). The main difference is that Jack lacks the belief that in playing the part of the servant he is embodying devotion to Christ, a belief that in Nashe's characterization marks the Anabaptists as deluded.

There are no characters in *The Unfortunate Traveller* who meet the scriptural criteria for the good servant: such service has no traction in the social world, which is the only realm in which humans can act. The Anabaptists are condemned not for being self-interested servants but for their hypocrisy and stupidity in pursuing self-interest under the cover of pious disinterestedness. "They did not serue God simplie, but that he should serue their turnes; and after that tenure are many content to serue as bondmen to saue the danger of hanging." So says Jack about the Ana-baptists. If we substitute Jack for "they" and the Earl of Surrey for God, we have an accurate prediction both of Jack's engagement with the earl and his movement toward a state of bondage. But because Jack embraces the aesthetics of service without any pretense to moral duty, his narrative flirts with danger but ends in comedy, unlike the Anabaptists, who meet the moralistic narrative end that their doctrine of service has, in a sense, laid out for them.

Nashe explores most intensely how aesthetic service both plays on patriarchal hierarchies and works against their interests in the episode in which Jack and the earl exchange identities. In *The Unfortunate Traveller*, to exchange identities is to engage in a performative commercial transaction that, at least in theory, allows both servant and master to profit from impersonating each other. The other side of the coin, however, is that neither owns the identity of master or servant, a dispossession that makes subject positions as insecure as they are mobile. Fittingly, servant and master change places in the company of the magician Cornelius Agrippa, who has just conjured the figure of Tully to an awed audience of scholars. Inspired by this impressive demonstration of counterfeiting, servant and master stage their own piece of theater: "By the waie as we went, my master and I agreed to change names. It was concluded betwixte us that I should be the Earle of Surrie, and he my man, onely because in his own person, which hee woulde not have reproched, hee meant to take more liberty of behavior: as for my cariage he knew hee was to tune it at a key, either high or low, as he list" (253). Surrey's "person" operates doubly here, alluding both to his body—with which he intends to take liberties when disguised as a servant—and to the noble persona that he wants to avoid tarnishing. The impetus for the exchange comes, then, from the earl, not Jack, and it follows the long tradition of gods and aristocrats who disguise themselves in humble form in order to pursue pleasures too low for their stations. Surrey assumes that he controls the other half of this transaction, believing that he can "tune" Jack's representation as if his servant were a musical instrument. The mutual performances of page and nobleman begin in circumscribed fashion, dictated by Surrey's certainty that the motivation and decision making rest all on his side. Though he puts on the servant's garb, he will remain the master in identity. The servant, by extension, remains the appendix to his content.

What actually occurs, of course, is that the consequences of the exchange far outstrip its intent.[15] Very quickly, Jack commissions Cornelius Agrippa to display an image of Surrey's love, Geraldine. When Surrey sees the image, he is compelled, "though he had taken upon him the condition of a servant" (254), to break out into verse. The moment issues from a typical confusion in servant-master imitations, for it is not clear whether Jack Wilton has acted *for* his master or *as* his master. Notwithstanding the fact that he is disguised as his master, does he continue to represent his master's interests in showing him Geraldine, or does he advance a self-interest, appropriating Geraldine as his own? Is he still the faithful servant, even when he plays the master, or has he appropriated the earl's "person" as his own? The vignette brings up anxieties rehearsed frequently in the didactic literature: the servant might only appear to serve his master's interests, disguising behind his dutiful exterior a subversive and self-interested will. Nashe translates the servant's opacity into a new idiom: if a master licenses his servant to impersonate him and has voluntarily forsaken the trappings of mastery, what control, if any, does he have over his servant's—now master's—performance? The performance that the earl thought to have managed becomes unmanageable as Jack Wilton's reproduction turns into an unauthorized production of mastery.

In suggesting that the servant's ability to produce mastery denaturalizes it, *The Unfortunate Traveller* makes aesthetics constitutive of subjectivity. To make this point, Nashe renders the earl and Jack's exchange of identities as a series of theatrical set pieces. Such moments of embedded theater both emphasize the performativity of service and mastery and exhibit the appropriative nature of prose fiction, which harnesses drama to its winding, dilatory narrative. In one revealing example, Jack and the earl stage a baroque scene in Venice, a parody of Italianate revenge tragedies. In the familiar plot they enact, the servingman plots with a courtesan and her pander to kill his master. Jack and the earl act their parts to the hilt, as the "master" confronts his faithless "servant," whom he has dubbed Brunquell, and his accomplices with a dream that foretells their murder of him.[16] The scene culminates with the master physically reprimanding his servant. As Jack narrates it,

> My servuant, or my master, which you will, I tooke roughlie by the coller, and threatned to run him through incontinent if he confest not the truth. He, as it were striken with remorse of conscience, (God be with him, for he could counterfeit most daintily), downe on his knees, askt me forgivenesse, and impeached *Tabitha* and *Petro de campo Frego* as guiltie of subornation. (257)

The miniature drama follows a moralistic trajectory: the master recognizes just at the crucial moment that his servant has been disguising his malevolent intentions from him and brings him to repentance. By presenting this plot in a generically self-conscious fashion and containing its dramatic conventions within a prose narrative, Nashe highlights its artifice, revealing the conventional, generically constructed formations of the servant who harbors a desire to overthrow hierarchy and the master who asserts his natural authority and calls the servant to conscience. What matters in the earl and Jack's performance is their ability to make the artificial seem real, at least real enough to fool the other unwitting participants. Jack's "My servuant, or my master, which you will," suggests that servant and master have been translated into fictional and theatrical roles and that mimicry and creativity have replaced duty and loyalty as reciprocal obligations of the servant-master relationship.

Like writers of didactic literature, Nashe recognizes that service consists of an externalized set of behaviors; unlike them, he perceives these behaviors as valuable currency in the circulatory economies in which service participates. The didactic literature puts great stock in the servant's spiritual and affective condition, the degree to which "*I serue because I loue*" (239), but Nashe indicates that such propositions do not have any subjective, social, or aesthetic value. After he officially loses the earl's sanction to impersonate him, Jack invests even more in the aesthetics of the role: "My pomp, my apparel, traine, and expence, was nothing inferior to his, my looks were as loftie, my wordes as magnificall" (267). As far as Jack Wilton is concerned, his interior state is beside the point. Surrey eventually discovers the perfidy of his servant, "whom hee little dreamed off had such arte in my budget, to separate the shadow from the bodie" (267). By using the conventional metaphor of the master as body and servant as shadow, Surrey falls back on the notion, which he now finds reassuring, that the master is the substantial entity and the servant his reproductive dependent. The lines allude indirectly to Plato's allegory of the cave in book 7 of *The Republic,* where the prisoners chained in place misperceive shadows cast on the cave wall as the things themselves.[17] The irony lies in the discomfiting acknowledgment that Jack produces the same artful effect in the role of duplicate Surrey as does Surrey himself. Jack's shadowy representation has become every bit as substantial as the earl's original body and in fact threatens to gain primacy over it. Once Surrey puts his "person" into circulation, it becomes impossible to reattach the role permanently to the body. To put it another way, when servant and master identities can be performed interchangeably, these identities become commodities that manifest in the aesthetic realm of sensation and perception: they are all exteriorized surface.

Eventually Jack and Surrey make another exchange and return to their original positions. But despite the apparent recuperation of hierarchy and Jack's resumption of his rightful station as "appendix or page," few readers will be fooled into thinking these moves are either permanent or internally verifiable. When confronted, Jack falls back on explanations that couch his traitorous behavior as exemplary aesthetic service, for "a noble mans glory appeareth in nothing so much as in the pompe of his attendants" (269). The earl pronounces himself grateful for the "honour" done his reputation, and Jack professes: "Lo, into my former state I return agayne; poore Jack Wilton and your servant am I, as I was at the beginning, and so wil I persever to my lives ending" (269). As Jonathan Crewe argues, it is no longer possible to ensure the stability of hierarchical position: "No ontological guarantees underpin the respective roles of and styles of master and servant."[18] This suspicion is almost immediately borne out by Surrey's return to England, which also signals his exit from the narrative. Meanwhile, Jack gets to keep the woman, Diamante, they had both pursued, Surrey through poetic verse and Jack through Nashe's prose: "My master beate the bush and kepte a coyle and a pratling, but I caught the birde: simplicitie and plainnes shall carrie it away in another world" (255). And of course, Jack gives the lie to his protestation that he will "persever" as Surrey's servant, taking up service roles that are increasingly contingent and commodified.

The Unfortunate Traveller moves from the episode in which Jack almost becomes an earl to episodes in which he adopts more marginal and abject service identities. The text traces seemingly contradictory narrative routes to upward and downward mobility and yet also manages to instantiate in Nashe's circuitous and iterative prose style a continuous circulation of subject positions. Jack's comment on the Anabaptists would have it that self-serving servants may end up committing themselves to the utmost servility: they "serue as bondmen to saue the danger of hanging" (239). In a sense, this is the condition in which Jack finds himself in later sections of the narrative, getting his just recompense for his failure to conform to the patriarchal ideology of service. Nashe traces the risks as well as the rewards for servants of putting their identities into performative circulation. No new material structures arise within Nashe's fictional world to replace the old ones that Jack, along with Surrey and others, have helped crumble, and thus Jack is obliged to live with the economic and subjective uncertainties that he colluded in creating. Literally falling through a trapdoor into the house of the Jew Zadoch, Jack finds himself subject to Roman law, which holds that "if anie man had a fellon falne into his hands, either by breaking into his house, or robbing him by the high-way, he might chuse whether he would make him his bond-man, or hang him" (304). Taking the first option, Zadoch sells Jack as a specimen for anatomical dissection to another Jew, Doctor Zacharie. Then the pope's concubine, Juliana, contrives to make Jack her sexual slave by banishing the Jews and seizing Zacharie's "territories, his goods, his mooueables, his chattels, and his seruants" (307). Jack's lover, Diamante, likewise becomes part of the Roman traffic in slaves, eventually becoming Juliana's "bond-woman" (314). Jack Wilton and Diamante are reduced by these misadventures to instrumental status. Rather than participating as agents of exchange in a commercial economy, they become the objects of commercial exchange; in the case of Jack's near brush with anatomization, he comes close to being transformed into an inert aesthetic body.

In detaching himself from the codified structure of courtly service, Jack seems finally to actualize the warnings of the didactic literature that deceptive, self-interested servants were destined to lose their personhoods. But Nashe refuses this easy answer, instead indicating that courtly service is subject to many of the same dangers and possibilities as are other service identities. Earlier, I mentioned that in Rome, Jack meets a nameless English earl (not Surrey), who has been banished from England and who offers bitter insights on travel as a form of enslavement. This earl exemplifies downward mobility; he describes himself as "an Earle borne by birth, but a begger now as thou seest" (302). Even a high-ranking aristocrat is not immune from social risk. Although his aim is to discourage Jack from traveling, the earl suggests that the condition of servile submission entailed by travel is no different from that experienced at court: "Rats and mice ingender by licking one another; he must licke, he must croutch, he must cog, lye, and prate, that either in the Court or a forren Countrey will ingender and come to preferment" (299). In either scenario of service, performances of artifice are necessary to gain advancement, and crucially to "ingender," a word that conjures both sexual reproduction and the production of new textual genres. The earl clearly intends "ingender" as a derogatory description, something practiced by vermin. But Jack realizes the productive potential of such modes of service, as does Nashe, who "breeds" a new form of fiction from moments where servants "cog, lye, and prate."

True to his form, Nashe does not preserve Jack and Diamante in objectified positions for long. Even when they are legally other people's property and utterly dispossessed, they still participate in an economy of performances that eventually leads to their liberation from slavery. In disguise as a supplicatory offering, Diamante is sent by the Jews to kill Juliana but quickly recognizes her opportunity and tells Juliana the truth about the plot, inciting Juliana to promise "though she were her bond-woman to be a mother vnto her" (314). Zadoch is brought to a gruesome execution by their collaborative agency, "in reuenge of two women, her selfe and her maide," though Nashe quickly reminds readers that Diamante, formerly a magnifico's wife, is no "authenticall maide" (316); she merely plays the part. In fact, it is Diamante's ability to perform the servant's role persuasively that gives her cover to reunite with Jack and plot their escape from Juliana, carrying with them with "all her iewels, plate, mony that was extant" (318).[19] As Julian Yates observes, Diamante is "the absolute likeness of her mistress in every situation"; she is, in fact, "mistres *fac totum*." Yates notes that the phrase connotes a technology of typesetting.[20] It also recalls the insult against Shakespeare as a *Johannes fac totum* and the possibility that Nashe might have been the author of *Greene's Groats-worth of Wit*. In chapter 1 I discussed the implications of considering Shakespeare's early comedies as self-conscious products of a servant who takes on everything for his master. Here in Nashe's fiction, the phrase is likewise associated with a servant who represents her mistress in all senses and gains unwonted agency as a result. In suggesting that Diamante provides a figure for Nashe's authorship, we are placing Nashe in close proximity with Shakespeare, in a way that Nashe was perhaps reluctant, and yet compelled, to admit.

Aesthetic service leads Jack and Diamante back into the circulatory material economy: "what defame will not golde salve?" (318) asks Jack rhetorically. Although he and Diamante are headed toward a comic ending, the iterative, excessive logic of the narrative requires it to linger with Juliana and her remaining servants: thus, we learn that when Juliana sends her servant to fetch a reviving dose of wine, the servant mistakenly brings her the poison that was supposed to have been used by Diamante to kill Juliana. This time, though in error, the poison does its job. For her punishment, the nameless servant is condemned to drink the rest of the draught. The poison works through a complex circuit of substitutions, performances, and exchanges of identity to kill the mistress and the servant, a suitable image for Nashe's use of prose fiction to dismantle hierarchy.

Challenging the Golden World

As Jack and his paramour turned wife flee from Italy to the king of England's camp in France, the narrative ends not with a gesture toward the renewal of moral and social norms but with the writer's plea to readers on aesthetic and commercial grounds: "All the conclusiue epilogue I wil make is this; that if herein I haue pleased anie, it shall animat mee to more paines in this kind" (328).[21] Jack's self-positioning in the closing sentences as servant to the reading public reminds readers that Jack's story is also Nashe's, not only because Nashe is Jack's creator but also because Jack's aesthetic service helps portray Nashe's concept of what it means to be an author.

In *The Unfortunate Traveller*, Nashe stakes a position against Sidney's *Defence of Poesy* and its construction of mimesis. For both writers, the poet's vocation is fundamentally imitative and transformative, but they differ in their respective understandings of the spheres in which mimesis works. As Mihoko Suzuki argues, "Sidney's analogy between the Maker and the second maker holds for Nashe as well, but unlike Sidney, Nashe . . . refuses to create an ideal golden world to transform the brazen in its image."[22] Instead, I would add, Nashe envisages transformations that work within the "brazen" world: not toward a utopian ideal or even toward an individual spiritual ideal, but on the level of material change that has no moral trajectory. Nashe's anti-Sidneian aesthetics generate a set of practices for prose fiction that encompass new relations between author, text, and readers.

Nashe approaches Sidney's poetic theory through the character of the Earl of Surrey, who is a complicated figure in *The Unfortunate Traveller*. Not only does the earl represent the courtly master and the aristocratic patron (standing in for Nashe's patron, the Earl of Southampton), but he also offers a poetic foil for prose fiction. By reminding readers that Surrey was one of Sidney's heroes and exemplars, Nashe is able to criticize Sidney indirectly. Surrey presents a historically distanced, safe target for satire. W. A. Sessions notes that Sidney had looked to Surrey as a progenitor of the new poetry he attempted to theorize: "In Sidney's classic inscription, Surrey offers 'many things tasting of a noble birth, and worthy of a noble mind'—a dual genealogy"; he is one of the few English poets Sidney finds worthy of praise.[23] In his sense of Surrey as embodying a certain ideal—not just of poetry, but also of the poet himself—Sidney both drew upon and helped sustain a cultural mythology of the heroic "poet-earl" that had built up around Surrey in the decades following his execution by Henry VIII.[24] Nashe debunks this image of Surrey, transposing the earl into a performative but often ineffectual figure.[25] What emerges most clearly in Nashe's depiction of the earl is the futility of attempts to re-create a golden world which, the text implies, never really existed in the first place.

In satirizing the earl, Nashe's prose fiction resists framing authorship in terms of moral and social authority. Jack's first encounter with Surrey parodies Sidney's lofty idea of the poet: "Iesu, I was perswaded I should not bee more glad to see heauen than I was to see him. O, it was a right noble Lord, liberalitie it self (if in this yron age there were any such creature as liberalitie left on the earth), a Prince in content because a Poet without peere" (241–42). Jack's use of a negative construction to compare Surrey favorably to "heauen," his characterization of the earl as "liberalitie it self" in the midst of an "yron age"—recalling Sidney's discussion in the *Defence of Poesy* of the barren state of English poetry—and the grandiloquent naming of Surrey, a noble peer, as a "prince" among poets and a poet without "peere," all signal an ironic interruption. Nashe has already established Jack Wilton as an irreverent and cynical observer of humanity and his motives as entirely self-interested. Not only is Jack's preferment of Surrey over heaven blasphemous, but it also privileges the earl's material body over the golden world. Moreover, the earl's "liberalitie" emphasizes the earl's ability to support Jack economically. Whereas the historical Earl of Surrey sought to develop new forms of poetry in order to reimagine and reinvigorate the role of the "old nobility," Nashe's Surrey is stripped of all political imperative and absorbed only in the conventions of courtly love and Petrarchan poetry, strategies which, as I have indicated, fail where his opportunistic servant succeeds.

By making a page his authorial stand-in, Nashe turns against itself the notion that aesthetic skill is linked to courtiership. Again, it was Sidney who had argued strongly for such a connection. In a 1580 letter to his uncle Leicester, Sidney commented that he was absent from court "since my only service is speech, and that is stopped."[26] While today's scholarly consensus on Sidney's career at court is that it was often markedly unsuccessful, the widespread eulogizing in the decade after his death represented Sidney as having attained an ideal of action that crossed between the court, his writings, and the battlefield.[27] Nashe himself participated in such eulogies. But his shaping of Surrey suggests quite another outlook. The idea that skilled performances constitute service is one that Nashe adopts in *The Unfortunate Traveller;* what he rejects is the implication, first, that aesthetic service should be practiced by and produce socially elite, courtly identities and, second, that poetry written under the auspices of courtly service and for a circumscribed readership of courtiers has an aesthetic worth that is morally sanctioned. Nashe's prose fiction, built on continual exchanges between masters and servants, patrons and readers, high and low genres, allows him to distribute aesthetic and social agency much more broadly and to take such exchanges, rather than morality, as the arbiter of value.

Nashe's elaborate description of a "summer banketting house" in Rome offers both his most pointed critique of Sidney's mimesis and his most vivid vision of the alternative he sought to cultivate in prose fiction.

There is a close resemblance between this episode in *The Unfortunate Traveller* and Nashe's 1591 preface to the first printed (but unauthorized) edition of *Astrophil and Stella*. In a preface ostensibly devoted to praising Sidney, Nashe remakes him in his own image, enacting a version of the servant-master exchange that he would flesh out in the later prose fiction.[28] He describes Sidney's lyric sequence as "this Theater of pleasure, for here you shal find a paper stage streud with pearle, an artificial heau'n to ouer-shadow the faire frame, & christal wals to encounter your curious eyes, while the tragicommedy of loue is performed by starlight."[29] Nashe insists on the decorative qualities of Sidney's poetry, its patently artificial delights. The conceit of the "paper stage" reminds readers that the sonnet sequence represents both a textual artifact and a theater, but there is also something disposable about a stage made of paper, foreshadowing Nashe's description of *The Unfortunate Traveller* as "wast paper." Finally, Nashe's generic classification of the drama that the text performs seems a strange one, given Sidney's disapproval of most current "tragi-comedies."[30] In its emphasis on visual sensation and luxury, ephemerality, and suspect generic mixing, Nashe's portrayal of Sidney's verse is a far cry from Sidney's theories in the *Defence of Poesy*. In particular, the passage flouts Sidney's injunction that poetry should "delight, to move men to take that goodness in hand, without which delight they would fly as from a stranger; and teach, to make them know that goodness whereunto they are moved."[31] While the *Defence* argues that pleasure helps inculcate "goodness," Nashe sees in *Astrophil and Stella* no such subordination of pleasure to a moral purpose.

Nashe returns to the "theater of pleasure" in *The Unfortunate Traveller*'s extended description of the banqueting house, but this time rather than "stand talking all this while in an other mans doore," Nashe appropriates the image for his own prose fiction.[32] Jack narrates: "I sawe a summer banketting house belonging to a merchaunt, that was the meruaile of the world, & could not be matcht except God should make another paradise. It was builte round of greene marble like a Theater with-out: within there was a heauen and earth comprehended both vnder one roofe" (282). Although the house is purported to encompass the wonders of both heaven and earth, its comparison to a theater undercuts its mystical quality and construes it as yet another site for performance. That it belongs to a merchant, rather than to a nobleman, enhances its status as a scene for, and artifact of, commerce.[33] In the reference to God as maker, Nashe both alludes to Sidney's conception of the poet as a "maker" who seconds God and renders the poet's creation as a material, worldly reproduction of paradise. In short, Nashe literalizes the golden world and turns it into a prototype for the public amphitheaters of London, designed to inspire awe—complete with a painted "heaven" on the underside of its roof—and open to all paying customers.

The banqueting house suggests that a simulacrum of the material world engenders the same aesthetic effects as does Sidney's morally infused counterpart. By representing mechanical birds in the house who trill in perpetual song, *The Unfortunate Traveller* allegorizes its own usurpation of Sidney's poetic mimesis. Nashe exposes the mechanical basis for the birds' apparently effortless lyricism:

> Who though there were bodies without soules, and sweete resembled substances without sense, yet by the mathematicall experimentes of long siluer pipes secretlye inrinded in the intrailes of the boughs whereon they sate, and vndiscerneablie convaid vnder their bellies into their small throats sloaping, they whistled and freely carold theyr naturall field note. (283)

An elaborate technological system fills in for the birds' absent "soules" and "sense." Yet their mechanization does not taint their startling effect. Nashe concludes: "But so closely were all these organizing implements obscured in the corpulent trunks of the trees, that euerie man there present renounst coniectures of art, and sayd it was done by inchantment" (284). Even or especially when the counterfeit reveals its falsity and emptiness, it conveys a powerful aesthetic value that spectators and auditors mistake, and also can substitute, for the workings of divine authority. By his own accounting in the preface to *Astrophil and Stella*, Nashe is a "witles youth" who may be "taxt with a margent note of presumption, for offering to put vp any motion of applause in the behalfe of so excellent a Poet."[34] Thus, he imagines himself through the eyes of a potential reader who jots down a marginal note censuring his unearned arrogance in writing an encomium to Sidney. But in *The Unfortunate Traveller*'s mechanical birds, as in Jack Wilton, Nashe dares to imagine that the servant has supplanted the master and that readers might collaborate, rather than stand against him, in this audacious exchange.

Louise Simons has argued that Nashe uses the birds to symbolize a type of inauthentic poetry from which he wishes to distance himself.[35] But I see the birds, ensconced within an artificial Eden, as representing Nashe's vision of how prose fiction works and what it does. Like Jack Wilton impersonating the Earl of Surrey, the birds seize the mastery that they are supposed merely to reflect. The fascination that they hold for fictional spectators and actual readers derives as much from the possible exposure of their cunningly hidden material apparatus as from the beauty of their song. This is precisely the calculus of artifice and revelation that Nashe uses in *The Unfortunate Traveller* to narrate Jack Wilton's fraudulent performances of service. Readers are invited to recognize themselves as the servant, who deceives, transforms, and is transformed, and as the master, who is deceived and transformed, thereby gaining the servant's ability to transform.[36] Like service in the text, the machinery that makes the birds sing is circuitous and circulatory: "Neyther went those siluer pipes straight, but, by many edged vnsundred writhings & crankled wanderinges a side, strayed from bough to bough into an hundred throats" (283). The elaborate scaffolding resists clear order and hierarchy; instead, the music issues from an intricate, sometimes seemingly aimless intertwining of the machinery's composite parts.[37] But there is more of a logic to its structure than first appears. What Nashe describes is an economy of air, propelled through pipes by a "great paire of belowes" (283), eventually issuing forth from the birds' throats in the form of song. Not only does this miniature economy act as a metaphor for the circulatory commercial economy through which service produces its aesthetic effects, but even more specifically, its peregrinating, dilatory form metaphorizes the formal qualities of Nashe's prose fiction.

The aesthetics of these birds are solidly material; although they conjure divinity, they work independently of it and perhaps even mock its absence. In so doing, they license their audiences to "mistake" art for God. In *The Unfortunate Traveller*, Nashe makes service the machine that enables this blasphemous exchange to occur. Sidney laments the hard times on which English poetry has fallen, "that base men with servile wits undertake it, who think it enough if they can be rewarded of the printer."[38] Nashe transforms servility into service and the printer's reward into prose fiction's justification.

CHAPTER THREE

~

"Play the Shoemaker"

Craft and Commerce in Deloney's *The Gentle Craft* and Dekker's *The Shoemaker's Holiday*

Thomas Nashe looked down on Thomas Deloney, at least in print. In *The Anatomie of Absurditie,* he mocks: "What politique Counsailour or valiant Souldier will ioy or glorie of this, in that some stitcher, Weauer, spendthrift, or Fidler, hath shuffled or slubberd vp a few ragged Rimes, in the memoriall of the ones prudence, or the others prowesse? It makes the learned sort to be silent, whe as they see vnlearned sots so insolent."[1] "Weaver" has often been noted as a direct dig at Deloney, who was a weaver by training.[2] And Deloney's *The Gentle Craft* (1597–98), a prose fiction with roots in early modern ballads and other popular litera-ture, would seem to be exactly the kind of work Nashe derided, a work written by a craftsman for the express purpose of mythologizing a shoe-makers' guild. As I discussed in chapter 2, Nashe develops an aesthetic form in *The Unfortunate Traveller* quite different from that proposed by Sidney in the *Defence of Poesy,* but his comment about Deloney betrays his own anxieties about social and generic mixing: weavers should not write about soldiers or, in the case of *The Gentle Craft,* about shoemak-ers who prove heroic soldiers. As so often with Nashe, his criticisms hit uncomfortably close to home. Although Nashe was "learned," he was hardly "silent," raising the question of whether Nashe identified rather more with Deloney than he was willing to say.

Whether or not Nashe recognized his affiliation with "vnlearned sots," their ranks were redefining the subject matter, style, and reception of lit-erature in the commercial marketplace. And they were doing so in two forms, prose fiction and drama, that were developing in tandem. In this chapter, I investigate how a prose fiction, Deloney's *The Gentle Craft,* part 1, and a closely related drama, Thomas Dekker's *The Shoemaker's Holiday* (1599), crafted innovative aesthetic forms out of the work of shoemakers. The two previous chapters have argued that Shakespeare, in drama, and Nashe, in prose fiction, portrayed service as exploiting fears about whether the servant who was licensed to act for his master might begin to act as him. Imagining service as an ambiguous representational practice allowed these authors to destabilize concepts of mastery and endow servants with new kinds of agency. I argue in this chapter that Deloney and Dekker take a further step in developing these insights. Both texts depict an incipient capitalist economy in which hierarchical servant-master bonds are not simply under duress but are being replaced by commercially oriented service relations. Thus, both texts explore the rise of an urban service sector in which servants in theory gain the potential for profit making and social advancement. In a circulatory economy, they suggest, performances of service can engender, rather than hinder, social mobility and agency for servants.

The idea that service is a positive force for self-identification is aesthetically formative for Deloney and Dekker; a transformed, and transforming, service presents opportunities for their popular, nonelite forms of literature to develop their own criteria of worth. Their conceptions of aesthetic value emerge in interaction with readers and audiences. When read side by side, *The Gentle Craft* and *The Shoemaker's Holiday* illustrate how prose fiction and drama jointly nurtured public reception as an important part of aesthetic self-definition. Both texts position themselves as servants to an expansive, socially varied range of consumers who, in paying money to buy prose fictions or attend plays, take up places either next to or formerly occupied by elite patrons. These new "masters"—diverse, anonymous, and rapidly growing in number—require new images to reflect and drive their aspirations. Deloney and Dekker each respond to this challenge by developing textual and formal strategies to cultivate a sense of readers and audiences as a public. Such strategies involve generic imitations, appropriations, and recombinations that blend socially high and low discourses and thereby create interwoven forms. The texts that result from this process act, in turn, as agentive servants who represent their masters doubly, both mirroring and inventing their self-images. Although *The Gentle Craft* was Dekker's main source for *The Shoemaker's Holiday*, the prose fiction is not a foil for the drama. Rather, the two forms work through a mutual investment in socioeconomic change and literary invention at the turn of the seventeenth century.

There are, of course, also significant differences in the ways that Deloney's prose and Dekker's drama shape their aesthetics in conversation with a nascent public.[3] In her influential study of craftsman literature, Laura Caroline Stevenson attributed to it an insufficiency in genre, arguing that there was no paradigm in the late sixteenth century to praise craftsmen, tradesmen, and merchants on their own terms. The result, she said, is that works such as Deloney's were forced to couch bourgeois accomplishments in terms of conservative aristocratic values.[4] But to view *The Gentle Craft* as somehow retrograde is to ignore Deloney's adaptive use of prose.[5] The text accumulates a series of sequential, progressive narratives that move from rural, historically bound scenarios, in which aristocrats and shoemakers engage in mutually beneficial exchanges of identity, toward a more contemporary urban history in which an apprentice, Simon Eyre, rises to become lord mayor of London. Merging and melding a variety of popular and print genres of service from the chivalric romance to the ballad, Deloney redefines service as an aspirational profession compatible with the emerging service sector and with traditional hierarchical modes. *The Gentle Craft* thus forms itself as a romance in which economically and socially diverse performances of service coexist.[6]

Deloney made aesthetic and social claims based on what Nashe deemed an "vnlearned" status. Alexandra Halasz has argued that "Deloney's books . . . generate an image of the public sphere that directly and indirectly challenges the claims of learning and learned men to a presiding or supervisory relation to public discourse."[7] She suggests that Deloney's public discourse figures the artisan-author's resistance to his dispossession by the Stationers' Company of control in the print marketplace.[8] In my reading, Deloney enacts authorial self-possession by representing social and generic exchanges that allow apprentices and journeymen to become viable, mobile subjects. Yet *The Gentle Craft* does not promote individual social advancement at the expense of those who remain in low-ranking service positions; rather, it suggests that the promotion of one shoemaker is the promotion of all. Strictly defined, the class thus demarcated is the Cordwainers' Guild; it is also adumbrated more broadly by Deloney in terms of artisanal servants. But the definition of a class has further extension—to the fiction's readers, who are invited to identify with Eyre *and* the apprentices he feasts. It is the connections that Deloney makes between individuals and through service that allows his readers to see themselves both as individual readers and as a self-identified public.

While Deloney draws on mixed service to generate new aesthetic forms and a new readership for prose fiction, Dekker imagines a dramatic form centered on the city. In *The Shoemaker's Holiday,* urban life, with theater at its center, redefines service in terms of commerce. The play features shoemakers who perform scenes of inclusive community and profit for clients who double as an audience. In this environment, identities and places are exchanged in the same way as capital and goods, with productive consequences both for individual mobility and the coalescing of urban community. The play has diverse intertexts, many of them filtered through Deloney's prose fiction. Dekker draws most heavily on Deloney's story of Simon Eyre, but he also borrows more subtly from *The Gentle Craft*'s other episodes, too. Yet the aesthetic effect is quite unlike Deloney's cobbling of genres; instead, Dekker compresses genres of service to create an impression of wholeness and unity. Thus, the play translates Deloney's progressive prose narrative into a fantasy of and for the public stage. Where Deloney builds through discrete yet thematically linked episodes toward a climactic vision of service, Dekker's dramatic form allows him to reveals fissures in the self-enclosed presentation of service. *The Shoemaker's Holiday* uses multiple plotting to dramatize both a dominant perspective on upwardly mobile service and a subordinate perspective on downwardly mobile service. Rather than narrate a genealogy, as *The Gentle Craft* does, Dekker's play alternately interweaves and separates contemporaneous narratives of service. Not all of Dekker's shoemakers profit in equal measure; the shift in structures of service inscribes new hierarchies of privilege to replace the old ones. As I will suggest later in the chapter, Dekker shows that servants, along with the public theater, are newly vulnerable to forms of capitalist dispossession.

"My Rude Worke": *The Gentle Craft*

The commercial achievements of *The Gentle Craft*, especially part 1, have been well rehearsed by Deloney's editors and critics.[9] The text's appeal owes much to its marketing to the Cordwainers' Guild.[10] But this explanation begs the question of *how* the book met its mark so successfully, and here I suggest we look to Deloney's deployment of the wide range of textual models and resources available to prose fiction and the advantage he takes of an absence of articulated rules and standards for prose. Despite its popularity in its own time, Deloney's work has been oddly marginalized, or omitted altogether, in the recent spate of studies on prose fiction.[11] It may not be surprising that Deloney has received such slight consideration; even by the loose standards applied to prose fiction, his texts can seem atypical and ill-fitting for their emphasis on craftwork and occupational identities. But it is precisely because *The Gentle Craft* does not fit readily into categories such as the prodigal narrative, the prose romance, or the coney-catching pamphlet that it displays the flexibility and adaptiveness of early modern prose fiction.

Like Shakespeare and Nashe, Deloney defines his aesthetics against some of the standard tenets of early modern poetic theory, which insists upon a stylistic and social decorum. His dedication to part 1 of *The Gentle Craft* offers his craftsmen, with their "gallant mind" and "high conceit," as models for aristocratic imitation (91), inverting the association of shoemakers, in particular, with base qualities.[12] The dedication to the recently uncovered 1599 edition underscores the status of shoemakers as exemplars; the author notes the Roman custom of paying textual tribute to "worthie & renowned menne," leaving out neither "the painter Apelles, Pigmalion the Carver, nor Arion the the [*sic*] Fidler," while in contrast "English men may be much blamed . . . that have suffred many men to passe unspoken of, in their sweete recording muses, which have as greatly deserved to be inrolled in the Register of Fame."[13]

In complicating the alignment of exemplarity with social status, Deloney presents an aesthetics of labor that includes and implicitly valorizes readers. In the dedication to part 2, Deloney advises "Courteous Readers" to "expect not herein to find any matter of light value, curiously pen'd with pickt words, or choise phrases, but a quaint and plaine discourse, best fitting matters of merriment, seeing we have no cause to talke of Courtiers or Scholers" (174). He relies on a similar tactic in the dedication to *Jack of Newbury* (1597), where he refers to the book as "my rude worke," written "in a plain and humble manner," even as he praises the "noble" class of clothiers (3). In both that text and *The Gentle Craft,* Deloney takes a jab at the elaborate courtly style of Lyly and his imitators and offers his own method as an antidote. The joining of "quaint and plaine," in particular, evokes an image of the book as a piece of superior craftsmanship: well-made, ingenious, even cunning, without being precious. By likening his text to the shoes that his fictional shoemakers fashion, Deloney literalizes Sidney's famous comparison of the poet to an "Artificer."[14] In the *Defence of Poesy,* Sidney argues that, in common with the poet, "the skill of each artificer stands in that *idea* or fore-conceit of the work, and not in the work itself."[15] Deloney subverts Sidney's emphasis on the conceptual design by putting a higher premium on the material product itself.

The metaphor of authorship as craftwork implies a sense in which the text is self-consciously cobbled or woven together from its materials. Deloney generated broad commercial appeal precisely by stitching together disconnected and detachable narratives. Because the text is composed of short, discrete episodes, it lent itself to being published in excerpted or abridged editions which brought it to a readership that was likely to include propertied, titled, and affluent readers as well as trades- men, apprentices, and servants.[16] *The Gentle Craft* owes explicit debts to chronicle histories, saints' tales, jestbooks, ballads, chivalric romance, pastoral literature, and conduct manuals.[17] One thing that these dispa- rate forms have in common is the thematic rendering of service, whether courtly, military, domestic, or commercial. In Deloney's fiction, combi- nations of these genres express the open-ended potential of service; the setting of *The Gentle Craft* slides effortlessly between the battlefield, the court, and the shoemaker's workshop, while a narrative thread is spun out here as courtly romance, there as fabliau. Aristotle's dramatic unities exert little pressure on the text, which arranges itself instead according to principles of accommodation and assimilation. At the same time, as my analysis will show, the narrative builds progressively, if not continuously, toward a realization of the social mobility that service can engender.[18]

Deloney's episodic structure advances an aesthetic strategy that both drives and derives from the marketplace imperative to sell books. Its discontinuity allows the text to proceed according to a logic of internal imitation: the text's constituent genres iterate and transform one another. *The Gentle Craft* bridges the gap between jesting maidservants and chi- valric knights, exploiting the shared cultural familiarity of the works that featured these characters. Tessa Watt has argued that this group of popu- lar works comprised a "'stock' of stories which endured over generations and approached what we might call 'folk stories.'"[19] As Watt illustrates, there was a continual transference of many of these works from one form to another, so that popular romances such as *Guy of Warwick* and *Bevis of Hampton,* which had been passed down in manuscript form as far back as the thirteenth century, appeared in expensive print versions as well as in abridged, cheap broadsides.[20] Deloney's text consolidates such textual conversions: the knight errant is sustained by witty shoemakers, while the apprentice's rise is narrated in the style of a chivalric romance. For example, Sir Hugh, the hero of the first episode of *The Gentle Craft,* is a direct descendant of knights such as Bevis and Guy. At the same time, the text relies heavily on the jest and "merry" traditions that feature in sixteenth-century jestbooks, ballads, and other brief fiction. Long Meg of Westminster, who appears as a heroine in part 2, was a courageous but indecorous maidservant who consistently outwitted her superiors. *The Gentle Craft* puts the likes of Sir Hugh and Long Meg into mutually transforming contact. Freely interweaving elements from the common cul- tural stock, Deloney advances a process of textual and cultural exchange already taking place in the sixteenth-century print marketplace.

The shoemaker was ideally suited to represent exchanges of the sort that structure *The Gentle Craft* and, in its turn, *The Shoemaker's Holiday*. Craftsmen, particularly the apprentices and journeymen to whom Deloney gives particular attention, typically held a stake in multiple forms of service at once. Although apprentices were bound to their masters for a specified period of time (usually five to seven years) and performed many of the functions of a domestic servant, they were ultimately being trained for a trade that would bring them into contact with industrial, commercial, and guild interests.[21] In Deloney's citation of an "old prouerb" about apprentices and journeymen who delight in their labors, the language registers an awareness of the varied components of shoemaking service: "They proue seruants kind and good,/That sing at their busines like birds in the wood" (140). In the sense of "a task appointed or undertaken," "busines" includes whatever jobs servants do at the behest of their masters.[22] At the same time, it is significant that the journeymen and apprentices "sing at *their* busines" and (a few sentences earlier) "followed *their* busines" (emphasis mine). In *The Gentle Craft,* service is certainly owed to the master shoemaker, but not solely and not in all cases as an end in itself: the "business" at hand refers also to the occupation of shoemaking itself.[23] This second definition situates masters as sometime pedagogues and intermediaries for servants, rather than as always the controlling subject/object of service. What is most striking about the work of shoemakers, as represented by Deloney, is that it negotiates between obligations to masters and clients and between personal, guild, and commercial forms of service. Thus, Deloney's shoemakers become figures who bridge patriarchal models of service and models increasingly inflected by capitalism.

In fashioning shoemakers into figures who exemplify a new flexibility in service, Deloney both manipulates and plays against popular stereotypes of the shoemaker as socially denigrated, a reputation that had a basis in the historical poverty of many shoemakers.[24] His use of the shoemakers' moniker, "the gentle craft," is instructive in this regard, for his strategy was to turn an identification often delivered tongue-in-cheek into proof of the value of shoemakers and their work—and, by extension, of his own textual production.[25] Texts immediately predating *The Gentle Craft* tend to paint shoemakers as rude and rustic figures. For example, in the anonymous play *George a Greene,* "the gentle craft" is used in a parodic way, and shoemakers are not shown earning or displaying any true gentility.[26] Other references are equally unflattering, often aligning shoemakers with marginal figures such as the rogue or tricky slave.[27]

Deloney makes hay out of such disparaging implications. By pretending that "the gentle craft" is meant to be taken in earnest and taking it as his title, Deloney magnifies shoemakers' praiseworthy attributes. In his text, the identification of shoemakers with poverty and low birth is an occasion to emphasize their humility and modesty and to show that these are "gentle" virtues that noblemen and gentlemen in disguise absorb precisely by putting themselves in the abject role of shoemaker. He makes much of their reputation as "good fellowes," known for liberality or generosity. Deloney does retain the popular notion of shoemakers as roguish and tricky; his shoemakers, including Simon Eyre and even the sainted Crispin brothers, repeatedly scheme their way out of trouble and outwit authority figures to get ahead. But their tricky means are recast in *The Gentle Craft* as advancing virtuous and beneficial ends, first, for the shoemaking fraternity, but also for London and the English nation.

The Gentle Craft also makes use of the reputation that shoemakers had for intellectualism. This perception may have been fed by their supposed physical weakness, often taking the form of lameness (adapted by Dekker in *The Shoemaker's Holiday*'s journeyman Ralph), which yields a sense that shoemakers succeed by virtue of their wits rather than physical strength. E. J. Hobsbawm and Joan Wallach Scott argue that the reputation of shoemakers for cerebral sophistication manifested itself in higher than usual rates of literacy, leading the authors to speculate that the "physically undemanding" nature of the work allowed plenty of time for shoemakers to read aloud in the group setting of the workshop.[28] It is plausible to imagine *The Gentle Craft* being read in this collective fashion. At the very least, the supposition that shoemakers are literate allows Deloney to strengthen his case for the gentility of his shoemakers.

The depiction of shoemakers as literate also connects to a broader image of their aesthetic facility, which most often took the form of the "merry shoemaker" motif. A stock figure in sixteenth-century print, the "merry shoemaker" was liable to break into song or dance—and to provide entertainment for royalty—at the slightest provocation. In the tale of *King Henry the VIII and a Cobler*—published in 1598, but possibly known to Deloney in earlier versions—the cobbler "began to be merry, and fell a singing his old Songs and Catches, which pleased the King very much, and made him laugh heartily."[29] Likewise, at the end of the prose romance *The famous Hystory off George a Greene*, "the shoo makers came and presented the Kinnge wth a coontry morryce dance . . . wch was so well ordered it mch pleased him."[30] Watt observes that it was not only in fiction that shoemakers had a reputation as performers; she cites evidence that "groups of craftsmen traveled as 'common Players of

Enterludes' during the spring and summer months" and that on at least one occasion the civic authorities in London were bothered enough by craftsmen ballad singers, especially tailors and shoemakers, that they issued a statute forbidding them to sing for profit.[31] In a move that Dekker would amplify for the theater, Deloney borrowed from historical and literary precedents to emphasize that shoemakers' musical and theatrical performances were a socially inclusive form of service, one that could cater to audiences from the king down to village inhabitants participating in guild pageants or Londoners gathering in public spaces.[32]

The Gentle Craft makes clear that the merry performances of shoemakers actively produce civic, religious, and nationalistic values. Caxton's *Golden Legend,* a Catholic hagiography informed by the conflict between Christian Britain and imperial Rome, is adapted by Deloney into generalized Christian mythology that the text represents as formative for the English nation. In this sense, the shoemakers' service has a more lofty aim than the making or selling of shoes, and the objects of their service are more expansive than individual masters or consumers. In suggesting that they ultimately serve such weighty causes as the city, the nation, or the Christian faith, Deloney endows "the gentle craft" with moral seriousness and power. Whatever the more equivocal features of shoemakers' reputations, Deloney could rely on readers having in mind a repertoire of images, which he highlights, exploits, plays down, and otherwise shapes into figures who are heroic, but also accessible, exemplars of service.

Deloney's shoemakers establish an alternative to the catastrophic telos outlined in the didactic literature of service. Deloney borrows many of his proverbial "truths" about servants and masters from this literature, but he also interrogates its often polarizing stance toward changes in service. In the introduction, I explored this literature's pervasive concern over the decay of hierarchical principles and its assertion that a crisis in service was pushing individuals out of service altogether. Michael Neill has summarized the condition of the "masterless" man as "something of an oxymoron, since service was presented as a condition so universal that properly to be a man was to be somebody's 'man.'"[33] The intimate relationship between service and subjectivity shifts in *The Gentle Craft.* In Deloney's fiction, it is possible to be both somebody's man and one's own. His stories about shoemakers accommodate both a respect for hierarchy and the desire for self-advancement. While stressing the importance of traditional traits such as loyalty and obedience, Deloney repeatedly gives examples of shoemakers who serve with their eyes cast both toward their masters and toward the main chance. Crispine and

Crispianus, princes disguised as apprentices, "both bent their whole minds to please their Master and Dame, refusing nothing that was put to them to doe" (119) even as they conceal their identities and their agendas. Deloney's shoemakers are always careful to situate themselves within a hierarchical framework, though their objectives stretch the limits of that framework and demonstrate its weaknesses. Far from predicting dramatic downward mobility, the canny, commercial self-interest of these craftsmen foretells their success, carrying with it a romantic, and yet also quotidian, vision of how the servant might redefine himself in a nascent capitalist economy. Yet, in *The Gentle Craft* the agency of servants is not only personal but societal as well. In promoting themselves, Deloney suggests, his heroes also promote the interests of the fraternity of shoemakers, which takes on a collective identity to which the text continually returns.

"A Shoemaker's Son Is a Prince Born"

The first two episodes of *The Gentle Craft*, part 1, establish mythological origins for shoemakers in the institution of the Cordwainers' Guild of London. In so doing, they trace an intertwined progression in generic hybridity and paradigms of service. With a doubled mandate of idealizing the history of shoemakers and justifying their present ambitions, these sections exhibit their diverse textual forebears even as they establish new generic and social arrangements. Deloney mythologizes artisanal history, but he also directs himself squarely to finding thematic and formal resolutions to the problems of service in the late sixteenth-century economy.

The tale of Sir Hugh and Winifred, which launches *The Gentle Craft*, depends on generic conversions, as the text absorbs and eventually transcends a spent chivalric romance narrative, a usurpation that signals Deloney's concern with elevating shoemaking service. The most explicit sources for the story are *The Story of Saint Ursula and the Virgins* and *The Life of Saint Winifred* from William Caxton's *Golden Legend* (1483), a translated collection of hagiographies that was reprinted numerous times in the sixteenth century. His service in love spurned by the pious Winifred, Sir Hugh becomes a knight in search of an errand; in a pale echo of Odysseus, he flees sirens and fights Cyclops, but he achieves no real distinction in battle or bravery. Chivalric and military service, not to mention courtly service, fail him. Whereas in Caxton's narrative the turning point is Ethereus's conversion to Christianity, in Deloney's it is an occupational conversion in which Hugh plays the shoemaker's role, implying that "the gentle craft" not only parallels religious service but also fulfills and perhaps even supplements it. While Winifred is persecuted for her Christian beliefs, Hugh "wrought in a Shoomakers shop, having learned that trade through the courteous directions of a kind Iourney-man, where hee remained the space of one whole yeere; in which time hee had gotten himselfe good apparell, and every thing comely and decent" (105). In undertaking this condensed apprenticeship, Sir Hugh performs a native resistance to the forces of foreign and heathen tyranny, an activism rooted in the quotidian labor of the shoemaker rather than in the travails of the wandering knight. As part of his and the text's conversion, Sir Hugh becomes a merry shoemaker, enthusiastically adopting the shoemakers' propensity for making music as he first composes a "pleasant Ditty" to Winifred and then, after joining her in prison, pens a ballad in praise of the gentle craft (106–7). It is no coincidence that Deloney was best known before 1596 as "the principal ballad maker in England."[34] Deloney's use of the merry shoemaker trope is weighted with an image of the author working through his ballad experience to construct a prose narrative.

It is in Hugh's ballad that *The Gentle Craft* first makes the claim that shoemaking ennobles both shoemakers and aristocrats. The ballad proclaims of Hugh's brethren shoemakers that "their minds doe mount in courtesie," and "their bodies are for Chivalrie" (108.4, 6), making them emblems of aristocratic heroism. The craft is a balm for gentlemen and noblemen in dire straits: "Yea sundry Princes sore distrest,/Shall seeke for succour by this Trade:/Whereby their greifes shall be redrest," while also providing an avenue for advancement: "And many men of fame likewise,/Shall from the Gentle Craft arise" (108.10–12; 14–15). Are, as seems likely, the "men of fame" a class of common shoemakers who make good on the trade's gentle reputation to ascend to positions of social prominence? Could the "Princes" also be the "men of fame"? Both possibilities are left intact by the ballad, and indeed the second comes into play in the succeeding episode. The lesson seems to be that even as gentlemen impart their nobility to shoemaking, they are ennobled by their participation in a gentle trade. Like other ballads in *The Gentle Craft*, Hugh's song offers an alternative, yet complementary, structure of narration. It provides a mode of reflection that in its celebratory premise is both flexible and inclusive, recasting Hugh's chivalric tale in familiar, homegrown terms. At the same time, by incorporating verse in a larger prose narrative, Deloney demonstrates the ability of prose fiction to appropriate and digest a variety of genres.[35] In order to portray service as mobile and unifying, the episode integrates discourses associated with divergent practices of service and shows the ways in which, like Sir Hugh and the journeymen shoemakers, they transform one another to forge a communal identity.

The narrative of Sir Hugh emphasizes his musical and literary performances; the next episode, which recounts the story of two princes and brothers, Crispine and Crispianus, who disguise themselves as shoemakers' apprentices, features performances that are theatrical and dissimulative. Shoemaking is represented early in the tale as a refuge for the young princes, whose mother fears that if they remain at court, they will be enslaved in a foreign land.[36] Playing on contemporary anxieties about Turks taking Christians into slavery, Deloney sets up "service" as a fortunate alternative: "Therfore suiting your selves in honest habites, seeke some poore service to sheild you from mischance, seeing necessity hath priviledged those places from Tyranny" (116).[37] The "privilege" of the shoemaker's hidden "places" derives ostensibly from their lowliness, which makes them invisible to the emperor's powerful eye; and yet, these places enjoy other kinds of privilege as well. Just as Sir Hugh's song promises that "many men of fame likewise,/Shall from the gentle craft arise," the Queen forecasts: "And so (my sons) the gracious Heavens may one day raise you to deserved dignity and honour" (116). Deloney overlays two mutually mimetic narratives, one in the romance tradition of disguised royalty and the other exploring the theme of meritorious upward mobility. What allows for the generic doubleness is the ambiguity attached to "deserved," which might imply either birth or worth as its source.

Consistent with this doubleness, the text merges the masquing of Crispine and Crispianus as apprentices with a historically grounded scenario, in which young men roam the countryside in search of work. The brothers identify themselves with this group when seeking an apprenticeship: "We are two poore boyes that want service, stript from our friends by the fury of these warres, and therefore are wee enforced succourlesse to crave service in any place" (118). Because this situation would have been familiar to many of Deloney's readers, the fact that neither the shoemaker, his wife, nor the journeymen question the brothers' story becomes a believable detail rather than a fantastic element. Crispine and Crispianus reward their master and mistress's munificence by performing the part of ideal apprentices. And yet, in keeping their princely identities hidden, they also live precisely the kind of double life against which conduct books on service vigilantly admonish. Although the shoemaker and his wife believe they "looke with honest true faces" (118), this transparency is an illusion. In concealing one set of purposes behind another, Crispine and Crispianus evoke the purported sinfulness of eye-service, defined in Ephesians as "seruice to the eye, as men pleasers," and the earned mistrust of servants' intentions.[38] Crispine almost fulfills the cultural fears for a canny and self-interested servant: on the sly, he woos, impregnates, and clandestinely marries (in that order) the Roman emperor's daughter. Apprentices in early modern England were forbid-den to marry during the tenure of their apprenticeship, and a master was held responsible if his servant fathered a child out of wedlock.[39] And indeed, the first reaction of Crispine's mistress to the news seems rooted in contemporary realities: "Ah thou whorson villaine, thou hast undone thy selfe, how wilt thou doe now? . . . Wee shall lose a good servant, so we shall" (131). The knowledge that Crispine is no ordinary apprentice threatens to disappear at this point in the narrative.

Crispine's recuperation is accomplished through a performance that inserts the disguised prince into a circulatory economy of shoemaking. Deloney seems largely to have invented this part of the story, in which Crispine not only has a sexual relationship with the princess Ursula but also becomes her favored shoemaker, all while being granted "oversight of his houshold, which place he guided with such discretion, as therby he got both the good will of his Master, and the love of the houshold" (126–27). His dual ascent through service in his master's household and through marriage to a royal woman who is also his client signifies the multiplicity of the apprentice's practices of service and the cultural nar-ratives told about them. Mihoko Suzuki has argued that the difficulty in sixteenth-century England in moving from the position of apprentice or journeyman to that of master translates into a fantasy of marrying the mistress, a device that Deloney is better known for using in *Jack of Newbury*, in which Jack effects the transition from servant to mas-ter by marrying his master's widow.[40] In *The Gentle Craft*, the widow has become a virginal princess, a metamorphosis of the common into the extraordinary that parallels the metamorphosis of apprentice into prince. There is a surface contradiction between a romance of promotion through erotic satisfaction and a mundane tale of promotion through persistently diligent labor, and yet in Crispine's story the two strands coexist comfortably.

Deloney strikingly juxtaposes courtly and commercial practices of service in narrating the mutual seduction of Crispine and Ursula. The rhetoric revolves around the crafting of shoes: "Now (quoth she) Ile shew thee, they are too low something in the instep; also the heel is bad, and besides that, they are too strait in the toes. You shall have a paire made (said he) shal fit you better, for none shall set a stitch in them but mine owne selfe" (121). Shoemaking here is not simply an elaborate metaphor for sex but the basis for the lovers' union. Crispine woos Ursula with his ability to generate a product made specially to fit her specifications and desires. Their interaction evokes the erotic dimension of retail service, particularly salient when the commodity is an expensive luxury item. An elaborate dance between shoemaker and client, in which desire is anticipated, created, and negotiated, is envisioned as part of the shoemaker's service. Recognizing the admixture of elements in his service, Ursula duly rewards Crispine, not only with her love but with "a handfull of gold" and a promise: "From henceforth let no man make my shooes but thy self" (122). The skilled artisanal servant makes a good husband. It is also true that the female customer is often conflated with capital and commodities; the princess appropriates this equation but also tries to dematerialize it, promising Crispine his "portion" in marriage: "thou shalt have a bag full of rare vertues." His joking refutation is telling, however: "Tru(e)ly Madam ... such coines goe not currant among Tanners; and I know, if I should goe therewith to the Market, it will buy me no soale leather" (123). As Ursula attempts to return to the language of the courtly romance, Crispine continues to insist on the importance of capital. In this scene, at least, Crispine sees both shoemaking and marriage in terms of commercial considerations. To ensure that both ventures are profitable, Crispine must perpetually circulate goods and capital. The text thus distances Crispine from the noncirculatory version of nobility into which he was born, while also separating him from the household servant whose position, also noncirculatory, depends on a personalized hierarchy.

While Crispine advances his position in a kind of courtly service sector, Crispianus is redefining military service through the identity of the apprentice. Deloney's praise of the shoemaker's valor on the battlefield counters what Linda Ann Hutjens has described as a tendency for early modern dramas to depict shoemakers as pathetic conscripts and "incompetent soldiers" (11).[41] By featuring Crispianus engaged in spectacular military exploits, Deloney popularizes a literary tradition in which the apprentice takes on the role of chivalric hero for the English nation. The seventeenth-century ballad and chapbook story, variously titled *The honour of an Apprentice of London* (1664) and *The Famous History of the Valiant London Prentice* (1693), may have appeared in print prior to *The Gentle Craft* in forms now lost; alternatively, it may have been indebted to Deloney's fiction. The narrative tells of a young English apprentice who proves his courage and strength in battle against the Turks, a subject also treated in Richard Johnson's *The Nine Worthies*

(1592) and Thomas Heywood's *The Four Prentices of London* (1592–94).[42] The respective heroes of these texts revitalize chivalry, reversing the trajectory of Sir Hugh by infusing soldiering with the ethos of the craftsman, the tradesman, and the servant.[43] The genre of the apprentice hero is beholden to chivalric romance but not subsumed by it, for it remakes the service of the knight-errant in contact with the prosaic, and literally prose, forms that Deloney introduces.

In tracing the parallel rises of Crispine and Crispianus, Deloney strengthens the theme that shoemaking provides a noble heritage, surpassing that of title and property.[44] According to romance conventions, the revelation of royal birth restores political, economic, and social order, but in this episode, the apprentice shoemaker generates a new order, one in which he is fit to be a prince, while the prince proves himself worthy to rule by serving an apprenticeship in both war and shop. Deloney complicates the structure of romance by portraying the brothers as "earning" rather than simply recovering their birthrights. "A Shoomakers son is a Prince borne" is the proverb that emerges at the end of the tale, as the child of Crispine and Ursula is revealed as being of royal parentage. The phrase has a double function, as do so many other examples of social and textual exchange in *The Gentle Craft*. On the one hand, it refers to a socially conservative closure, in which once the brothers' identities are known, "all the controversie was ended" (137); in this sense, Crispine's son literally is "a prince born." On the other hand, it confirms that shoemakers deserve the same status as the nobility, a move that diminishes the significance of birth.[45] The textual and social exchanges signified by the proverb and by the episode as a whole suggest the emergence of a circulatory economy of service, one that Deloney invites readers to enter from vantage points ranging from aristocrat to apprentice.

Courtly, military, household, and commercial paradigms of service all remain active at the end of the narrative of Crispine and Crispianus, but it is telling that the final emphasis is on the celebration of Saint Crispin's Day by future generations of shoemakers, and in particular, on the ballad that retells the brothers' story in simple verse. The song downplays their royal birth and reinterprets Crispine as an ordinary shoemaker:

> Her Shoomaker most daintily
> had got her Maidenhead.
> But he at length so wisely wrought,
> as does the Story tell:
> Her fathers right good will he got,
> and every thing was well. (139.1–6)

This version of the story invites readers to see themselves reflected in Crispine and Crispine in them. The distance between Crispine, Crispianus, and their shoemaker brethren is elided once again with the episode's ballad frame. As at the end of Sir Hugh's episode, priority is placed on a collective identification that crosses social and generic boundaries.

The most pointed meaning of "A Shoomakers son is a Prince borne" comes into play in the final episode of part 1, where the story of Simon Eyre tackles both the social mobility and the nascent class consciousness developed more tentatively in the first two tales. Here, for the first time, Deloney locates service in an openly urban and commercial realm. The text depicts Eyre, a figure with roots in chronicle histories, as using his considerable aesthetic skills to dive into the city's burgeoning capitalist economy. Precisely because Simon Eyre's dramatic rise was out of reach for most apprentices and servants, his story becomes a romance about and for them, one that transforms insecurity into mobile opportunity. Even as the episode seems to pit individual advancement against the interests of the fraternity of shoemakers, it announces their reconciliation.

Simon Eyre's trajectory highlights the shoemaker's ability to move adeptly between paradigms of service. Like Crispine and Crispianus, Simon Eyre seems at first to have walked straight off the pages of a conduct manual. One of the story's important influences is the legend of Dick Whittington, the mercer's apprentice who became lord mayor and who was the subject of laudatory ballads.[46] Steve Rappaport notes that one of the morals of the Whittington story as told in early modern print is that following the rules pays off: "It was *because* of these acts of obedience that he won fortune and fame."[47] By the same logic, Deloney takes care to show that Simon Eyre adheres meticulously to the bonds of apprenticeship; he takes delight in his work and fulfills the full term of his obligation to his master before making a suitable marriage and setting up his own shop. These traits are introduced early on, when the young apprentice finds himself short of money at a weekly breakfast for apprentices. Eyre makes an oath to his comrades that if they will "pardon me at this time, and excuse me for my part of the shot, I do here vow unto you, that if ever I come to be Lord Maior of this City, I will give a breakfast unto all the Prentices in *London*" (140). Simon Eyre's story unfolds toward the conclusion that Eyre prophesizes, and he ultimately fulfills his promise. At its close, the narrative circles back to its beginnings, confirming a hierarchical reciprocity between the positions of servant and master.

Side by side with this portrait of the conventionally respectful servant is a story of how the shoemaker uses aesthetic service to transcend hierarchical constraints and reap the benefits of participation in the new service sector. Eyre's opportunity is spurred by the chance docking of a ship "laden with all kind of Lawnes and Cambrickes, and other linnen cloth: which commodities at that time were in London very scant, and exceeding deare" (141). Because he lacks capital, he is compelled to repeat his earlier pledge that he will return the investment of others with interest, with the difference that now he secures the necessary investment by assuming two disguises—first that of an alderman's factor and then that of an alderman himself, exactly the role he hopes to inhabit. Eyre's wife assures him that the absence of ready capital should not hinder his ability to make a deal with the ship's captain: "Every man that beholds a man in the face, knows not what he hath in his purse" (144). She substitutes the purse for the heart, economic interiority for spiritual, and as she does so suggests that the servant's interior privacy is not a sin but an advantage. At the same time, she acknowledges the power of aesthetics: although the purse is recognized as the location of real value, the face, as a synecdoche for appearance, attains value through its ability to deceive the spectator. In order for Eyre to step fully into a new economic and social role, Deloney suggests, he must first imitate it. While service manuals derogate the servant's capacity to mutate, manipulate, and emulate, *The Gentle Craft* turns these into positive attributes by indicating that service exists in relation to the marketplace as well as in relation to a patriarchal master. Having complicated the objectives and objects of service, Deloney invites his readers to interpret Eyre's dissembling as both necessary and appropriate for participation in a capitalist economy.

As his advancement progresses, Eyre distances himself from the running of his household and becomes a "Merchant" (149), a position that gives him entrée into the economic and civic elite. Without seeming contradiction, however, the text imagines that Eyre's commercial service enhances the interests of apprentices and shoemakers, rather than threatening them through a disregard of traditional values. The final lines of part 1 gesture to the future: "Then after this, Sir Simon Eyer builded *Leaden-Hall,* appointing that in the middest thereof, there should be a Market kept every Monday for Leather, where the Shoomakers of *London,* for their more ease, might buy of the Tanners, without seeking any further" (169). The embrace of the market economy is the culmination of a gradual shift from the rural pastoral milieu of the Sir Hugh episode to the courtly and military settings of Crispine and Crispianus to an urban environment in which service is ever less centered on the servant-master relationship and more on relationships derived from the market. The "ease" of commodity and capital circulation at Leaden-Hall is presented as the outgrowth of Eyre's success and, by extension, of his facility at maneuvering within a circulatory economy. Eyre's material achievements, wrought through his adapting and adaptable service, ultimately redound to the benefit of the shoemakers who will use the new market.

Deloney generates a circulatory form for prose fiction as well, allowing the chivalric and courtly contexts of romance to be reworked under the influence of texts like John Stow's urban chronicle, *Survey of London* (1598).[48] Stow's Eyre is a draper, not a shoemaker, and his philanthropic tendencies are recounted briefly: "*Simon Eyre* Draper, Maior 1446. builded the Leaden hall for a common Garner of corne to the use of the Citie, and left five thousand markes to charitable uses."[49] Deloney interprets Stow's allusion to economic reciprocity broadly, suggesting that Eyre's success in the service sector provides both immediate benefits and a template for the ordinary shoemaker. He also absorbs from Stow a framing of the tale as a recent and accessible history. Now abandoning altogether the traditional romance contexts for heroic service, Deloney ventures—like Eyre—into a milieu where heroism is a decidedly quotidian affair. The environs of the Conduit, the shoemaker's shop, and the lord mayor's house become the sites for a romance of service and commerce. In contrast to the preceding episodes, the narrative requires no superimposition of apprentice upon nobleman, or shoemaking upon chivalry. One straightforward, unadorned story is told in this final episode, and yet the fantasy of social transformation occurring as a result of a transformed and transforming service is undeniably acute.

Whereas in the preceding episodes separate intertexts can be identified fairly easily, in the Simon Eyre episode genres are more completely assimilated. It is surprising at first to discover that the tale lacks the ballads and songs so prominent elsewhere in part 1, but it is as if these texts have finally been so thoroughly digested that their visible traces have disappeared. In the transformation of service and social identity, stretching from Sir Hugh to Simon Eyre, part 1 of *The Gentle Craft* thus allegorizes the process by which prose fiction gains a formal identity. Rather than tracing the progress of one shoemaker throughout, Deloney uses an episodic strategy that encourages selective and flexible reading. At the same time, the structure invites extended, progressive reading, as each narrative imitates and alters its predecessor, reiterating generic mixtures and adding new components. The text enacts the narrative of its own development in this accumulative, gradual fashion, one that stresses the reconciliation and coexistence, not exclusion and replacement, of paradigms of service and literary genres.

Deloney offers his readers an image of the text itself as seen through the lens of service. He poses himself and his text as servants in a commercial economy, occupying positions analogous to those of the shoemaker heroes who fill the book's pages. The work's title refers to the craft of writing as well as to the craft of shoemaking, with the implication that the author who writes within a marketplace rapidly growing in influence faces many of the same potential rewards and challenges as do Deloney's fictional shoemakers. In both cases, servants are increasingly free, even obligated, to construct a reputable, profitable self-image. Both also have the opportunity to construct images of their "masters," which in Deloney's case are called into self-recognition as mobile subjects and members of a reading public.

"Play the Shoemaker": *The Shoemaker's Holiday*

Dekker shared with Deloney an abiding interest in fashioning a public aesthetic. Indeed, Dekker had considerable experience designing public entertainments that could appeal across ideological, social, and economic divides.[50] *The Shoemaker's Holiday* was no exception. It was performed by the Admiral's Men at the Rose Theatre in 1599 and in front of the queen at court on January 1, 1600.[51] The play's early performance history represents the bridging of audiences, readers, and groups of consumers that is reflected in the play.

Dekker's direction of *The Shoemaker's Holiday* to several constituencies is clear in the first printed edition of the play, dated 1600. The prefatory matter includes not only the prologue delivered at the court performance but also a dedication to shoemakers which demonstrates Dekker's appeal to a readership broader than the exclusive court audience implied by its prologue. The dedication does not, as Deloney's does, directly target the shoemakers' guild, but it does work on a guild principle by encouraging shoemakers of varied ranks to feel included in its address: "To all good fellows, professors of the gentle craft, of what degree soever."[52] It calls readers "kind gentlemen and honest boon companions," a phrasing that stresses the inherent gentility of shoemaking and also implies a companionate bond between playwright and readers. The emphasis throughout is on mirth and merriment: "the mirth and pleasant matter by her Highness graciously accepted," "the merriments that passed in Eyre's house," and "nothing is purposed but mirth. Mirth lengtheneth long life, which with all other blessings I heartily wish you" (5–6, 15, 18–20). In these repeated allusions, Dekker implies the

play's allegiance with jests, ballads, and other popular forms of entertainment meant to be consumed and enjoyed. Among other coming
attractions listed is the scene in which Lacy "served the Mayor and his
household with shoes" (14). "To serve" has the double connotation of
producing shoes for the lord mayor and serving him with a trick, a pun
that makes Lacy into a jestbook figure. The preview concludes with a
reminder of the "two merry three-man's songs" that were also printed
in the prefatory matter of the book (17), an allusion to the shoemakers' reputation for singing in public. The dedication announces the play's
solidarity with a set of textual discourses with which artisanal servants
were associated not only as audiences but as producers, too. A readership or audience that contains such servants will be capable of its own
aesthetic interventions.

The workmanlike prose of the dedication stands in marked contrast
to the elaborate verse of the prologue, "as it was pronounced before
the Queen's Majesty." A footnote in the New Mermaids edition speculates, on the basis of "prostrate thus" (8), that the whole cast might have
knelt onstage while one player delivered the verses, an image that fits the
tone of exaggerated deference that the prologue strikes (5n5). Whereas
the dedication suggests that the servant is liable to trick the master, the
prologue returns to a neofeudal paradigm of service. The players are
Elizabeth's "meanest vassals," who fear "to sink into the bottom of dis-
grace/By our imperfect pastimes" (4, 5, 6–7). In proffering these images
of humility, even abasement, the prologue suggests that the play is a serious, if unworthy, labor of service, designed to affirm Queen Elizabeth's
singular mastery through the power of her "celestial breath" to "send
us life, or sentence us to death" (17, 18). The verses also support the
traditional understanding that servants are subjectively dispossessed.
The players are totally dependent on the queen's favor: "to ourselves
ourselves no help can bring" (11). With this plea, the prologue invites
the queen to position herself as the absent center of the play's urban
location. Even though the king of England does not appear as a character until nearly the end, the prologue implicitly puts the city under the
queen's royal governance.

A few moments in the prologue complicate the queen's mastery and
redistribute at least some agency to servants. First, there is the subtle
acknowledgment that as a woman, Elizabeth has a layered identity, for
she is presented not only as the feudal lord but also as a prototype for
the Petrarchan courtly mistress, "dear goddess, wonder of all eyes," with
"life-breathing stars your sun-like eyes" capable of bestowing on her servants "One gracious smile" (4, 16, 17). Such images make the queen as

much the object of the players' gaze as she is their spectator. Dekker insinuates that a royal audience is not safe from direct engagement: servant players can admire—and even stare at—the queen, and only at her peril may her "saint-like ears" "refuse the tribute of our begging tongues" (12, 14). Elizabeth is a mistress, then, who has something in common with other playgoers: she has at least one role to play, if not more.

The dedication and prologue propose two genres of service, the first based on apprenticeship and guild fraternity and the second on court patronage and a patriarchal hierarchy. In some ways, then, the challenge Dekker set himself was to develop a dramatic form that could reconcile two such disparate approaches. Yet, with its suggestion that servants and masters intermingle both onstage and in the audience, the front matter provides its own solution. The mutual imitations of servants and masters break down boundaries between the fictions onstage and the "real" social dynamics within the theater. The play imagines itself participating in a fantasy of community in which the theater acts not only as the forum but also the agent of social cohesion. In *The Shoemaker's Holiday*, Dekker's public aesthetic is one that contains competing genres of service.

If Dekker's dramatic form accommodates multiple genres of service, the play's shoemakers are generically capacious as well. To serve successfully in *The Shoemaker's Holiday* is to perform exchanges of identity that have both textual and economic registers. The main exchange, which occurs between the shoemaker Simon Eyre and the aristocrat Rowland Lacy, makes both characters profitable by virtue of, not despite, their generically rich role-playing. What matters more than the original social position of the shoemaker is his ability to circulate, an aesthetic act that simultaneously endows him with economic agency.[53] Dekker's shoemakers learn to represent themselves as capital and thereby learn how to multiply their capital.

Although an economy predicated on displacements and replacements might result in social dislocation, Dekker imagines instead that shoemakers' exchanges produce a cohesive community in which all subjects have the opportunity to play servants and to profit. Or, rather, we can say that Dekker almost expels the threat of dislocation, for in some moments, and especially in those that feature the journeyman Ralph, Dekker provides a glimpse of the abjection and exclusion that might confront servants in the new economy. The play thus demonstrates liabilities as well as rewards in the growing interdependence of aesthetics and capital. Metadramatically, too, Dekker envisages the rich possibilities of exploiting this connection, but he also sees clearly the vulnerability of the theater's, and especially the playwright's, identifications with service.

It has been obvious to most readers of *The Shoemaker's Holiday* that Simon Eyre benefits from imitating and impersonating his social superiors, for by doing so he gets the credit necessary to transform himself from an artisan to a merchant and from thence into a position of civic authority. Less obvious are the benefits that the aristocrat, Sir Rowland Lacy, gains in playing the shoemaker. Yet if we want to understand the far-reaching claims that Dekker makes for service, we need to pay attention to the ways in which elite subjects gain new purchase in capitalist economies by performing service roles. In developing the Lacy disguise plot, Dekker followed in Deloney's footsteps: Lacy occupies the niche filled in *The Gentle Craft* by Sir Hugh and Crispine and Crispianus. Both texts participated in a broader literary interrogation of mastery, which as I have argued in previous chapters was often embodied in the master who imitates his servant. What Dekker makes explicit is that when the master expands his performative range, he benefits not only subjectively but economically, too.[54] As in Shakespeare's *The Two Gentlemen of Verona*, discussed in chapter 1, performances of service do not preclude performances of mastery but prove mutually enhancing. The dramatic logic in *The Shoemaker's Holiday* is additive. Thus, Dekker shows Lacy cultivating a layered persona, at once servant and master, which speaks to several audiences simultaneously and in the process invokes a heterogeneous theatrical public.

Lacy's soliloquy early in the play explains that he is inventing the persona of a journeyman Dutch shoemaker, Hans, so that he can be near his forbidden lover, Rose Oatley. The speech is phrased as appeals to different constituents in the audience. He begins by evoking Ovidian metamorphosis: "How many shapes have gods and kings devised/Thereby to compass their desirèd loves!" (3.1–2). His assumed role merely "clothe[s] his cunning" (3.4), shrouding a set of intentions and desires that remains unchanged. It is love that has driven Lacy to "change/High birth to bareness, and a noble mind/To the mean semblance of a shoemaker!" (3.10–12). The imagery allows a courtly audience to comprehend Lacy's shoemaking performance as a version of pastoral masquing, the gentleman dressed in shepherd's weeds to court a woman below his station. In this reading, he dresses the craft with his still fundamentally aristocratic presence. But the soliloquy also gives an audience in which there were numbers of artisans and apprentices reason to believe that by performing the shoemaker's role, Lacy is receiving an education in a new urban gentility.[55] He says, "I know the trade," and announces his intention to work with Eyre. And he ends with a populist motto for shoemaking: "Do Fortune what she can,/the Gentle Craft is living for a man!" (3.23–24). Although Lacy regards the labors of shoemaking simply as a way to while away the time not spent wooing Rose, those same labors become an important source for his aesthetic and economic development. In fact, his uncle, the Earl of Lincoln, discloses that Lacy first learned the shoe-making trade in Wittenberg as a result of having squandered his uncle's money abroad and become a "bankrupt presence" (1.28). Shoemaking is presented as a viable economic alternative to the cycle of inheritance and consumption that characterizes the aristocracy. The soliloquy thus offers a dual impression—Lacy is performing a low station; Lacy is earning a more authentic basis for high station—which brings together generic influences associated with elite and more popular traditions in the com-pact form of a single speech.

As Hans, Lacy enters a world that his aristocratic family adamantly opposes, in terms that conflate erotic and commercial pursuits with aesthetic artifice. Lacy's uncle, the Earl of Lincoln, forbids him from courting Rose Oatley, the daughter of the lord mayor: "I would not have you cast an amorous eye/Upon so mean a project as the love/Of a gay, wanton, painted citizen" (1.75–77). The reference to Rose as a "proj-ect" evokes the word's definition as "a practical scheme for exploiting material things."[56] Lincoln's description makes Rose the capitalist enter-prise and the thing exploited, both equally unfitted to a nobleman. She becomes a totem of the artisanal and entrepreneurial service that Lacy practices as a shoemaker. She also becomes Lacy's client. As was the case with *The Gentle Craft*'s Ursula, the role of courtly mistress is changed by its interaction with commerce, though in Rose's case her position as the daughter of an elite citizen is already generically complex. The mixed courtly and commercial dynamics of service signal both her dis-empowerment (she is commoditized and exchanged) and empowerment (she tells her shoemaker lover how to serve her). While Lacy's disapprov-ing uncle objects to the performed erotics of commercial service, Rose is drawn to them, as she urges Lacy to stay in character: "Come, come, be Hans still—play the shoemaker./Pull on my shoe" (15.27–28). In the same vein, her father, Oatley, addresses "Hans": "Fit my daughter well, and she shall please well" (15.34–35). The double entendres suggest that the eroticism of the shoemaker's service is marketable and transforma-tive of the shoemaker's financial and romantic status. Moreover, the pun on "fit" implies that Lacy's service achieves an aesthetic decorum pleas-ing to audiences. This kind of decorum results from a generic and social mixing frowned upon in early modern poetic theory and disparaged by

Dekker's blocking figures of authority from either side of the courtly/civic divide.

Lacy's downwardly mobile impersonation is especially effective when it joins with Simon Eyre's upwardly mobile one. Their performances converge in Eyre's disguise as an alderman, through which Eyre "earns" the good credit necessary to purchase the ship's contents that make his fortune. By arranging the meeting for Eyre and lending him the funds to use as a deposit for the goods, Lacy precipitates Eyre's rapid climb through the city hierarchy, first to sheriff and ultimately to the lofty position of lord mayor. Lacy may be a false servant, but he also proves loyal, expedient, and creative, the kind of servant who not only fulfills his master's commands but in anticipating his master's desires also gives shape to them. In other words, Lacy is a prototype for the aesthetic servant, and although the audience knows that it's all an act, what matters for Eyre is that Lacy has the capital and plays the part. Acting as a go-between with the Dutch captain, Lacy stages a bravura performance of Hans, his alien shoemaker persona, to seal the deal. Just as Lacy does with the journeyman's subordinate position, so he puts to use the seeming disadvantage of foreign status. Historically, immigrant shoemakers attracted a great deal of antipathy from the shoemakers' guild, whose control over the industry they threatened.[57] But Dekker remakes the alien shoemaker as a theatrical role, defusing the threat and yet at the same time allowing Lacy to exploit the mimetic exchange of identity for his and Eyre's agendas. The success of his performance yields rewards not only for Eyre but for Lacy, too, who secures in Eyre a powerful new ally, on whom he calls later to secure a pardon from the king for his inappropriate marriage. Acting as a servant, Lacy assists both his master and himself in trying out alternative, potentially profitable identities.

Lacy's layering of servant and master, alien and native-born, artisanal and gentle adapts Deloney's sequential prose fiction to the simultaneity of dramatic image making. Brian Walsh and Jonathan Gil Harris have each commented on *The Shoemaker's Holiday*'s complicated temporality, the ways in which, Walsh says, the play locates the construction of historicity in a theatrical present, or the ways in which, according to Harris, the image of Ludgate conveys "competing temporal economies" that alternately assert historical continuity and rupture.[58] Lacy's synchronous performance as servant and master exemplifies the temporal conflations characteristic of Dekker's dramatic form. Thus, Lacy does not leave behind the position of the master when he adopts the persona of Hans, nor does Hans disappear once Lacy is again "himself" in the final scene. They remain mutually transforming, and disturbing, roles for Lacy, and as is appropriate for a text that uses the past as an image of the future, the play refuses to make an ultimate choice between these roles.

Temporal compression occurs as well in Simon Eyre's transforming impersonation. While Deloney outlined a series of steps that Eyre took to approach his rise in status—playing the alderman's factor and only later the alderman himself—Dekker dramatizes the process in a single scene in which Eyre's journeymen help costume him for the performance. When Eyre asks his men how he looks, Hodge responds, "Why, now you look like yourself, master!" and Firk adds that "my master looks like a threadbare cloak new turned and dressed. Lord, lord, to see what good raiment doth!" (7.114, 117–18). The alderman's costume has the power to make Eyre self-identical, as if Eyre's recognition of his true identity has to catch up with his clothing, instead of vice versa. Peter Stallybrass's now classic point that clothing in early modern England signified both lines of dependency and their violation resonates in Eyre's dressing up: "In the transfer of clothes, identities are transferred from an aristocrat to an actor, from an actor to a master, from a master to an apprentice."[59] Simon Eyre's costuming transgresses against hierarchy, and yet Dekker features it as a revelation of a new economy, in which the servant can achieve mastery by performing versatile roles. One of these roles is the commodity, as represented by the identification of Eyre with his "guarded gown and damask cassock" (105–6), a description which cannot help but remind us of the "cambric" (3), expensive white linen, included among the ship's luxury commodities that he purchases. In this scene, Eyre puts himself into economic circulation, consolidating in the visual image of his costume the fantasy that service can result in a transformation of identity. Given the fact that he dresses onstage, presumably Eyre wears his shoemaker's garb below his new gowns; his servant identity may be obscured, but it remains an informing presence, as the closing scenes work hard to show. Like Lacy's, Eyre's exchange of servant and master roles is not a onetime occurrence but an ongoing process. By the same circulatory logic, it is not that Eyre comes to occupy Lacy's place but rather that the place has itself been displaced: neither Lacy nor Eyre will play the master in a "pure" courtly or aristocratic mold.

Lacy and Eyre singly and jointly engage in exchanges wrought by aesthetic service. There is a third figure who participates in exchanges with each of them: the journeyman Ralph. In the dramatic structure of the play, Ralph is a foil not only to Eyre but also to Lacy. Both sets of foils juxtapose the play's fantasy of service with an understanding of its limitations. New alignments of wealth and status appear, but so do new patterns of stratification. Whereas Deloney uses the divergence of military service from shoemaking to trace parallel paths through heroic apprenticeship to nobility, Dekker uses it to widen an existing gulf between the aristocrat and the journeyman. Ironically, the gulf is widened by an exchange between them: Ralph essentially takes Lacy's place in the military, lacking the money and influence that enable Lacy to dodge his service. And Lacy literally takes Ralph's place as Eyre's journeyman. Their exchange puts Lacy into the circulatory economy and removes Ralph from it.

One important aspect of the exchange between Lacy and Ralph, then, is that it fails to yield the benefits for Ralph that it does for Lacy. Appropriately, it is Lacy who refuses the pleas of Simon Eyre and the other shoemakers to exempt Ralph from military service. Addressing Lacy, Firk says, "Truly, . . . you shall do God good service to let Ralph and his wife stay together" (1.138–39). But this model of service is not what Lacy has in mind: "Truly, my friends, it lies not in my power./The Londoners are pressed, paid and set forth/By the Lord Mayor. I cannot change a man" (1.146–48). The last phrase, in particular, takes on an ironic resonance, for "changing" is precisely what Lacy is doing throughout. Hearing this disingenuous answer, audiences would have affiliated Lacy with the trope of eye-service in the didactic literature and the connotations eye-service raised of the deceitful aesthetic servant. Lacy does not pattern his conduct on service to God; rather, as both aristocrat and journeyman, he is slippery, fraudulent, and self-serving. He is that against which the didactic literature of service stridently and repeatedly warns, but in the world of *The Shoemaker's Holiday*, his histrionic service combines with his access to capital to improve on his initial position in the play. Ralph, on the other hand, remains bound to patriarchal service relations that especially in the opening scene fail to protect him.

Deloney treats war as an occasion for Crispianus to show the heroic potential of the apprentice shoemaker, but Dekker does not represent the wars in France at all, let alone give Ralph the chance to earn glory in battle. Despite Eyre's jocular comparisons of Ralph to legendary war heroes such as Hector of Troy and a member of "Prince Arthur's Round Table" (167–68), Ralph's military service does not elevate him to the status of an apprentice hero but simply excludes him from London's commercial economy. In Dekker's adaptation, England's pride revolves around the commercial and mercantile practices situated in London. Military service is no avenue for glory or for profit; it is simply the fate of those who cannot avoid it.

Ralph's sojourn in the wars is also contrasted to his master Simon Eyre's rapid ascent into civic government, which occurs mostly during

Ralph's absence. The contrast between Ralph's downward spiral and Eyre's upward mobility registers the historical discrepancies between, on the one hand, medium or large householders, who, like Eyre at the beginning of the play, owned an establishment with a number of journeymen and apprentices working under them, and on the other hand, journeymen, who, like Ralph, had little control over the terms of their employment and often little hope of attaining the status of master or householder. Though journeymen were not subject to the same strictures as apprentices, they were semidependent members of the households who remained under the authority of their masters.[60] Steve Rappaport's research on brewers, butchers, and coopers in the 1550s indicates that for almost two-thirds of journeymen in these occupations, "journeywork was not only the beginning but also the end of their occupational careers."[61] In light of this evidence, neither Ralph's adherence to patriarchal mastery nor his flirtation with unemployment is unlikely. Dekker reveals a break between material possession and dispossession that refuses to be elided, notwithstanding the powerful fantasy of such elision that the play proposes.[62] Patently more improbable than Ralph's travails is the double ascent of Eyre and "Hans," and this is precisely where Dekker suggests that the theater and theatricality enter, resolving historical contradictions between the servant's position and profit on the level of individual character as well as on the formal and institutional levels of drama to which I will return.

The plot of *The Shoemaker's Holiday* sets out to reintegrate dispossessed servants like Ralph into the circulatory commercial economy it depicts. Such reintegration is necessary in order for Dekker to portray convincingly the play's fictional community as a model for a public audience. Service, the play needs to insist, creates mobility not at the cost of common welfare but to its advantage. To that end, Jane, Ralph's wife, makes a successful transition to a form of service suited to the new economy. Ralph asks his master and mistress to provide for Jane while he is away: "As you have always been a friend to me,/So in mine absence think upon my wife" (1.203–4). Eyre promises to set Jane to work at spinning and weaving in his household. But there is no further word of her—she disappears from the stage as completely as her husband—until Ralph returns to London and it is revealed that she and Margery had had an argument that resulted in Jane being turned out of the house. Temporarily, she exemplifies the unmooring that contemporaries feared would occur when individuals went "out of service." And yet, when she finally reappears, she has not drifted down the social scale into vagrancy or prostitution, for instance; instead, she is working in a sempster's shop, selling "calico, or lawn,/Fine cambric shirts, or bands" (12.22–23), upscale commodities of the sort that that Eyre purchased and that epitomize the increased circulation of capital and commodities. According to Fiona McNeill, sempsters and spinsters occupied a precarious position in the occupational hierarchy: they "embodied the lowest level of legitimate unmastered employment for a poor 'maid' in London before she became criminally masterless."[63] But Jane does not sew so much as sell, giving her a role in the profitable exchange of services and commodities. Jane's new occupation seems representative of the kind of service that was in demand. The fact that her client, the "city gentleman" Hammon, woos her as if she were one of the fine cloths she sells only reemphasizes the link between sexual and commercial desire that features as well in Lacy's courtship of Rose. While Ralph migrates outside the limits of the community, Jane adapts her service within it to survive.[64]

Ralph's return to the play in scene 10 is heralded by the stage direction "*Enter Ralph being lame.*" His injury is immediately the occasion for Margery Eyre's double entendre, "I am sorry, Ralph, to see thee impotent" (10.66), gesturing at the damage war has done to his masculinity as well as his physical well-being.[65] Lameness was associated culturally with shoemakers, and Dekker here suggests that Ralph has developed into a shoemaker as represented in the popular imagination: incompetent at soldiering, infirm, poverty-stricken, helpless. But Dekker also newly aligns Ralph with shoemakers' conventional cleverness and trickiness, attributes that were earlier withheld from him. In a scene staged by Firk, Ralph takes Hammond's place at the wedding altar, preventing Hammond from marrying Jane and securing his reunion with his wife. In this version of the exchange of identities, the journeyman replaces the gentleman. Like Eyre, Ralph performs his new (and old) part as a way of embodying it: he recounts that when he first saw Jane again, he "stroked upon her shoes" and she sighed that "thou art somewhat like" her husband (18.7–8, 10–11). The scene demonstrates that even marginal shoemakers can intervene in London's theater of service.

Dekker takes this point only so far, confirming a persistent aesthetic and socioeconomic discrepancy between shoemakers. While Ralph's performance hinges on a replacement, it ultimately does no more than restore his original place. The play frames the scene as a resolution to Ralph's subplot, but it is accomplished through preserving the status quo rather than through personal advancement. Ralph still resists some of the implications of commerce. In contrast to Eyre's willing self-commodification, Ralph pointedly refuses to "sell" his wife to Hammond:

"Dost thou think a shoemaker is so base to be a bawd to his own wife for commodity?" (18.84–85). Firk pronounces: "A shoemaker sell his flesh and blood—O indignity!" (18.88), after the audience has watched Simon Eyre essentially selling his own "flesh and blood" and winning dignity as a consequence. Ralph is reinstated without question into the guild of shoemakers—on his reappearance, Hodge reassures him, "Thou shalt never see a shoemaker want bread, though he have but three fingers on a hand" (10.80–82)—and his marriage is rescued from near extinction, but he is one of those who are promised that they will not be left behind, rather than those who thrust themselves into the vanguard of capitalist service relations.

The shoemaker's holiday of the play's title is the crowning performance of social inclusion. At its center is Eyre's performance of the merry shoemaker trope, which Dekker represents as a means to reconcile the warring interests of court and city. The theater into which Eyre's Leaden Hall transforms in the final scene accommodates all the play's factions, from royalty to apprentices. The king, for one, arrives at the lord mayor's house in keen anticipation of the entertainment he is about to receive, confiding to his nobleman that "I am with child till I behold this huff cap," and even issuing an order to ensure that the show will go on: "Let someone give him notice 'tis our pleasure/That he put on his wonted merriment" (19.10, 14–15). Eyre and his shoemakers create a theater in which the king can seal the city's bond of love.

Dekker distills his aesthetic vision for drama into Simon Eyre's final staging of the merry shoemaker and the effects it produces on his audiences. His performance amounts to two short speeches but is rapturously received. Eyre's theme is to mock himself as "a very boy, a stripling, a younker" (21.20), a simple, lusty shoemaker. The joke works largely because of our knowledge, shared by the king and others onstage, that Eyre is not young and is anything but simple. The discrepancy between the callow image of himself that Eyre perpetrates and his sophisticated manipulation of the urban economy is never sharper than at this moment. Eyre is a developed character who does not reduce to the "merry shoemaker" type but, rather, includes that figure in his repertory of service. Dekker suggests that the successful servant in the new urban economy absorbs preexisting types and texts of service, a formula that applies to his own drama as well. Eyre's appropriation of a stock narrative, already disseminated in multiple forms through ballads, other plays, and prose, exemplifies Dekker's seamless integration of textual genres. Eyre's success, which is also Dekker's, derives from the ability to exchange generically shaped identities and, crucially, to allow them to coexist in a theatrical character and, even more specifically, in a dramatic image—Eyre layering the alderman's gown over what Lacy called "the mean semblance of a shoemaker" (3.12).

The theater of service culminates in this moment of the play, when a generically rich performance of service signifies to different constituencies and at the same time emphasizes the audience's common identity. Eyre says that the purpose of his mirth is to convince the king to "let care vanish" (21.33). Following the textual antecedent of the merry shoemaker and the tradition of the court fool, Eyre's great service to his monarch is to distract from the burdens of governance. Once that criterion is satisfied, he mobilizes the performance in the interest of the shoemakers' guild. Eyre uses the king's appreciation to request a reciprocal gift: "I for them all on both my knees do entreat that for the honour of poor Simon Eyre and the good of his brethren, these mad knaves, your Grace would vouchsafe some privilege to my new Leaden Hall, that it may be lawful for us to buy and sell leather there two days a week" (21.153–58). The king immediately grants Eyre's wish. A performance that slakes the sovereign's thirst for popular entertainment also meets the needs of the City's commercial economy, transforming the deferential kneeling of the prologue into a strategic and self-interested, if still respectful, gesture.[66] In this moment, Eyre's service both constitutes and displays the power of the theater to create an image of community from audiences' conflicting interests. Such moments are at the heart of Dekker's public aesthetic, one that elicits or even requires audiences to participate in performances of service and mastery which, in turn, drive the economy.

The Theater of Service

If, as *The Shoemaker's Holiday* represents it, aesthetics are a crucial component of service's potential for profit, then the service economy becomes ever more interdependent with an aesthetics of service, onstage and off, in the Rose Theatre, where the play was first performed, as well as in other London theaters. *The Shoemaker's Holiday* allows us to consider the theater not only as a site where service was represented but also as a workplace where service occurred. The material conditions of service in the theater, which like those in the economy more generally were shifting toward capitalism, directly shaped Dekker's aesthetic possibilities.

The Shoemaker's Holiday depicts an economy in which there is a continual circulation between identities and genres of service; a similar circulation took place between service in the trades and in the theater, thanks to their common reliance on guild structures. The evidence suggests that theatrical and artisanal forms of service were tightly interwoven in the working lives of many individuals whom we associate with early modern playing companies: some workers in the theater derived the benefits of their freedom from a livery company without actually practicing nontheatrical trades, while others left the theater to practice a trade full-time or moved back and forth between theatrical and nontheatrical worlds.[67] In writing about the profit that theatrical shoemaking opens to Eyre and Lacy, Dekker comments on something more than a metaphoric resemblance between playing and shoemaking; he portrays traits such as adaptability, versatility, and histrionic skill as maximizing the personal benefits of service across its many spheres of practice.

The interpenetration of theatrical and guild service complicated the definition of the master, a move that opened new possibilities for servant agency. An apprentice might be legally bound to a freeman of a livery company who was also affiliated with a playing company. That same apprentice might serve some or all of his apprenticeship working in the theater under the tutelage of a group of players. David Kathman's account of an apprentice and boy actor named Thomas Holcombe notes that although he was bound by John Heminges, his expenses were seemingly distributed among the King's Men sharers.[68] Another way to conceive of the sharing of service comes from Philip Henslowe's diary. Henslowe, the owner of the Rose playhouse and financier for the Admiral's Men, recorded in December 1597 that he had purchased the rights to an apprentice—a boy named James Bristow—from one of his players; presumably Henslowe then leased Bristow's work out to the Admiral's Men.[69] In these scenarios, the apprentice has several masters, some of whom were fungible and some of whom were contextually specific. The apprentice's legal master might not be his everyday master, and he might have more than one everyday master, either within a playing company or between theater and trade.

Even nonapprentice players might enter into bonds of service in which the master was an ambiguous, multiple presence. Henslowe recorded a series of bonds in 1597–98 in which players for the Admiral's Men signed exclusive contracts with him. The language varied from bond to bond but was often phrased explicitly in terms of service, as in this note concerning the player Richard Alleyne:

Memorandom that this 25 of Marche 1598 Richard Alleyne came
& bownde hime seallfe vnto me for ij yeares in & asumsette as a
hiered servante with ij syngell pence & to contenew frome the daye

aboue written vnto the eand & tearme of ij yeares yf he do not per-
forme this covenant then he to forfette for the breache of yt fortye
powndes & wittnes to this

> Wm Borne.
> Thomas Dowton.
> Gabrell Spencer.
> Robart Shawe.
> Richard Jonnes.[70]

Carol Chillington Rutter notes that it is impossible to know what authorization Henslowe had to generate these bonds or how binding they
actually were, especially because he signed for the company members
who were the alleged signatories.[71] In any case, what did it mean for a
landlord to commit a player as his "hiered servante"? Formally, players
owed their labor to, and derived their income from, the playing company, whether in the form of profit shares or set wages. Playwrights,
including Dekker, likewise worked for the company, not the playhouse
owner. However, the bonds between Henslowe and players—and on at
least one occasion, a playwright: Thomas Heywood—hint at a more tan-
gled web of service and mastery in the theater. Henslowe consistently
loaned money to playing companies who mounted productions at the
Rose, most prominently the Admiral's Men. Henslowe's adoption of
the rhetoric of mastery indicates that individuals who served the company, their patron, and the playgoing public also owed service to him
as the owner of the playhouse.[72] Despite Henslowe's attempts to gain
control over members of the Admiral's Men, the proliferation of mastery in the theater suggests that there were openings—supported by the
documentary record—for playwrights and players to exploit competing
paradigms of service and thereby to carve out economic and subjective
agency. Such openings helped model Dekker's portrayal of service in *The
Shoemaker's Holiday*.

The idea that changes in service nurtured by an urban, commercial,
and theatrical economy benefit the servant, as well as the multiple masters
and audiences whom he serves, is only sharpened by Dekker's treatment
of the moments when the fantasy fails. Dekker's own playwriting career
was pocked with moments of economic failure. Sole authorship of a play
could earn him six or seven pounds; the partial work he did on the vast
majority of plays with which his name was associated earned him com-
mensurately smaller amounts. By comparison to the wages that most
workers in London earned in a year, the compensation for playwriting
was generous, provided that the playwright produced work at a steady

and continual rate. Dekker did more than that, writing at a terrific speed. R. L. Smallwood and Stanley Wells estimate that from 1598 to 1603, the six-year span that encompasses the writing of *The Shoemaker's Holiday*, Dekker worked on more than fifty plays, usually in collaboration with others.[73] But despite his productivity and an adequate income, Dekker could not fend off poverty. He was sent to debtors' prison on multiple occasions. In 1598 and 1599, the latter occasion only a few months before Dekker submitted the manuscript for *The Shoemaker's Holiday*, Henslowe gave money to have him released.[74] Dekker had a firsthand understanding of how difficult it could be to make one's way as a servant unbound from paternal structures of service and obliged continually to negotiate the conditions of his service.

Dekker's industrious but indebted relation to Henslowe and to the Admiral's Men tells a story of theatrical service closer to the journey-man Ralph's marginal plot of struggle for sustenance than to Simon Eyre's dominant plot of exuberant social and economic transformation. Dekker's tenuous career is a reminder that at the edges of the play's celebration of aesthetic service lurks the threat of dissipation. Even in the affirming final scene, there are reminders of why a fantasy of urban economy and community might have been so urgently needed and so popularly received in early modern London. As the shoemakers, includ-ing Ralph, file in, the king announces that "we will incorporate a new supply" of soldiers to avenge the country's losses on the battlefield (21.139). Dekker gives little reason to think that Ralph, lucky enough to survive his first tour of duty, will escape reconscription and just as little reason to believe that Lacy will lack for the resources to avoid, a second time, fulfilling the onerous duties of military service. *The Shoe-maker's Holiday* endorses the efficacy of service in an urban commercial economy, which satisfies the demands of king and apprentices alike, at the same time that it measures with cold-eyed precision the exclusions that underlie this economy. In doing so, the play evinces how willful and fragile the basis is for the theater of service it portrays and embodies.

Reading a book and going to a play are two radically different experi-ences, but they were a little less so in early modern England. The close relationship between Deloney's prose fiction and Dekker's drama has a lot to teach us about how the two forms worked analogously, even cooperatively, to develop public receptions for their performances. This chapter has sought to illustrate how service not only helped these two authors imagine publics for their works but also provided a common thread that linked prose fiction to drama. Each author wove a dis-tinct pattern with that thread, Deloney pulling the generic and social exchanges exemplified by service through a detachable, but also accumulating, sequence of episodes and Dekker weaving a single textured fabric out of similar exchanges. Deloney encourages individual reading decisions, and yet he also pushes readers to see themselves as having a collective, unifying interest in the narrative momentum that service generates toward mobility and nobility. Dekker shows his awareness of socially distinct audiences but then puts them in a theatrical space where, like Deloney's readers, they become aware of their common investment in aesthetic service. The receptions of both *The Gentle Craft* and *The Shoemaker's Holiday* depended on the public's economic power, and both texts made the public feel as if it played an essential role in powerful performances of service.

CHAPTER FOUR

~

"Iterate the Work"

The Alchemist and Ben Jonson's Labors of Service

In the previous chapter, I argued that Thomas Deloney and Thomas Dekker activated fantasies about service in a nascent capitalist economy, fantasies that were as much about the roles that prose fiction and drama played in a transitional economy as about servants themselves. Ben Jonson follows in Deloney's and Dekker's footsteps, but he weighs the effects of aesthetic service differently. While *The Gentle Craft* and *The Shoemaker's Holiday* suggest that capitalism enables performances of service that in turn generate mobility and profit, Jonson's *The Alchemist* (1610–11) explores the possibility that this "new" service, with its attendant hopes and desires, may actually be pulled back toward the "old" patriarchal service. But these retrograde qualities hardly signify that Jonson wishes to abandon service as an image for authorial and textual self-fashioning. To the contrary, service articulates Jonson's aesthetics.

In *The Alchemist*, Jonson integrated sides of his authorial persona that have long struck commentators as contradictory or even incoherent. A writer who, as Laurie Ellinghausen has recently shown, both disdained and identified with the common laborer, who advertised his elite learning and stressed his affiliations with the court, and yet who also composed plays in which disreputable servants, con men, and rogues consistently outwit their social superiors, Jonson seems to stake out irreconcilable social and aesthetic positions.[1] In this chapter, I argue that Jonson uses service to negotiate such extremes, for he imagines that servants navigate between self-effacement and self-assertion, servile copying and inventive creation, low status and high. Servants embody simultaneously the idleness of the rogue, the toil of the laborer, the pretensions of the courtier, and the ambition of the urban entrepreneur. These qualities describe Jonson's writing, which likewise canvasses many corners of the culture and takes on multiple personae to speak to various readerships and audiences. The servant, in short, is the ungainly, often misshapen, but vigorous society that the author sets out to represent; the servant is also the author who represents that society to itself.[2]

I discuss *The Alchemist* alongside the *Discoveries* and several poems in order to argue that service was a trope that endured throughout Jonson's career, bridging textual genres and cultures of reception. In all these texts, Jonson mediates patronage and the marketplace, reflecting the large-scale transition in conceptions of authorship. He does not reject patronage; indeed, he draws as much from patronage relationships as he can. Rather, the servant's subjective and aesthetic agency transforms patronage by putting it into conversation with capitalist modes of service. Jonson creates a vocabulary of service that intermingles modes of address from theatrical performance and print production. Reconstructing authorial and textual service through capitalism, Jonson builds on the public aesthetic that, as I argued in chapter 3, Deloney's *The Gentle Craft* and Dekker's *The Shoemaker's Holiday* each developed. Even when he retreats from the marketplace, he remains irrevocably engaged with it.

The Alchemist is my starting point because it was written during a time in Jonson's career when he managed service across a range of textual and theatrical contexts. The decade from 1606 to 1616 was when Jonson's writing for the public stage flourished; it was also, arguably, the period of greatest diversity in his output. In this span, Jonson wrote six plays, nine court masques, and lyric poetry that included "To Penshurst," written the same year as *The Alchemist*. He moved with facility between neofeudal and capitalist modes of service, between its courtly and urban sites, between its most elite and most disreputable practitioners.[3] Jonson represents his service in *The Alchemist* through his rogue protagonists, who mount self-consciously aesthetic performances of service that extract money from a deluded clientele. The alchemy of the play's title becomes a metaphor for the transformative potential of aesthetic service, which promises to turn rogues into capitalist entrepreneurs and masters into clients, and ultimately, gulls. The vision of the author's service as roguish and fraudulent, flexible and exuberant, appears in many of his other works, even later in his career when he wrote relatively little for the theater. In these texts, servants prove skilled at manipulating their masters, often through impersonations and other misrepresentations. He infuses the relationship between author, text, and patron with images of service he developed in the public theater. These images derive in turn from the material conditions of service in the early modern theater, which underwrite Jonson's aesthetic service.

There is another side to Jonson's ambitious agenda for service. Servants emerge in *The Alchemist*, and more generally in Jonson's corpus, as vulnerable figures, whose machinations often reap few material benefits and who are bound more tightly to servitude than their irreverent, gleeful performances might portend. Jonson's rogues in *The Alchemist* fail by play's end to keep the money they have "earned" or to rise in social status. Capitalism ultimately reinforces their marginal service positions and does not allow them to invest in ventures in which their money, rather than their person, performs labor. In the texts that I analyze, Jonson returns repeatedly to the motif of economic, social, and textual dispossession that newly capitalist forms of service provoke. Representing the rogue, Jonson implies that imposture and marginality are equally attributes of the early modern author, who reaches for a subject position and socioeconomic standing that remain perpetually just out of reach. The challenge that Jonson sets for himself is to suggest that even a disenfranchised service is aesthetically productive, which in turn reinvigorates the hope for economic and social gain. It is this iterative cycle, alternately bold and abject, clear-sighted and deluded, self-possessed and dispossessed, that defines Jonson's authorship.

I shift the emphasis of recent criticism to suggest that Jonson's internal debate over authorial self-possession and dispossession was not primarily about how to claim ownership but about how to capitalize on the potential of service and cope with its limitations. Jonson was not striving to break free from service as much as he was grappling with its changing meanings for his authorial identity, textual form, and public reception. Joseph Loewenstein and Bruce Boehrer have each encouraged us to think of Jonson as one of the first authors to assert in open, even fierce terms the burgeoning stakes of intellectual property. In Loewenstein's formulation, the book-buying public becomes a crucial determinant of Jonson's "possessive authorship," which Loewenstein uses to designate both the author's subjective self-possession and the intellectual property rights that print culture was gradually making available to authors.[4] As Loewenstein brilliantly shows, Jonson's self-presentations are freighted with anxiety, insecurity, and dispossession as well as with claims to ownership and autonomy. My point is that Jonson expresses such tensions through representations of service rather than through representations of mastery. The question of plagiarism in Jonson's works is one area where conflicting ideas about the author's proprietary rights are particularly vexing. Boehrer has pointed out that Jonson often did not practice what he preached about intellectual property, imitating copiously from the works of others.[5] For Boehrer, the issues raised by plagiarism speak to a larger contradiction: "Poets should not be bound to laws because, apparently, they 'fulfill' those laws anyway and in fact define the law for others; to this extent, the poetic freedom that Jonson advocates turns out to be servitude writ large."[6] Boehrer describes servitude as a condition that Jonson tries and fails to transcend. I propose that changing paradigms of service allow Jonson to imagine new authorial productions and identities. These aesthetic possibilities are predicated on a new "poetic freedom" and subjectivity that service expresses rather than stifles.

Rogues who Serve: *The Alchemist*

In *The Alchemist*, Jonson's rogues try to reinvent themselves as agents in a market economy of investment and profit. But the play gradually unfolds their continued dependence on service, the very category, ironically, that their peers try to seal off from them by designating them as rogues. Thus, the rogues are not considered legitimate enough to be servants, nor do they want to be servants. But service turns out to be precisely *what* they do and all they *can* do by play's end. Jonson dramatizes the immense socioeconomic pressures that service was under and shows both the desire and disillusionment that such instability engendered.

Appropriately for a text sensitive both to the conventional attributes of service and to the regularity with which such conventions were violated, *The Alchemist* opens with a cultural cliché about the dangers of leaving a servant idle. The plague having descended upon London, a master, Lovewit, leaves his house in the city to the care of his butler. But his trust proves to be misplaced:

> Ease him corrupted, and gave means to know
> A cheater and his punk, who, now brought low,
> Leaving their narrow practice, were become
> Cozeners at large; and only wanting some
> House to set up, with him they here contract,
> Each for a share, and all begin to act. (1.1.3–8)[7]

The transition from definable "practice" to wide-ranging criminal enterprise is disposed of quickly: the butler, Face, merges seamlessly with the "cozeners," Subtle and Dol Common. Together, the three move beyond petty crime to pursue a more expansive scheme. "The Argument," a brief piece in verse that precedes the prologue, promises that idleness and criminality will be transformed into a livelihood that somehow entails freedom from labor.[8] On a first reading, *The Alchemist* might thus seem to be about redefining work in terms of an emerging capitalist ethos, one that provides greater opportunity for subjects on the periphery of the economy to gain productive entry.

At stake in the rogues' scheme is the possibility of detaching work from service. These two concepts were closely intertwined in early modern England. Although work, like service, has varied connotations, the sense in which I use it here is: "Action involving effort or exertion directed to a definite end, esp. as a means of gaining one's livelihood; labour, toil; (one's) regular occupation or employment."[9] The emphasis lies both on the actions involved, "labour" and "toil," and on the ends to which labor is directed: the "livelihood" that enables individuals to sustain themselves. If we probe the employments that relied on labor of some sort and provided sustenance, we discover that they entailed in most cases the practice of service. To put it another way, most working conditions involved a service relationship, whether comprising the relation of the household servant to his master, the apprentice to his master, the day laborer to the farmer, or the page to the courtier.[10] Thus, service provided the framework in which a great deal of early modern work transpired and within which requirements work was understood. With the service relationship came the servant's obligation to perform labor: under the supervision of, on behalf of, or to the benefit of the master. In the case of *The Alchemist,* service is performed by entrepreneurial con men and a woman for a group of "clients" who end up assuming some of the more traditional functions of the master. In trying to avoid work, Face, Dol, and Subtle signal their desire to escape the durable bonds of service.

Yet in *The Alchemist,* service proves indispensable to the livelihoods, and perhaps even the survival, of these marginal figures. The play implies a division between older forms of work entrenched in service, which it associates with subservience, physicality, and toil, and newer forms of work, which produce profit seemingly without labor. It then shows these categories collapsing back into each other. *The Alchemist* balances an emergent capitalist fantasy with an entrenched narrative in which patriarchal service renews its claims on the rogue characters. In theory, the transition to capitalism enhanced the possibilities for individual advancement and weakened patriarchal structures; in a capitalist economy, anyone could seek profit, as the rogues do, for example, by taking shares in a venture. However, Jonson suggests that in a milieu of seemingly limitless opportunism, some restrictions still obtain, for as

the play illustrates, those who lack the capital to control labor are ultimately excluded from investment and ownership and resigned to labor
for others.[11] Whereas Jonson's rival, Dekker, had a decade earlier in *The
Shoemaker's Holiday* envisioned a new kind of servant seizing advantage
in a bustling urban economy, Jonson's characters, who seem at first blush
extraordinarily uninhibited by principles of decorum, move toward a
more conservative, if unwilled, stance on service.[12]

Service in *The Alchemist* is entangled with service relations in the theater that Jonson experienced as a playwright and sometime actor. The
play delights openly in its metatheatrical dimensions; most pointedly, the
Blackfriars house in which all the action is set refers transparently to
the Blackfriars playhouse in which the play was performed. However,
shareholders in licensed London theatrical companies such as the King's
Men, who commissioned *The Alchemist,* were no rogues. If Lovewit's
masterless house conjures newly available economic subject positions
only to show the limits of that imagining, Jonson is quick to remind his
audiences of both the analogies to and distinctions from the theatrical
workplace they are visiting. The history of the early modern theater suggests a complexity in perceptions of the link between service and work
that the drama, particularly in its final acts, both embodies and evades.
Examining that history in relation to *The Alchemist* illuminates how
Jonson conceived of service and authorship according to competing
models that invited upward mobility and deferred it, that detached from
the materiality of labor and reconfirmed it.

Alchemy is the governing conceit of the play, and its theatrical power
derives from its mutable meanings. It functions as a prime business
motive for the rogues; it also often demands extenuating labor. Face,
Subtle, and Dol establish an alchemical enterprise that lures people with
the promise of great wealth and social prestige. No chemical alchemy
takes place, the rogues' gamble being that their customers will pay in
advance for their services. As their scheme requires, the rogues are under
immense pressure to juggle the multiplying demands made by an ever-
increasing number of aspirants, with the result that they are forced to
work harder and harder to maintain their fraudulent enterprise. The
distance, illusory to begin with, between simulated and actual labor collapses altogether as they struggle to satisfy their clients' expectations. As
Jonson foretells in the last line of "The Argument," their goal of getting
rich at the expense of others finally evaporates altogether, the flurry of
roguish labor—"casting figures, telling fortunes, news,/Selling of flies,
flat bawdry" (10–11)—along with the rogues themselves, disappearing in
"fume[s]" (12). Master Lovewit's return at the end of act 4 precipitates

the rogues' reversion to low status. While Face, back in the role of household servant, gets to share at least some of the proceeds from the cons with his master, Subtle and Dol are left with nothing.

Alchemy is also Jonson's metaphor for the desire to inflate oneself—subjectively, economically, and socially—that drives rogues and gulls alike, and a joke about the extremity of self-delusion they endorse in this pursuit.[13] Throughout, Jonson plays on the applicability of alchemical terms and concepts to the private and cultural imaginings of his characters. "Projection," for example, which refers to a technical stage in the transmutation of base metal into gold, also describes the cognitive process by which longings express themselves as a tangible, if ultimately unrealized, outcome. Moreover, a "project" referred, in Joan Thirsk's words, to "a practical scheme for exploiting material things," precisely the sort of capitalist enterprise upon which the rogues embark.[14] For transformation to "project" itself long enough for the gulls to keep investing their money in the rogues' venture, alchemy's lack of substance—its essential nonbeing—must be balanced with its continually deferred promise. The gull Mammon asks Subtle, "When do you make projection?" and is met with a characteristic response: "Son, be not hasty" (2.3.101–2). Although they manipulate the meanings of alchemy, Face, Subtle, and Dol, no less than their gulls, fall victim to its allure. The rogues wish to convert their human acts of labor into work performed by their capital, not by themselves. But their projection, like their project, ends up only reasserting their participation in labor. Subtle may put off Mammon by professing the need to "iterate the work" (2.3.106), but his words later take on an unwanted resonance as Subtle and his partners unceasingly repeat their machinations with alchemical props and their encounters with increasingly dissatisfied clients. Jonson exposes a persistent gap between the dream of "a work" that creates profit without human labor and the reality of difficult and toilsome labor that cannot be relied upon to produce any profit at all.[15] Trapped by the incommensurability of alchemical desire and the difficult labors that desire entails, the rogues in fact have more to lose than anyone else.[16]

Subtle, Face, and Dol would have been legible to audiences from their first appearance onstage as rogues, who avoided legitimate forms of labor largely by refusing service. A more economically sensitive interpretation is that such figures had a fluctuating relation to service during a period when long-term service offered increasingly uncertain prospects. When Subtle accuses Face of having been merely "the good,/Honest, plain, livery-three-pound-thrum" (1.1.15–16), he is gesturing toward the familiar type of the domestic servant. This is hardly the only prototype of service encountered in the play, however; Dol and Subtle have also engaged in service, albeit in less permanent positions in which compensation was correspondingly unpredictable.[17] Dol's main employment is as a prostitute, while Subtle has apparently flitted from one "course" (5.4.146) or subsistence scheme to another. What Face calls "your conjuring, cozening, and your dozens of trades" (1.1.40) might have been inscribed in popular rogue literature as a willful rebellion against gainful, steady employment, but recent scholarship has confirmed that the pull of necessity is a more realistic explanation.[18] Face's recollection of Subtle standing on a street corner, sniffing pies he cannot afford to buy, "like the father of hunger" (1.1.27), tells that story clearly. Shifts in the labor market, together with the rise of monetary exchange, spawned what Patricia Fumerton has usefully defined as an "economy of 'unsettledness,'" a de facto community that included "not only the legally vagrant, but also the 'respectable' yet unstable servant and apprentice classes," continually on the move, sometimes geographically and other times simply occupationally, piecing together survival through ad hoc combinations of licit and illicit work.[19] Understanding the play's scenario in an unstable economic context allows us to read the rogues setting up house as just another move in an ongoing dialectic between constraint and opportunity for those engaged in, or at the margins of, service; if for Face his master's departure gives him a chance to improve his economic status, for Subtle and Dol it surely also augurs a comparatively stable interlude in their itinerant existences.[20]

Jonson's audiences would have been familiar with the type of the lazy and avaricious rogue popular in "coney-catching" literature, whose objective is to avoid honest labor at all costs and accrue wealth through dishonest means. In *A Caveat for Common Cursitors,* for example, Thomas Harman sketches a typical portrait of a rogue, dubbed an "upright man," as a former soldier or "serving-man, and weary of welldoing, shaking off all pain, doth choose him this idle life."[21] In a bit of circular logic, another sixteenth-century commentator hypothesizes that rogues do not work "by reason their sinews are so benumbed and stiff through idleness as their limbs, being put to any hard labour, will grieve them beyond measure. So as they will rather hazard their lives than work."[22] The rhetoric of avoidance that runs through rogue literature serves as an important background for contemporary assumptions about rogues in *The Alchemist;* their plot, audiences know without having to be told, is premised on an evasion of rigid hierarchical structures of authority and of moral conventions of industry and diligence. As I discussed in chapter 3, although Deloney's aspiring shoemakers in *The Gentle*

Craft sometimes mount dishonest performances to accomplish their aims, they are always careful to maintain the decorum of their honest service occupations. Jonson's characters, on the other hand, transgress openly against the doctrine of labor and the patriarchal conventions of service. In this sense, they are the antithesis of the recipients of relief described in a parish document: "they are laborious and painfull and by reason of their hard charge of children they are not able to maintayne their familie by their hard labour.' "[23]

One of Jonson's characteristic ironies is that the rogues' desire to be both idle and rich, when taken on its merits, is almost identical to the hopes expressed by their victims. What is suspect in such a sentiment when expressed by Face, Subtle, and Dol—or their antecedents in rogue literature—is their egregiously forthright attempt to violate their rightful occupational and social stations.[24] As Jonson intimates, the sin of transgressive desire is committed equally by the gulls, among them a lawyer's clerk, a druggist, a country yeoman, and a pair of Anabaptists. All of these figures fantasize about achieving powerful positions, and all attempt to realize their fantasies by procuring "magical" enhancements to their material goods, their personal abilities, or their professional status. The agents of the gulls' illicit advancement are, however, the rogues, and it is they who conveniently shoulder the burden of responsibility for the social and commercial aspirations of more "legitimate" members of society. In this way, as Craig Dionne argues about the coney-catching texts, "the otherness of underworld villainy gives voice to the anxieties of a social disruption brought about by the very practices that empowered London's new corporate class: self-advancement through histrionic manipulation of the social and linguistic registers of court and state."[25] Face and his partners serve as representations of the culture's ambivalence about the changing criteria undergirding elite status.

These socioeconomic anxieties center in *The Alchemist* on how work in an urban, commercial space is being recalibrated to emphasize mobility and ambition over the idealized goals of the servant, which are limited to self-preservation and sustenance. Self-advancement is the driving motive for Jonson's characters, irrespective of their initial access to economic and social capital, and it is precisely the apparent cross-class availability of profit that Jonson highlights, and undermines, so effectively. The discourse of "venture," used by both gulls and rogues, indicates the nature of the work that these characters imagine themselves performing. The vision is already present in "The Argument," with the mention of each rogue "contract[ing]" for a "share" of the investment. Early on, Dol refers to the relationship between the coconspirators as the "venture tripartite" (1.1.13). Her rhetorical questions, "All things in common?/Without priority?" (1.1.135–36), imply a contractual agreement that has established equal shares of investment and profit. Work is transformed from labor conducted at the orders and on behalf of a master to a collaborative project undertaken on the initiative and for the benefit of shareholders. Mammon plays up the distinction between the "venture" and other kinds of work when he articulates his relationship to the coveted philosopher's stone. After his friend Surly opines that the man who acquires the stone must be "one free from mortal sin," Mammon counters, "But I buy it;/My venture brings it me" (2.2.99; 2.2.100–101). The humor lies in Mammon's unabashed substitution of money for morality, but equally telling is his substitution of venture for labor. There is no suggestion that Mammon expects to do anything in particular; his commitment to the work of the venture is secured, rather, by his monetary investment and the personal risk it signifies. Once initiated, the venture becomes the actor, that which "brings" and labors on the investor's behalf.

Mammon's vision of the venture not only promises but requires the absence of industry and diligence. It is the antithesis to Deloney's insistence that servants who wish to advance their positions must perform the patriarchal ideal of service. Jonson's characters instead try to make their capital perform in their place. The fungibility of servants and commodities that I have analyzed in other chapters translates in *The Alchemist* to the possibility that money might substitute for service. In suggesting this prospect, Jonson taps into the fear that commerce, trade, and other kinds of capitalist enterprise might subvert the economic and social virtues that commentators on service saw as increasingly endangered. The detachment of capitalist work from labor in *The Alchemist* is evident not only in the implications of the "venture" but in its sometime synonym, the word "work," which appears thirty times in the play, most often in reference to grand alchemical projects. Representative is Subtle's pronouncement: "This is the day, I am to perfect for him/The *magisterium*, our great work, the stone" (1.4.13–14). Defined less by occupational labor than by creative and contractual outcome, the work described by both rogues and gulls centers on a projection of hopes and gains, a perfect analogue for, or even a realization of, commercial enterprise.[26] Seven mentions of "work" come as verbs. These uses enhance the capitalist redefinition of work and tend to occur at moments when Jonson's characters are advising one another or themselves about how to produce transformative or manipulative effects in other people and things. Mammon imagines making Dol into his consort and showing her off at court: "Set all the eyes/Of court afire, like a burning glass,/And work 'em into cinders" (4.1.139–41); while Dol teases Mammon, "you are pleased, sir,/To work on the ambition of our sex" (4.1.129–30). To "work" or "work on" something or someone is an essentially self-serving act designed to advance a larger project. Far from connoting laborious activity or adherence to duty, it entails subverting societal expectations and circumventing moral requirements in order to accrue capital.

As it turns out, Face, Subtle, and Dol have not exactly liberated themselves from labor; on the contrary, they are entangled in precisely the toil, subservience, and dependency from which they sought to escape. Face exposes this irony in one of his rants against Subtle: "You must have stuff, brought home to you, to work on?/And, yet, you think, I am at no expense,/In searching out these veins, then following 'em,/Then trying 'em out" (1.3.104–7). Although the stress on capital investment—here, "expense"—remains, Face gives an early reminder that the grandiose illusion that they are projecting entails tangible labor. The raw material or "stuff" of their schemes, namely, the gulls, must be identified, pursued, and lured to the house. Face wants to show Subtle that such efforts require not only money but also the fulfillment of a series of delimited, disciplined tasks. Indeed, the rogues are forced to labor ever more intensively as the conflicting demands of the gulls multiply, ratcheting up the effort needed to keep the facade of the great work intact. By act 3, Face is evincing frustration at labors that have failed to "yield us grains," using an extended metaphor in which he is the "mill-jade," or horse whose laborious, circular march powers a grain mill (3.3.6, 3.3.5). We are always behind the scenes with the rogues, and the result is that we may be struck more by the sheer drudgery involved in keeping such complex schemes afloat than by the thrill of getting a glimpse into London's underworld.[27]

The exposure of the rogues' labor heralds the return of service in *The Alchemist*, although it would be more accurate to say that service never really left the picture, for it becomes evident that the rogues' plans are predicated upon serving gulls. In the intent of the rogues, "to serve" means to trick or to dupe, but in carrying out this intent, the rogues end up serving the gulls in a more conventional fashion. The relationships the rogues establish with their proposed victims both mimic and merge with the bond of servant and master. The venture depends upon appearing to cater to the gulls' desires, and the appearance must be sustained, the rogues soon find, through performances of service built upon labor. As the pace quickens to a frenzy in acts 3 and 4, the rogues are at the beck and call of their gulls, improvising "some device" (3.5.57) to keep each one placated. From the rogues' perspective, they are juggling a set of false hopes along with the exits and entrances of the gulls. Yet Jonson also displays the perspective of the gulls, who often act just like satisfied masters. In his dealings with Sir Epicure Mammon, Face insists, "I have blown, sir,/Hard, for your worship" (2.2.21–22). Mammon, in response, is so pleased with Face's services that he promises him exalted positions as "master/of my seraglio" (2.2.32–33) and a "lord's vermin" (2.3.330) once the philosopher's stone comes to fruition. To serve their own pleasurable delusions, the gulls require the rogues to play service roles that in turn allow them to play the role of the master. What Mammon promises Face is not the transcendence of service but simply more exalted service positions. Here, the eye-service condemned in the didactic literature of service as performative and deceitful makes possible actual service, further blurring the distinction between the aesthetic and the "real."

On some level, the rogues seem to recognize the hold that service has over them. Even in their role-playing, they never stray too far from service positions. Face alternates between turns as "suburb-captain" (a general purveyor of vice in the Liberties) and as the alchemist's servant, Lungs. In impersonating a doctor of alchemy, Subtle appropriates a somewhat higher rank; but although the gulls accord an obsequious reverence to the "cunning-man" (1.2.8), he is soon revealed to be more like a pander or pimp, managing an illicit but highly sought-after service, than the scholarly master to whom he bears a passing resemblance. He is also briefly disguised in act 3, scene 4 as "a Priest of Fairy," a minister of the "Aunt of Fairy" from whom Dapper hopes to inherit a fortune. It as if Face and Subtle do not dare to play more elevated social roles in the Blackfriars house where they encounter their clients.

The case of Dol needs to be treated separately for a moment, since she alone projects herself into aristocratic or royal identities. Her primary service position, that of the prostitute who caters to men with money, titled or not, gives her an access to a sexual and marital economy that seems briefly to offer the possibility of upward mobility and a transformation from marginal servant to elite wife. But the promise retreats, like the rogues' other dreams, into an illusion. Ultimately, Dol's relationship to service proves as intractable as her male counterparts'.

In acts 2 through 4, Dol appears mostly as a lord's sister wooed by Mammon, while in act 5, she takes the part of the Fairy Queen to the hapless Dapper. Both are coded, or euphemized, versions of prostitution, an occupation that, as Jean Howard has suggested, "figures a market economy that like it knows no boundaries."[28] Dol's fluidity gestures to the lack of a firm divide between prostitution and other forms of service available to women in the lower ranks of society.[29] Accordingly, her labors encompass, but are not limited to, the sale of her body. She is clearly an equal sharer in the "venture tripartite" and takes as active a role as her male partners in managing the business; indeed, she is listed in the *dramatis personae* as "their colleague." She halts the feud in act 1, scene 1 that threatens to dissolve the venture; she provides crucial communication between the enterprise and its clientele ("I have told 'em, in a voice,/Thorough the trunk, like one of your familiars," [1.4.4–5]); and she plots to relieve Dame Pliant of her jewels (4.4.74). Moreover, Dol's prostitution, as the play portrays it, involves meticulous planning that goes beyond sexual activities. In readying herself for a sexual encounter, Face notes that "she must prepare perfumes, delicate linen,/The bath in chief, a banquet, and her wit" (3.3.20–21). It is evident from such examples that prostitution is part of broader commercial prospects.

The prostitute's lack of circumspection applies as well, Howard maintains, to her ability to work her trade virtually anywhere and in virtually any guise. Dol bears out these truisms as she plies her sexual wares in Lovewit's "respectable" Blackfriars house and in disguise as a noblewoman. There is an implied exchange value between Dol's props and skills and those possessed by women of high rank who similarly rely on personal and luxurious enticements to woo suitors in the marriage market. Prostitution proves particularly malleable for Dol, allowing her both to engage in multiple facets of the commercial economy and to translate herself believably from a woman of sexual and other petty commerce to a virginal lord's sister involved in an elite marital commerce.[30] The interchange between gender and economics allows Dol to impersonate classed identities that are beyond the imaginations of Face and Subtle. In this way, Dol recalls the increasingly commercialized female servant, whose threat of disorderly independence, as Michelle Dowd has shown, is managed through upwardly mobile marriage.[31] Dol is a servant who almost crosses between the "shadow" service economy and the legitimate, sanctioned marriage economy, in which she could play the wife's part, analogous to the servant's and yet importantly distinguished by marriage's ability to raise a woman's socioeconomic position.

But as Jonson would have it, Dol's narrative trajectory resists marriage. Her meetings with Mammon mimic those of a woman of elite status, without actually securing her such status through marriage. Despite her flexibility, Dol is limited, as are her male counterparts, by her marginality: she is the prostitute whom it was feared other female servants might become. It is the wealthy widow, Dame Pliant, rather than she, who marries at the end of the play. Dame Pliant is, after all, "a rich one" (5.3.86), while Dol evidently possesses little beyond the "velvet gown" (5.4.134) with which she is ultimately sent packing. Impersonation never yields to transformation for the rogues in *The Alchemist,* and finally Dol is no exception. She may imitate Queen Elizabeth in the role of the Fairy Queen, but while the performance parodically suggests an identification between queen and whore, it does not serve Dol's advancement. Her role points to continuities between women of disparate economic status while restoring the boundaries between them.[32]

In *The Alchemist,* the changing prospects of service in the early seventeenth-century urban economy reassert distinctions that keep the most vulnerable members of the service economy on the periphery. By recasting service as capitalist enterprise, Dol, Subtle, and Face attempt to turn masters into clients, convert their masters' interest and profit into their own, and eliminate labor in favor of a self-acting "venture." But what quickly emerges is that their only access to the capitalist sphere comes through the skills in service that they already have. In this way, their histrionic and proliferating performances of service become recursive, failing to generate capital and keeping them in the subordinate position of servants in the patriarchal mold. The rogues are not the only disappointed aspirants in the play; most of the gulls are also sent away empty-handed. The difference is that the gulls by and large already have a foothold in society: they have capital to invest in their ventures, whereas those who possess little to begin with remain dispossessed.[33] Although critics have associated performance, disguise, and role-playing with social mobility, the efficacy of such methods proves limited in this play. Marginality begets marginality, and the servant who takes on a variety of capitalist roles produces rich theatrical pleasures but little material gain.

It is no accident that Face makes a literal return to servitude when Lovewit arrives at the end of act 4 to reclaim his house. The circular logic that Jonson traces demands that Face must ultimately scrape together an appeal to his master's largesse to save his place. By leveraging his influence with Lovewit, Face manages to defraud his coconspirators and hold onto the "pelf" that the three had stolen from the gulls. Yet he does so at the cost of a far more valuable prize: the widow, Dame Pliant, whom he had intended to marry himself. Because Lovewit's social and economic authority trump his servant's, the latter must surrender his best hope for advancement to his master. The disguise of the Spanish don that he had planned to wear to fool the widow into marriage is worn by Lovewit instead, affirming that elite disguises are more efficacious for those whose status is already assured. Lovewit reinforces hierarchical privilege when in his final speech he promises to show his gratitude to Face "and help his fortune" (5.5.151). Face himself tells the audience that "this pelf,/Which I have got, if you do quit me, rests/To feast you often, and invite new guests" (5.5.163–65). The audience is left to wonder whether Face's newly acquired capital will finally allow him to leave his master's service and establish his own household and hospitality or, as seems more likely, leave him bound to the master at whose pleasure he keeps his hard-won treasure.

Jonson's Theatrical Service

If Face, Subtle, and Dol try with mixed results to perform capitalism by "acting" on their shares, thus hoping to transform their relationship to labor and profit, capitalism was being performed in London theaters daily in ways that were transforming the relationship between labor and profit. Just two years before the first performance of *The Alchemist,* the King's Men assumed occupancy of the indoor Blackfriars playhouse. The collaborative nature of the rogues' shareholding, as well as the fact that in *The Alchemist* rogues and gulls are ultimately engaged (even if sometimes unwittingly) in a shared venture, offers a striking parallel to the innovative business arrangement that the King's Men had culti- vated since 1594, when a group of players and theater entrepreneurs took shares to form a company then called the Lord Chamberlain's Men. Based on the shareholding principle, in 1599 the Burbage brothers formed a core group of "housekeepers" who together bore the risks and rewards of building the Globe theater and eventually of taking over the Blackfriars playhouse. For those who owned shares, and especially for housekeepers, to work for the King's Men was to participate in a capi- talist venture akin to that imagined by Jonson's characters. Indeed, the highest levels of the company were occupied increasingly by the house- keepers, who could expect significantly greater profits than standard company shareholders.[34]

For other members of a playing company, enjoying the fruits of a cap- italist economy could not be taken for granted. The ranks were filled by hired hands who worked steadily or occasionally, as players or behind the scenes, in exchange for "wages . . . paid by the year or the week or even the day."[35] Near the bottom of this continuum, comparisons to Fumerton's "unsettled" subjects become apt. As Natasha Korda has sug- gested about the theater, with particular reference to women's work, its location "on the cusp of formal and informal market activities" made it amenable to exactly the kind of marginal, mixed service activities that are the territory of Face, Subtle, and Dol in *The Alchemist*.[36]

In some ways, then, *The Alchemist* can be read as an allegory for entrenched hierarchical divisions between capitalists and servants in London theaters of the early seventeenth century.[37] But while divisions certainly did reproduce themselves within the playing companies, they were neither stable nor predictable. For instance, the emphasis on monetary investment and reward hides from view the labors that most sharers in the early seventeenth century continued to perform, whether acting in plays or managing the company's affairs.[38] The King's Men's housekeepers who collaborated on the Globe doubled the roles of "impresario–playhouse-landlord and player–tenant."[39] For a housekeeper at once to occupy the position of employer and employee, manager and worker, property owner and renter, master and servant, was to break down boundaries between these categories, not stiffen them.

The documentary evidence on the King's Men supports the varied nature of early modern work in and for the theater, which was grounded in labor that made good on an investment, transforming it from inert to active status. Along with Jonson, the London theater was becoming "professionalized," which entailed finding new ways to authorize and legitimate the work of its practitioners. Even so, spectators of different ranks within the theater saw no contradiction in, and in some cases relied materially on, inhabiting more than one occupational position, just as the players and other workers in the theater did.[40] Company records indicate that Face was played consecutively by two housekeepers–sharers in the King's Men: Nathan Field (also at various times a boy player and playwright) from 1615 through 1619, and Joseph Taylor after 1619. Lovewit was likely played by Robert Benfield, who began as a hired man and evolved first into a sharer and by the 1630s into a housekeeper.[41] Unlike Face and Lovewit, the players behind these roles did not revert to a strict occupational stratification; rather, they were men who ascended the ranks of company hierarchy, who likely did or had done manual and physical labor, who learned parts and donned costumes, and who did or would make investments that rendered them property owners and stakeholders. Their fluid histories suggest that the same subject might in the course of a working life be a Face and a Lovewit, sometimes both at once.

Such histories also remind us of Jonson's multiple relationships to service. In his younger years he followed his stepfather's precedent and trained as a bricklayer's apprentice before joining the military for "service in the Low Countries" and then touring as a journeyman player.[42] Traces of Jonson's beginnings in artisanal service stayed with him, not least in the fact, as David Kathman observes, that he was free of the tilers and bricklayers and thought enough of his membership to pay his dues to the company for quite some time after he established himself as a writer.[43] Like other playwrights, Jonson was part of the expanding market economy, receiving a fee for each play text that he wrote, collaborated on, or revised. His masques and other royal entertainments were likewise paid by commission. Both kinds of dramatic composition intersected with Jonson's appeals to patronage, his cultivation of influential backers and friends who could support his endeavors in theater and print.

Jonson drew on his biographically diverse perspectives on service to cultivate a hybrid, often conflicted self-image. His addresses to patrons frequently cast the author as a servant, and yet, as Loewenstein argues in reference to *Cynthia's Revels* (1600) and Jonson's court masques, they "express a desire not merely for patronage but for a patronage that would function as a controlled economy, and one in which poet, not the patron, determines the structure of exchange."[44] Jonson's self-construction as a servant who negotiates his own terms appears in his epigram "To Fine Grand." The epigram's conceit is that it functions as a "borrowers letter," tallying up all the poetic services the author has proffered to his patron, including "a jest," "a tale or two," an "imprese," or motto, for the courtier to use "at tilt," and "an *epitaph* on my lords cock" (*BJ* 8:51.3, 5, 7, 15, 18). The list of reductive, parodic poetic genres culminates in the last line in an injunction, "pay me quickly," and a threat, "or Ile pay you" (*BJ* 8:51.22). The relationship between poet and patron is rendered not just crassly commercial but also coercive. This servant clearly feels empowered to bully his master, knowing that the patron owes his fashionable, literate reputation to him: "the world must know your greatnesse is my debtor" (*BJ* 8:51.4). Thus, the particular currency of the author's services gives him commercial bargaining power, even as he evinces scorn for the "vile verses" that Fine Grand required, which "cost me more paine" than if he had "made 'hem good" (*BJ* 8:51.19, 20). The image is of painstaking labor performed for a master whom one despises and yet must serve anyway. It is strikingly reminiscent of the work that *The Alchemist*'s rogues undertake with a blend of reluctance and enthusiasm.

The prefatory matter to early printed editions of *The Alchemist* reiterates the ambivalence, mixed with opportunism, of the author's foray into commercial service. Jonson was an innovator in composing front matter for plays, seizing the opportunity to frame his plays—as he says in his dedication "To the Reader," which appears in the quarto edition but not the folio—as texts designed for the "understander" (1). In "To the Reader," Jonson distinguishes his desired reader from the "pretender," who, like Fine Grand, is warned to "beware at what hands thou receivest thy commodity, for thou wert never more fair in the way to be cozened (than in this age) in poetry, especially in plays" (2–4). Although the ostensible purpose of the dedication is to contrast Jonson with playwrights who "cozen," the prefiguring of Face, Subtle, and Dol, described as "Cozeners at large" in "The Argument," is unmistakable, as is the suggestion that Jonson is likening his authorship to the rogues' deceitful practices. If the analogy holds, the status of the "understander" will be difficult, perhaps even impossible, for the reader to achieve, which leaves him or her in the position of the audiences addressed in the prologue. In these verses, Jonson at once addresses the audience as "Judging spectators" (3) and implicates them as unwitting targets of the satire they witness onstage:

> If there be any, that will sit so nigh
> Unto the stream, to look what it doth run,
> They shall find things, they'd think, or wish, were done;
> They are so natural follies, but so shown.
> As even the doers may see, and yet not own. (20–24)

The trouble is that no matter how closely the spectators apply *The Alchemist*'s lessons, they will be deceived by the way in which the author represents follies, and they will fail to acknowledge their susceptibility to the very vices and weaknesses that they believe they are well equipped to recognize. Many critics have read Jonson as seeking to hone a readership that he imagines as superior to the theatergoing public, but the textual dedication and the theatrical prologue tread some of the same ground. Readers and audiences always end up as the gulls, most emphatically at the moment when they are invited to see themselves as discerning patrons. In entering the marketplace of the theater and the book, they are transformed into a clientele and made correspondingly vulnerable to the ministrations of the tricky, self-serving servant.

Jonson's rhetorical cozenage casts doubt on the flattering, even obsequious tone of the dedication to Lady Mary Wroth that appears, with variations, in both the quarto and folio editions. In the quarto, the author presents "offerings" of sacrificial zeal at the altar of his noble patroness. He asserts that "it is your value of it, which remembers, where, when, and to whom it was first kindled" (13–15). On the face of it, the author resorts to the submissive posture of the courtly servant applying for patronage. Wroth is the arbiter of "value" and the dispenser of the sound "judgment" (17) that will nurture the printed book. But what secures Wroth from the tenuous position of the dedication's "understander" or the prologue's "judging spectators"? She has no rhetorical ground to stand on which is not already tainted, at least in the quarto, by the comparison of masters to gulls and authors to roguelike servants. The unsettledness of this patronage relation is enhanced by the last sentence, which indicates that "this," nominally Jonson's offering, is "forbidden to speak more; lest it talk, or look like one of the ambitious faces of the time: who, the more they paint, are the less themselves" (17–20). It only requires a little confusion in assigning a referent to "this" to construe Wroth herself as the silenced party, warned to stay away from cosmetics or other modes of aspirational, commercial artifice. Even Jonson's straightforward appeal for patronage yields commercial implications, making masters vulnerable to the self-deception that goes hand in hand with allowing oneself to be "catered to" in a capitalist economy.

While the rogue characters in *The Alchemist* do not enjoy the fruits of their labors, the textual front matter offers a more encouraging perspective for the aspiring servant. Face and his colleagues are emboldened by the advent of a commercial economy but are ultimately restricted to subservient service roles. Service is equally inescapable in the terms laid out in the prefatory text, but with the important difference that Jonson here highlights the opportunities for the author as servant to manipulate the service relation to his own profit. In creating new combinations of patronage and commercial models of service, he stresses that the author can simultaneously claim a disparaged social persona and assert control over his services. He may act the rogue without suffering the rogue's liabilities. In Jonson's projection here, the author surmounts many of the obstacles that confront servants without capital.

Service and Imitation in the *Discoveries*

In his compilation of critical reflections, *Timber or Discoveries,* Jonson returns again and again to service to generate images of authorship and aesthetics. His allusions to service in the text borrow from elite and humble, courtly and urban, respectable and illicit contexts. Like the other authors I discuss, Jonson draws on multiple categories of service to show their cross-pollination. What coheres the *Discoveries'* fragmented reflections on service is Jonson's attention to its imitative properties. The *Discoveries* is itself a work of imitation. In the style of the commonplace book, the text variously reproduces, translates, and adapts material from classical, Continental, and English sources. The textual structure is imitative, too: proximate passages, often taken from different authors, echo and distort one another. Jonson suggests that writing is a form of imitative service that creates the potential for both authorial self-possession and dispossession. The *Discoveries* uses service to explore the vacillations between these two extreme subject positions.

Because there is very little in the *Discoveries* that is wholly original to Jonson, he has often been accused of hypocrisy in drawing a strict line between moderate and immoderate forms of authorial imitation. But while that line does prove notoriously unstable, Jonson's self-conscious method shows him putting the theories he cites into practice, as he continually renegotiates the tenuous border between judgment and oblivion. The text condemns imposture as "a specious thing," that remains "ever asham'd of the light" (*BJ* 8:570), and elsewhere it considers the problems of theatrical impersonation:

> *I have* considered, our whole life is like a *Play:* wherein every man, forgetfull of himselfe, is in travaile with expression of another. Nay, wee so insist in imitating others, as wee cannot (when it is necessary) returne to our selves: like Children, that imitate the vices of *Stammerers* so long, till at last they become such; and make the habit to another nature, as it is never forgotten. (*BJ* 8:597)

The fear of losing oneself through habitual imitation lurks at the core of Jonson's disapproval. Heedless imitation carries the threat of self-nullification and exemplifies an unthinking embrace of lower impulses. To imitate others in this way is to serve the wrong master: "But wee make our selves slaves to our pleasures; and wee serve *Fame,* and Ambition, which is an equall slavery" (*BJ* 8:606). "Slavery" is the abyss into which service falls when passion, here described as the desire for reputation and advancement, dominates over reason. The author who wants to achieve these social registers of success above all else is in danger of imitating his master too closely, thereby dispossessing himself.

In a number of places, however, Jonson displays a more congenial attitude toward textual imitation. He observes that the habitual nature of imitation is an asset to the young writer in developing his own authority and voice: "The third requisite in our *Poet,* or Maker, is *Imitation,* to bee able to convert the substance, or Riches of an other Poet, to his owne use. To make choise of one excellent man above the rest, and so to follow him, till he grow very *Hee:* or so like him, as the Copie may be mistaken for the Principall" (*BJ* 8:638). As long as he takes care to "digest" the appropriated material, that is, to absorb it self-consciously and with confirmation of its excellence, he may safely impersonate it, even to the point of indistinguishability, as Jonson presumably sees himself doing in the process of selection and assemblage in the *Discoveries*.[45] In short, the poet's is "an Art of imitation, or faining; expressing the life of man in fit measure, numbers, and harmony, according to *Aristotle*" (*BJ* 8:635). The word "faining" pulls readers back toward the sphere of social impersonation and deception in which *The Alchemist*'s servants act and which Jonson represents pejoratively in the passage on theatrical imitation. That "faining" operates as a praiseworthy modifier for the author's work means that the relationship between service and imitation, which might at first seem to be regarded dubiously, requires more careful attention. George Rowe argues perceptively that despite Jonson's vehemence against the blurring of subject and object that occurs in imitation, Jonson also imparts the sense that "To live is to adopt roles, or rather . . . to imitate."[46] What is fascinating in Jonson's text, as well as in Rowe's comment, is that Jonson slides so effortlessly between social, theatrical, and authorial modes of imitation that even commentators do not observe the distinctions among them. For Jonson, "To live is . . . to imitate," to be sure, but he suggests equally that to write is to imitate and to act is to imitate. Just as the rogues in *The Alchemist* collapse a fraudulent aesthetic service with the material practice of service, so the *Discoveries* collapses spheres of imitation to show that aesthetics cannot be separated from material life.

The collapse can be witnessed from other standpoints, too. On several occasions, Jonson turns to extended metaphors or similes to illustrate that poets occupy the positions of servants. In one such passage, poetry becomes the master and the professional author a put-upon servant:

> Poetry, in this latter Age, hath prov'd but a meane Mistresse, to such as have wholly addicted themselves to her, or give their names up to her family. They who have but saluted her on the by, and now and then tendred their visits, shee hath done much for, and advanced in the way of their owne professions (both the *Law,* and the *Gospel*) beyond all they could have hoped, or done for themselves, without her favour. Wherein she doth emulate the judicious, but preposterous bounty of the times Grandes: who accumulate all they can upon the *Parasite,* or *Fresh-man* in their friendship; but thinke an old Client, or honest servant, bound by his place to write, and starve. (*BJ* 8:583)

Jonson does not seem to have a direct source for this passage. There may be an echo of Sidney calling England "so hard a stepmother to poets," but Jonson transfers the familial relation to service and makes poetry itself, rather than the nation, the figure of cruel authority.[47] The connotations of a female mistress allow Jonson to play on erotic, as well as social and occupational, forms of subjugation. In comparing the mistress to the "times Grandes," he implies poetry's noble status but also its fatal trendiness, as the mistress, perhaps turned prostitute, bestows her favors and the promise of advancement on undeserving "parasites," novices, and those who need her patronage the least. Meanwhile, the "old client" and the "honest servant," those servants who persist in the patriarchal mold, have only penury in reward for their labor and loyalty. According to Jonson's analogy, the true poet's lot is that of the many servants whose unfair treatment at the hands of their masters bears witness to the breakdown in the patriarchal institution of service. The insistence, here and elsewhere in the *Discoveries,* that the poet dwells in poverty reminds us that Jonson was at times drawn to identify with a type of servant that he sees as outmoded but admirable.[48]

The identification between author and the traditional servant is complicated by the knowledge that Jonson was hardly bound to the acceptance of marginality and abjectness signaled in the foregoing passage. It is revealing that the passage that follows, which begins: "*Indeed, the multitude commend Writers, as they doe Fencers, or Wrestlers*" appears almost word for word in *The Alchemist*'s "To the Reader," where Jonson equivocates about his similarity to "cozening" rogues. The possibility that even the true poet might play the part of the self-serving, unethical servant returns in the *Discoveries,* in a passage adopted from Machiavelli, when Jonson gives counsel to a prince on how to judge his advisors and followers. According to Jonson and Machiavelli, selfish servants come in two varieties. The first is lazy and in thrall to base emotions. The second "remove themselves upon craft, and designe (as the *Architects* say) with a premeditated thought to their owne, rather their *Princes* profit. Such let the *Prince* take heed of, and not doubt to reckon in the List of his open enemies" (*BJ* 8:598). Although Jonson does not use the term, these servants are drawn as practitioners of "eye-service," along the lines of the epistemologically suspect servants portrayed in didactic literature and the rogues who perform service in bad faith in *The Alchemist*.[49] Jonson condemns the servant who seeks primarily his own profit and who for that reason merely imitates the true servant. The self-interested servant fits the profile of unhealthy imitation described elsewhere by Jonson, insofar as he is "in travaile with expression of another." But is he also "forgetfull of himselfe"? If anything, he proves too mindful of his self. And if we place beside the untrustworthy servant the dictum that the poet should take "the substance, or Riches of an other Poet, to his owne use," with the goal of becoming "so like him, as the Copie may be mistaken for the Principall," does it not suggest that the good poet, himself a kind of servant, is counseled to do exactly as the bad servant does? The poet shares with the slippery servant an emphasis on "craft," and while the poet is supposed to use it as a "true Artificer" would, the servant's cunning and trickiness inevitably creep in as well.

Because Jonson does not distinguish either between material and aesthetic service or between social and authorial imitation, he allows the poet to slip between roles, inhabiting at some moments the persona of the faithful servant who abjures commerce and the seeking of profit and at other moments the persona of the faithless servant who embraces concepts of profit and use that belong to the new capitalist economy. Figures of service help Jonson express his vision of authorship as straddling patronage and commerce, patriarchal traditions and an emerging affect of the public as "master." Interwoven with issues about authorship are aesthetic ones: for Jonson, service communicates a complex attitude toward poetry as a form or outgrowth of *imitatio*, the humanist pedagogy of imitation I discussed in the introduction. Where on the continuum between the reproduction of approved sources and their transformation should poetic production lie? Does taking another's work "to his owne use" entail a betrayal of one's "master," the textual authority one takes as an exemplar? Or should the poet regard such authorities more in the light of the theatergoing or book-buying public, as entities to which one pays homage but which are simultaneously fleeced for the poet's gain? And what does it mean for poetic imitation to yield one's "owne use"? Is the objective solely to achieve a kind of self-ownership, as some critics on Jonson have asserted, or is there an acknowledgment that the poet remains a servant, who "uses" his master's material and tries to glean a profit from it but who is nevertheless never fully autonomous or self-possessing? The pressing questions raised in the *Discoveries* about the author's work are generated through the same thematics and images of service that Jonson puts onstage in *The Alchemist*. In both texts, one written for theatrical performance and the book trade and the other published only after his death, Jonson shows that aesthetic creation always has social and public dimensions, a fact that has profound implications for the author's understanding of who he is and what he does.

"Broome's Sweepings": Service in the Later Jonson

The story of Jonson's later career, as it has often been told, is one of retrenchment in the face of the "multitudes," against whom he fulminates in the *Discoveries* and the dedication in the quarto edition of *The Alchemist,* in favor of the readerly "understander" he evokes in the latter. As Loewenstein points out, however, writing for the theater and print publication were mutually supportive propositions for Jonson, precisely because they had evolved into competing options: "when he prepares a script for the press, the preparation explores and evaluates the theater, from which the script is wrested, and the press, to which it is entrusted."[50] Writing more for patrons and print, and less for the theater, trends that marked the second half of Jonson's career, did not mean that he detached from the growing commercial orientation of service. On the contrary, his later writings are especially preoccupied with their uneasy location in the interstices of older and newer paradigms of service. This preoccupation was only heightened by Jonson's largely unsuccessful plays of the 1620s and '30s. Print publication allowed Jonson to reflect on playwriting, as in "Ode to Himself," attached as an epilogue to *The New Inn* (1629). The verses are an often-cited testament to Jonson's frustration with popular taste and the vagaries of writing for the theater, and indeed, they do attempt to draw a firm distinction between Jonson and his former servant turned playwright, Richard Brome. On that basis, the poem opposes Jonson to the degraded environs of seventeenth-century theater. And yet, in this and other later poetry, he seems inexorably drawn back to the servant's position in ways that reveal how the public and commercial nature of the theater continued to inflect his authorship.

In stressing his disdain for the current state of the theater—"Come leave the loathed stage," the poem begins—Jonson turns to a literal servant-master relationship.[51] In the second stanza of "Ode to Himself," he tries to convince himself to abandon the theater once and for all: "'Twere simple fury, still thyself to waste/On such as have no taste;" (*CP* 13–14). This prepares the way for a description of the waste material that passes for drama in the current theatrical climate, culminating in a bitter indictment:

> Broome's sweepings do as well
> There as his master's meal;
> For who the relish of these guests will fit
> Needs set them but the alms-basket of wit. (*CP* 27–30)

Jonson is referring to, and punning on, Richard Brome's name. His servant's refuselike "sweepings" and "alms-basket of wit," images that summon, respectively, the humble labor of domestic servitude and the debasement of public charity, cannot compare to the master's rich provisions. Meanwhile, Jonson uses domestic mastery to symbolize, and reinforce, his artistic mastery. The servant is slotted into a pale imitative position from which Jonson is at pains to detach himself. Yet Jonson's mastery goes unrewarded, and in the last two stanzas, he resolves to "leave things so prostitute,/And take th'Alcaic lute" (*CP* 41–42). While Brome remains strictly earthbound, tied to the everyday tools of the servant's trade, Jonson imagines himself by the end of the poem as transcendent, singing "the glories of thy King" (*CP* 52) and striking envy in his detractors' hearts. But his triumph is in the realm of the future imaginary, and the poem ends up reinforcing that theatrical service provides resources to the author, for as the poem freely acknowledges, "Broome's sweepings" satisfy playgoers and, by extension, fill the theater's coffers.

Jonson returned to the theme in verses attached to Brome's published play *The Northern Lasse* (1632). They realign Jonson with the servant and take a more sympathetic stance toward Brome than does "Ode to Himself." The poem is addressed: "To my old Faithfull Seruant: and (by his continu'd Vertue) my louing Friend: the Author of this Work, M. RICH. BROME." Brome's role as servant still comes first, though he has by now earned the appellation of friend as well. Jonson begins by reminding Brome of their previous relationship:

> I Had you for a Seruant, once, Dick Brome;
> And you perform'd a Seruants faithfull parts:
> Now, you are got into a nearer roome,
> Of Fellowship, professing my old Arts. (*BJ* 8:409.1–4)

The first two lines establish Brome as the "faithfull" servant, but even here, some doubt, expressed in the theatrical language of "perform'd" and "parts," surrounds Brome's sincerity. Did Brome merely impersonate the good servant, all the while harboring secret ambitions, like Face or Subtle? The significant change occurs in the third line, as Brome moves to a "nearer roome." In the *Discoveries*, Jonson uses an architectural simile to convey his adherence to the Unity of Action: "Wee conclude the fable, to be the *imitation* of one perfect, and intire Action; as one perfect, and intire place is requir'd to a building" (*BJ* 8:645). *The Alchemist* puts this theory into practice, for Lovewit's house instantiates the play's tight comic form.[52] In "To my old Faithfull Seruant," Brome's movement to a "nearer" room confirms his ascent from servant, who would have lodged farther away from his master, to playwright.

Brome's advancement from servant to master is not simply a metaphor for his achievement of aesthetic maturity but also a register of the theatrical apprenticeship Brome performed as Jonson's servant. The new relationship between Jonson and Brome is figured in terms of "fellowship," evoking a guild fraternity. "Fellowship" recollects Jonson's participation in the tilers and bricklayers' guild and invites readers to make the connection between trade guilds and the guild structure that was strongly implicated in theatrical work. Brome is praised for having "seru'd your time/A Prentise-ship" (*BJ* 8:409.9–10), in contrast to the current crop of playwrights whom Jonson lambastes in the latter half of the poem for failing to submit themselves to a disciplined training in their "trade" (*BJ* 8: 409.13). If Brome has achieved fellowship with Jonson, like Deloney's apprentices in *The Gentle Craft*, he has done so by working his way up through a traditional hierarchy of service, scrupulously observing the outward proprieties of apprenticeship, though also like Deloney's characters, he may have practiced strategy to get ahead. Even with its more generous attitude toward Brome, the verses are careful to maintain a hierarchical distinction that echoes the servant-master disparity. "My old Arts" remain Jonson's provenance, which Brome has taken upon himself to "profess," while elsewhere he reminds the younger playwright, in case he has forgotten, that "I, your *Master* first did teach the Age" (*BJ* 8:409.8) the "Comick Lawes" (*BJ* 8:409.7) that Brome applies now to modest success. Jonson is still Brome's master as well as the self-proclaimed master of playwriting.

"Ode to Himself" and "To my old Faithfull Seruant" might be taken to demonstrate that Jonson has left behind his identification with servants. However, the consciousness that very little separates Jonson from his former servant is embedded not far from the surface. In "To my old Faithfull Seruant," Jonson describes himself as having come up through the apprenticeship and guild system. In former times, he says, "Men tooke up trades/That knew the Crafts they had bin bred in, right" (*BJ* 8:409.13–14), crafts like those practiced by the "bilbo-smith," "physician," and "cobler" (*BJ* 8:409.15, 16, 17).[53] Brome's modest beginnings repeat Jonson's own, so that in highlighting Brome's ascension through an uneasy melding of faithful and opportunistic service, Jonson reflects on his own authorial trajectory. The servant behind the master constantly rearticulates himself. Jonson makes his acrimony grist for the poetic mill. The contingency of authorial mastery remains, and what rushes in to fill the vacuum is the servant: impersonating, imitating, transgressing, and creating.

The late poem "Epistle to my Lady Covell" finds Jonson near the end of his career still working at the same knot of service that preoccupied him in *The Alchemist*, now translated from an urban, commercial context to a private, courtly realm. Despite these differences, Jonson invests the patronage relationship with commercial and theatrical qualities. "You won not Verses, Madam, you won mee," the first line announces, going on to state: "So have you gain'd a Servant, and a Muse" (*BJ* 8:230.5). Although the poet quickly attempts to excuse himself from service on the basis of his age and unwieldy corporeality, the ultimate message about the servant and the muse, as Richard Helgerson notes, amounts to: "Get one . . . and you get the other."[54] Another way of putting it is that for Jonson, his muse *is* a servant. He conjures the image of an ethereal, feminine familiar: "One can tread the Aire,/and stroke the water, nimble, chast, and faire,/Sleep in a Virgins bosome without feare" (*BJ* 8:230.13–15). This muse is also a jester and entertainer, "to make you merry on the Dressing stoole,/A mornings" (*BJ* 8:230.21–22). The combination of sensual, even erotic intimacy, luxury, and the sensation of mastery that Jonson's muse will deliver to Lady Covell brings us back once again to the rogues' exorbitant promises to their clients in *The Alchemist*, and outward from there to the deceptive promises made to Jonson's audiences and readers. The vision is that service caters to the master's most deeply held desires, and although the arena has changed drastically from Lovewit's urban house and the London theaters, the terms in which Jonson makes his supplication are strikingly similar. As is usual with Jonson, he moves into an economic register to figure the exchange of services: "I can lose none in tendring these to you./I gaine, in having leave to keep my Day,/And should grow rich, had I much more to pay" (*BJ* 8:230.28–30). The lines invert the expected direction of payment by suggesting that it is the poet who pays the patron and gains immaterial virtues as a result. Yet, Jonson's tongue seems firmly in cheek, for readers know that he hopes to "grow rich" materially from his tender of verses to Lady Covell. And if the poem's addressee gets this joke, does she suspect as well that she is being sold a gulling muse? The muse is much more tempting a servant than Jonson himself, "laden with Bellie" (*BJ* 8:230.9), and in fact she becomes a proxy for the author's deceitful service. The servant figure whom Jonson portrays in the "Epistle" is characteristically self-possessed, displaying economic and subjective agency. He is also dispossessed, for he has been supplanted in the lucrative role of servant by his own muse.

If Jonson's muse is a servant, it is also true that the servant is his muse. In the works this chapter has examined, servants of even the most peripheral or humble status have functions that are expressly performa-tive and authorial, imitative and creative. The reason that Jonson returns throughout his career and across genres to an identification with service is that it provides extraordinary resources for his quest to define author-ship and literary production under the rapidly changing socioeconomic conditions of the early seventeenth century. An important part of this definitional project is comprehending the transition from patronage to public consumption of texts. I have suggested that service helps Jonson explore how the author's relation to audiences and readers participates in this transition. Although it is tempting to harness this narrative to argue that Jonson progressed toward mastery and complete self-possession, his representations of service show such aspirations to be illusory. Jonson realized that early modern authors were cast as servants and that they thus depended on a dispossession that, ironically, gave new fuel to their creative imitations.

⁓

CHAPTER FIVE

Tragicomic Service

The Winter's Tale and *The Tempest*

William Shakespeare was famously Ben Jonson's target in *Bartholomew Fair* (1614) for his production of "Tales, Tempests, and such like droller-ies" (*BF* induction, 125). Jonson's induction contractually stipulates that his play will not contain a "servant-monster," nor will he "mix his head with other men's heels" to give the audience the "jigs and dances" it so desires (*BF* 122–23, 126, 127). Jonson associates Shakespeare's foray into tragicomedy with degrading combinations of character and form: the tragicomic servant is lowered—or displays his low status—in merg-ing with the subhuman, while the tragicomic form debases authorial wit (the "head") with entertainments that pander to audiences ("other men's heels"). Jonson makes the monstrous servant the prototype for a dra-matic form that fails to observe the boundaries between higher faculties and lower instincts.

The irony of his criticism is that, as I discussed in chapter 4, Jon-son was no stranger to servants who skirted the margins and lowest depths of the human in the attempt to elevate themselves. The "servant-monster" could describe more broadly the servant rogues who populate *The Alchemist* and even the figure of Jonson, who in "Epistle to my Lady Covell" is "tardie, cold,/Unprofitable Chattell" (*BJ* 8:230.7–8). One can imagine Prospero speaking this phrase about Caliban. In fact, Jonson and Shakespeare shared a preoccupation with servants who were more than one thing at once, who could occupy roles both agentive and instrumen-tal. Both playwrights wrote dramas in which capitalist forms of service generate a logic of constant circulation and substitution, creating new subject positions but also new forms of subjugation for servants. Jonson may have objected to the literal manifestation of the "servant-monster," but he, like Shakespeare, used service as the basis for an aesthetic that generated and required public reception.

In chapter 1, I argued that Shakespeare's early comedies *The Comedy of Errors* and *The Two Gentlemen of Verona* draw on Shakespeare's relationship to the theatrical apprentice system to develop new aesthetic possibilities for drama. In this chapter, I suggest that Shakespeare's late tragicomedies *The Winter's Tale* (1610–11) and *The Tempest* (1610–11) reveal his continued investment in service at the end of his career. In the almost two decades between these two pairs of plays, Shakespeare had become the most prominent playwright on the theatrical scene. He had advanced his economic and social position and was by the close of his career "a man of considerable property and fame."[1] During the same span of time, the other authors I have discussed—Thomas Nashe, Thomas Deloney, Thomas Dekker, and Ben Jonson—made service the basis for their own innovations to dramatic and prose form. Although by 1610 Shakespeare occupied a masterful position, he nevertheless sustained his identification with service. In *The Winter's Tale* and *The Tempest*, Shakespeare turned the resources of service toward what was for him a new genre: the tragicomedy.

This chapter argues that Shakespeare uses service to represent the value of what Sidney called the "mongrel tragi-comedy" and Jonson the "servant-monster."[2] Shakespeare takes the implication that tragicomedy is a mismatched, disunified form and, as Deloney and Dekker did, turns it into an aesthetic that privileges the mixing of genres and servants. *The Winter's Tale* and *The Tempest* demonstrate how distinct, even opposed categories of service circulate and engage in exchanges endemic to a capitalist economy. The rogue Autolycus, in *The Winter's Tale,* and the slave Caliban, in *The Tempest,* mount effective performances of courtly service, while the courtiers in *The Winter's Tale* are skilled at playing the rogue's part. Capitalist discourses of service thereby infiltrate and alter the discourses of courtly service. The increased inequities of capitalism also feature in the two plays. Shakespeare portrays extreme disparities between his tragicomic servants: they are either elite and courtly or they are illicit, abject, and enslaved. There are no aspiring shoemakers in these plays. Yet just as taxonomies of service break down, so the servants develop subjectivities that derive from their aesthetic agency rather than from their social positions. Courtly and marginal servants collaborate to produce the "paradoxical unity" of tragicomedy.[3] The imitative and transformational qualities of service are a model for tragicomic form.

The Winter's Tale and *The Tempest* consolidate Shakespeare's claims for the public nature of the theater. The plays' early performance histories indicate productions in courtly and urban, private and public contexts. *The Winter's Tale* was performed at the Globe in May 1611, at court the same year, and at court again during the Christmas season of 1612–13. On both the court occasions, *The Tempest* was performed as well.[4] And it was likely, according to Andrew Gurr, that *The Tempest* was originally written to be performed at Blackfriars.[5] Shakespeare's tragicomedies cultivate a sense of broad-based theatergoing publics, of which the court was only one constituent. The image of the playwright that emerges from the tragicomedies is similarly versatile and wide-ranging. Shakespeare represents himself through his servants as a figure whose varied, even motley, attributes render him uniquely able to enter into exchanges of service with various and diverse audiences. The tragicomedies advance the argument set forth in the early comedies for the transformative power of the theater, a power that makes common cause between the theater's economic potential and its aesthetics. Shakespeare constructs a heterogeneous dramatic form that defines public reception in the widest possible terms.

In making these claims for the theater, Shakespeare addresses the ethical stakes of aesthetic service. To undertake a performance of service, both in the tragicomedies and in the theater itself, requires ethical judgments about how to interpret the master's command and how to act in response to it. To put it differently, representing a master opens possibilities for economic, social, and subjective agency that come with responsibilities. *The Winter's Tale* depicts its servants—Camillo, Paulina, and Autolycus—converting their sovereigns' unethical commands into ethical outcomes. They do so by exploiting a theatrical space in which they realize the potentially transformative effects of their performances on others. As Valerie Forman has pointed out, tragicomedy is at its core "a genre about the transformation of genre," one that poses the question of how comedy can be produced from tragedy. Forman argues that tragicomedy is structured on the principle of global capitalist investment, which necessitates an initial loss that is expected to grow on its return.[6] In weighing the ethics of their aesthetic service, the servants act as agents of this economic and generic transaction. Asserting that the theater spurs ethical reflection, Shakespeare rebuts the didactic literature of service, which portrays the aesthetic servant as self-promoting and deceitful. Shakespeare reconciles these dissimulative traits with an ethical project of reform; in the tragicomedies, servants are simultaneously self-serving and other-directed, dishonest and loyal. According to this logic, the theater at once deceives its audiences with feigned illusions and enables their scrutiny of themselves and recognition of others. Shakespeare's tragicomedies suggest that the social experience of playgoing is also an ethical one.

The Tempest, to which I turn in the concluding section, highlights ethics by representing the emerging discourse of slavery as the potential future of service. Shakespeare interweaves slavery with familiar metropolitan discourses of service. On the one hand, this porousness signals servants' new vulnerability in the global capitalist economy that was beginning to take shape in the early seventeenth century. On the other hand, Shakespeare insists that Ariel's and Caliban's performances of service, as in other texts I have discussed, unsettle mastery and form viable subject positions. *The Tempest* suggests that to serve is to be a subject and thus to be human. Shakespeare calls on his audiences, in turn, to engage ethically with the servants they watch onstage.

Courtiers and Rogues in *The Book of the Courtier* and *A Caveat for Common Cursitors*

In *The Winter's Tale,* Leontes's desires present an urgent ethical problem. On the dubious evidence of "the infection of my brains/And hard'ning of my brows" (1.2.147–48), Leontes determines that his wife, Hermione, has had an affair with his best friend, Polixenes, and that their newborn daughter is a product of this infidelity. He orders the condemnation and death of his wife and daughter, and he relies on servants to translate this order into action. However, the servants do not bring Leontes's will to fruition, nor do they carry out Polixenes's will later in the play. Instead, Shakespeare's elite courtiers and marginal rogue cooperatively exploit the space that exists between the master's order and the servant's fulfillment of it. In patriarchal ideologies of service, the servant is supposed to bridge the gap by acting as a mimetic reproduction of the master. But the injunction to act for the master gives the servant a representational license that *The Winter's Tale*'s servants seize. As Richard Strier has argued, in Shakespearean scenarios where the master acts as a tyrant and issues immoral commands, the most moral service is disobedient service.[7] Shakespeare manifests the ethical nature of such service in the servants' self-consciously aesthetic performances and suggests that these performances occur most effectively in socially hybrid collaborations.

Rarely have critics analyzed Camillo, Paulina, and Autolycus jointly. Paulina and Autolycus have each come in for a good deal of attention, the former for staging crucial interruptions of patriarchy and the latter for representing the protean author or burgeoning print culture.[8] Camillo, on the other hand, has tended to disappear from critical scrutiny, although he offers one of Shakespeare's most complex portrayals of the courtier.[9] Most critics, with one notable exception, have duplicated the play's apparent separation of Autolycus from the court.[10] Yet if we perceive that Autolycus plays service roles that are full of artifice, in both senses of the word, then we invite a connection to Camillo and Paulina, each of whom integrates artifice with service. In redirecting Leontes's and Polixenes's tragic desires to comic outcomes, courtiers and rogue become increasingly intertwined. The courtiers reveal their debt to discourses of the rogue, while the rogue increasingly reveals his dependence on discourses of the court.

In order to create such intersections, Shakespeare incorporates and blends the genres of courtier and rogue literature. In so doing, he suggests that courtiers and rogues are closer in their approach to service than readers might suspect. Two prominent examples of these genres, Baldesar Castiglione's *Book of the Courtier* (1516–18) and Thomas Harman's *A Caveat for Common Cursitors, Vulgarly Called Vagabonds* (1566), highlight the overlapping requirements for the successful courtier and rogue which Shakespeare exploits in *The Winter's Tale*. Both texts represent their subjects as using the mimetic quality of service: courtiers are expected to imitate their masters but also to generate a model for their masters to emulate; and Harman's rogues often imitate "true" servants to further their schemes. The courtier and the rogue both cultivate aesthetic skills because in their otherwise wildly disparate spheres, successful self-presentation is paramount to making a profit, although of course the nature of that profit can be defined in varying terms.

Castiglione assumes the interpenetration of aesthetics and service. His courtiers recognize that imitations cross between art and life, making humanist *imitatio* a model for social imitation. Sounding like Jonson in his writings on *imitatio* in the *Discoveries,* Castiglione's Ferdinand Fergoso maintains that the key to success in writing is selecting a model worthy of emulation: "one has to decide to imitate someone who by common consent is accepted as sound, and to employ him continuously as a guide and protection against hostile critics" (*BC,* 73).[11] The mimetic principle also guides courtly service: the aspiring courtier is advised to "make a constant effort to imitate, and, if possible, exactly reproduce his master" (*BC,* 66). Just as the writer improves his artistry by internalizing classical models, so the courtier becomes a more perfect example of his vocation by replicating his master. Aesthetic facility is not only analogized to social skills, it is the most important component of these skills.[12]

The question of how closely an imitation should hew to the original, both in art and life, troubles Castiglione's text as it troubled Jonson's. In a passage on the necessity of changes in the vernacular language, the same figure who counsels the courtier to reproduce his master warns against excessive fidelity to classical authorities: "So by insisting on imitating the ancients we fail to imitate them" (*BC*, 76), since even those ancient writers exercised judgment about when to imitate and when to depart from their forebears. The exercise of judgment is essential to selecting one's models and choosing how one uses them. Such discretion is also a matter of discussion when it comes to the courtier's attitude toward imitating his master, and the answers are not always clear. Some of Castiglione's courtiers advise a servant who finds himself in the employ of a "wicked and malignant" master to leave immediately, while others find this solution impractical, for "in this matter courtiers are like caged birds" (*BC*, 130). The courtier Federico has the last word: "What you must do . . . is to obey your lord in everything that redounds to his profit and honour, but not as regards things that bring him loss and shame" (*BC*, 131). His interlocutors are unsatisfied, wanting to know how the courtier distinguishes "what is really good from what merely appears to be" (*BC*, 131). But Federico refuses any response beyond this dictum: "let everything be decided by your discretion" (*BC*, 131). This scenario echoes in the stark dilemma faced by the kings' servants in *The Winter's Tale* of how to tell the "really good" from that which masquerades as the good. The indescribable quality of the courtier's discretion is in fact aesthetic, in the sense that it requires the exercise of interpretive judgment. Refusing to make such hard choices in service is presented as both an aesthetic and ethical failure.

The Book of the Courtier goes even further in its recommendations in cases where the master is following a misguided course. At these moments, it is incumbent on the courtier to reverse the course of imitation and become the pedagogue, albeit one who teaches through aesthetic means:

> In this way, the courtier will be able to lead his prince along the stern path of virtue, adorning it, however, with shady fronds and strewing it with gay flowers to lessen the tedium of an arduous journey for one whose endurance is slight; and so now with music, now with arms and horses, at other times with verse or with conversations about love, and with all the means these gentlemen have suggested, he will be able to keep the prince continually absorbed in innocent pleasures, while also, as I have said, always accompanying these beguilements with emphasis on some virtuous habit, and in that way practicing a healthy deception like a shrewd doctor who spreads some sweet liquid on the rim of a cup when he wants a frail and sickly child to take a bitter medicine. (*BC*, 288–89)

The courtier's art deceives in order to cure, a medical metaphor that Shakespeare adopts to represent the physic that *The Winter's Tale*'s courtiers apply to their diseased king. Thus, courtiers are called upon to generate performances of service, sometimes literal ones, that intervene in scenes of unethical command.

The mingled ethics and aesthetics of Castiglione's courtiers require policing sometimes unreliable social boundaries. Federico draws a firm line around the courtier's acceptable comportment, cautioning that he must not "act like a peasant who stinks of the soil a mile off. For a man of this sort can never hope to become a good courtier and indeed can be given no occupation other than looking after the farm animals" (*BC*, 147). The courtier must be at pains to avoid acting like someone who engages in physical labor. But later, when Bernardo discusses the courtier's use of humor and jokes, he recounts a practical joke that crosses the line between courtier and peasant. In the anecdote, a peasant impersonates a "real" courtier so convincingly that two noble ladies of the court can hardly be persuaded of his true identity. Bernardo attributes the peasant's success initially to his muteness: "He was so well attired in his livery and so elegantly decked out that, although he was only accustomed to looking after cattle and knew no other profession, by anyone not hearing him speak he would have been taken for a very fine gentleman indeed" (*BC*, 188–89). But even when they finally hear him speak, the two women imagine that he is merely impersonating a rough peasant: "Just imagine! How well he mimics the language!" (*BC*, 189). Though they have mistaken the nature of the impersonator and his impersonation, the women pinpoint the source of discomfort in the practical joke, for "mimicry" is a crucial aspect of the courtier's vocation. At the same time, the joke confirms the courtier's susceptibility to fraudulent performances. Because the courtier depends on externalized performance, even a peasant can present himself as a believable courtier, his rustic quirks perceived as just another manifestation of courtly mimesis. The aesthetic qualities that make the courtier successful also make him vulnerable to socially threatening impostures.[13] As I will show shortly, Shakespeare adapts this point in *The Winter's Tale* to suggest, first, that making aesthetic, ethically difficult decisions in courtly service also requires taking considerable social risks; and second, that sometimes making such decisions is enhanced by taking social risks.

While Castiglione suggests that courtiers are vulnerable to roguish influences, Harman's *A Caveat for Common Cursitors* shows that rogues are liable to become servants. The aesthetic and ethical stakes of service are heightened for rogues, as they are for courtiers. Castiglione's comparison of courtiers to "caged birds" has particular resonance with the representation of rogues as lacking control over their engagement with service, a haplessness that inflects Shakespeare's characterization of Autolycus. Harman's text recognizes the universal, sometimes suffocating quality that clung to service in the period and the way in which it claimed even marginal subjects. In *The Winter's Tale*, Autolycus's emancipation from service gradually reveals itself as an illusion, just as Harman's rogues are often unwillingly consigned to service, or at least to acting the part of the servant.[14] At the same time, to be "out of service" is sometimes presented as a necessity rather than a choice. Where courtiers are threatened by the ease with which it is possible to simulate their positions, rogues are threatened by the power of service norms to co-opt their oppositional positions or, conversely, to keep them bound in opposition. The rogue's choice, according to Harman and Shakespeare both, would have been familiar to Jonson: not whether or not to serve but how best to handle service.

A Caveat for Common Cursitors describes rogues negotiating with service in several ways: through their blatant rejection of a servant's occupation, their inadequacy to it, their counterfeit performances of the servant's role, and their movement in and out of service. These narrative threads overlap and intertwine; no single stance toward service is permanent or irrevocable. In his catalogue of rogues, Harman refers to Rufflers as "the out-casts of serving-men" who have chosen a life of idleness and beggary over honest service.[15] Similarly, some Upright Men are "serving-men, artificers, and laboring men, traded up in husbandry, . . . not minding to get their living with the sweat of their face" (CC, 116). And Dells, whom Harman characterizes as young girls who have not yet become sexually active, often flee service to escape "some sharp mistress that they serve" (CC, 144). Thus, Harman implies that rogues eschew service, in which they would earn an "honest" living by placing the master's interest before their own, in favor of direct self-interest, even if in the case of the Dells self-interest shades into self-preservation. The plaint of a walking Mort reveals a more complicated motivation. She tells Harman that she has no choice but to engage in illicit behavior because "None will take me into service. But I labor in harvest-time honestly" (CC, 139). Her statement, though Harman regards it skeptically, fits with the evidence of a surplus of laborers and a surge in unemployment across rural England during the sixteenth century. The Mort presents her options as severely curtailed and expresses the desire to practice service when the opportunity arises. Her words suggest that she does not deliberately maintain a permanent position outside of service. Even as Harman's text works to position rogues and vagabonds outside the structures of service, it cannot help but reveal the ways in which rogues could be—or wished to be— servants.

Harman struggles to distinguish between the counterfeit and real service of rogues. He doubts that the walking Mort has really labored for the harvest: "I think but a while with honesty," he tells her (CC, 139). In other cases, Harman describes how rogues imitate service to further criminal schemes.[16] To gain the trust of a intended victim, two rufflers disguise themselves as master and servant, "the one mannerly waiting on the other as [if] one had been the master, and the other the man, or servant, carrying his master's cloak" (CC, 116). The thieves' impersonations exploit the conventionality and credibility of the servant-master relationship; in so doing, Harman insinuates, they mock those roles. When they find one last coin buried deep in the victim's purse, the "gentleman thief" announces sardonically, "Good lord, what a world is this! How may . . . a man believe or trust in the same?" (CC, 116). The rufflers perform their parts with a winking self-consciousness that reminds us that service is always an aesthetic performance. In this example, the performance is decidedly unethical.

There are moments, however, when the rogues' performances of service are less clearly fraudulent. Harman narrates a common ploy in which an Upright Man would descend on "a poor husbandman's house" and "stoutly demand his charity, either shewing how he hath served in the wars, and there maimed, either that he seeketh service, and saith he would be glad to take pain for his living, although he meaneth nothing less" (CC, 117). The visit allows the rogue to scour the house for portable property, which Harman assures his readers that he and his confederates will filch on a return trip. But the text glosses over the service for which the rogues contract, though it does mention that they refuse food and drink, taking only money as recompense, which perhaps points to their doing some temporary service for the household. Harman is forced to acknowledge that some will "have good credit" in a certain shire, "where they work a month in a place or more, and will for that time behave themselves very honestly and painfully and may at any time for their good usage have work of them" (CC, 118). It is difficult, in short, for Harman to assert that the rogues' service is merely a manipulative act, particularly when their self-interested aims are filtered through "honest" work. The rogues' counterfeit performances of service merge in Harman's account with actual labor, raising the question of where the line can be drawn between these two modes of engagement.

Harman's text represents downward mobility in the form of a servant turned rogue. Identifying a problem treated in the didactic literature of service, *A Caveat* attributes servants' precipitous descents to the dangers of obeying immoral commands, exactly the peril that Shakespeare's courtiers face. Harman relates the anecdote of a former courtly servant: "This Stradling saith he was the Lord Stourton's man, and, when he was executed, for very pensiveness of mind, he fell out of his wit, and so continued a year after and more" (CC, 128). Stradling's tale had a possible basis in fact. A Baron Stouton was convicted in 1577 of contracting his servants to murder two of his neighbors.[17] Stradling performs the horrific personal consequences of his mimetic act, his incoherence of speech and uncontrollable palsy signifying the self-destruction that ensues from his transparent reproduction of his master. In standing in for his master, he has lost himself. Harman's Stradling shows that a servant's overly dogmatic imitation turns him into a rogue. As in *The Book of the Courtier*, the servant is called upon to make an ethical judgment in acting on his master's orders. Stradling's failure to do so thrusts him outside of service altogether. His story plays a variant on an early modern proverb about the vulnerability of servants' positions: "*An olde Seruingman, a young Begger.*"[18]

The ethical significance of aesthetic service is especially pronounced at either extreme of the social spectrum, at points where the possibilities and limits of service are tested. The decisions that Castiglione's courtiers make in the course of service affect the sphere of political governance. The attitude of Harman's rogues toward service has a direct effect on social stability. In this sense, both courtiers and rogues possess a strong agency which derives from their interpretations of service. Castiglione and Harman also indicate the considerable risks that such interpretations entail for servants. *The Winter's Tale* is alert to both of these points. Shakespeare portrays courtiers and rogues not only acting like one another but also interacting with one another. The play dramatizes the risks that elite and marginal servants confront and suggests that when they join together, they display a socially mixed agency that creates powerful effects.

The Tragicomic Space of Service: *The Winter's Tale*

The Winter's Tale establishes from its earliest scenes the difficulty of the courtier's position when confronted with a master who issues unethical orders, in this case a master who wants to erase the difference between himself and others and yet is terrified of the consequences. Leontes first demands of Camillo that he confirm an adulterous relationship between Hermione and Polixenes. Underlining and preceding this demand is the desire that those with whom he is most intimate serve as duplications of him. As act 1, scene 2 shows, that demand is inscribed not only as fantasy but also as its opposite, the nightmare of too much similitude. Polixenes's nostalgic image of him and Leontes as "twinned lambs" (1.2.69) describes a lost childhood ideal but also gives backing to Leontes's belief that Polixenes has taken his place with his wife.[19] Hermione, meanwhile, is enjoined to act as Leontes's representative in winning Polixenes's assent to stay longer in Sicilia, but her very success as acting as her husband's proxy again invites his suspicion. Finally, Mamillius presents a visual "copy" (1.2.124) of his father, which proves insufficient to reassure Leontes of his paternity because he does not trust the mimetic faculties on which he has staked everything. In fact, the more closely his friend, wife, and son mirror him, the more wildly distrustful he becomes. The self that he wants to see mirrored back to him only becomes more elusive in the glimpses that these others provide of it.

Camillo represents Leontes's final hope—and perhaps his greatest fear—of finding self-assurance in another's imitation of him. Camillo is present from the beginning of act 1, scene 2, but he does not speak until Leontes has exhausted his other mimetic options. As if Shakespeare is gesturing at an equivalence between son and servant, Leontes moves seamlessly from questioning his paternity of Mamillius to seeking affirmation in Camillo.[20] Patriarchal ideologies give Leontes ample justification to look to his servant for a reproductive image of himself. But when Leontes begins sounding him out about Hermione's and Polixenes's behavior and receives no confirmation of his suspicion, it soon becomes clear to him that Camillo will not provide such assurance. Leontes's reaction is swift:

> I have trusted thee, Camillo,
> With all the nearest things to my heart, as well
> My chamber-counsels, wherein, priest-like, thou
> Hast cleansed my bosom, I from thee departed
> Thy penitent reformed. But we have been
> Deceived in thy integrity, deceived
> In that which seems so. (1.2.237–43)

Camillo is cast as both a priest figure who absolved his master's sins and a feminized love object, the recipient of Leontes's most intimate secrets. Though they seem to look back on a quality of their relationship now lost, the lines also anticipate the roles that Camillo and Paulina will later play in relation to their masters, fostering confession and repentance rather than iterating their sins. Leontes's characterization of Camillo as "priest-like" contradicts his desire for Camillo to mimic his suspicions, suggesting that even Leontes is unsure about what he wants from his courtier.

The courtier's duty as outlined by Castiglione is to make a judgment about when it is appropriate to imitate his master, when to refuse imitation and instead instruct his master in a better course of action, and when to disobey orders and even leave the master's service entirely. Shakespeare shows Camillo following this fraught process. Midway through their encounter, Camillo refuses imitation, in language that evokes both the master's conventional expectation and his atypical denial: "You never spoke what did become you less/Than this, which to reiterate were sin/As deep as that, though true" (1.2.284–86).[21] Camillo represents an antithesis to the servant described in the service treatise signed by "I. M.," *A Health to the Gentmanly Profession of Servingmen*, one who saves his master from his enemies by dressing in his clothes. He "furnished him selfe with Maisters' apparrell, feigning to be hee, even offerying him selfe to the death for his Maisters safetie."[22] This story glorifies the servant who impersonates his master in order to rescue him; in doing so, the servant bridges his master's desire and its fruition. Camillo, too, is expected to stand in for his master against his enemies, but Shakespeare puts this moment in Castiglione's context rather than in I. M.'s. Camillo tries to take the position of pedagogue, as he advises Leontes to "be cured/Of this diseased opinion," (1.2.298–99) but to no avail. When Leontes orders him to poison Polixenes with a poisoned draught of wine, Camillo steps over the line to disobedience and desertion. But what is most striking is that he phrases his defiance deceptively, so that Leontes believes it to signal acceptance. Of Polixenes, Camillo swears, "If from me he have wholesome beverage,/Account me not your servant" (1.2.347–48). With this equivocation, Camillo shows his willingness to make an ethical judgment that is simultaneously an aesthetic one. Shakespeare acknowledges Camillo's desire for self-preservation and makes it compatible with his disinterested motive to save Leontes from dishonor and Polixenes and Hermione from false punishment. A hallmark of both courtier and rogue in this play is that they express through aesthetics both self-interested and selfless intentions.

Shakespeare outlines a healthier model for the servant-master relationship in the one sketched between Camillo and his new master Polixenes. Here, the servant's mimesis transforms his master, as Polixenes acknowledges: "Your changed complexions are to me a mirror/Which shows me mine changed, too," an image in which Camillo occupies both a reflective and a pedagogical position (1.2.381–82). By the end of act 1, scene 2, Polixenes is promising to "respect thee as a father" (1.2.461) if Camillo will guide him safely out of Sicilia. For the moment, at least, Camillo's service elevates him to the level of a king. Once Paulina has begun to reeducate Leontes, he too sees Camillo's opposition as more valuable than the self-projection he first sought. "How he glisters/Through my rust!" (3.2.168–69). Shakespeare plants the seeds for the servants' redemption of tragedy in act 1, even before the full implications of tragedy have unfolded, for it is here that Shakespeare depicts Camillo as driving the wedge that only the servant can between the king's distorted desires and their disastrous realization.

In the play's later acts, Camillo takes on the roles of playwright, player, and theatrical impresario that prove essential to the play's conversion from tragedy to comedy. When the play catches up to him in Bohemia, it is immediately clear that in the intervening sixteen years he has remained a guiding force for Polixenes, who testifies:

> The need I have of thee thine own goodness hath made. . . . Thou, having made me businesses which none without thee can sufficiently manage, must either stay to execute them thyself or take away with thee the very services thou hast done; which if I have not enough considered—as too much I cannot—to be more thankful to thee shall be my study, and my profit therein, the heaping friendships. (4.2.9–16)

The passage constructs Polixenes as the emulator and Camillo as the exemplar. Twice Polixenes says that Camillo has "made" things: first, in fostering Polixenes's dependence on him, and second, in making "businesses" for Polixenes that cannot continue in Camillo's absence. Rather than merely executing the prince's will, Camillo has gained the prerogative to fashion it as well. David Schalkwyk notes perceptively that Polixenes's rhetorical shift from "profit" to "friendship" "trumps a commodified concept of service with an appeal to an affective one."[23] But despite Polixenes's perspective, Camillo's aesthetic service has commercial implications, as he approaches the project of saving Florizel and Perdita from Polixenes's wrath from the perspective of one who expertly manages a business, in particular, a theatrical production. He scripts an encounter in Sicilia between Florizel and Leontes, down to the last detail of speech and mannerism: "The manner of your bearing towards him, with/What you, as from your father, shall deliver—/Things known betwixt us three—I'll write you down" (4.4.546–48). The goal is to make Leontes believe "that you have your father's bosom there,/And speak his very heart" (4.4.551–52). As Polixenes's closest advisor, Camillo has unique access to Polixenes's "heart" and the privilege to "speak" it. But the script he writes for Florizel does not, in fact, speak for Polixenes, who expressly opposes Florizel's intent; rather, it substitutes Camillo's language for his master's. He goes so far as to improvise a costume for Florizel: "It shall be so my care/To have you royally appointed as if/The scene you play were mine" (4.4.580–82). It is clear that the scene is indeed Camillo's own, although his framing of the declaration with "as if" reminds us of his necessary estrangement from the appearance of ownership.

Camillo creates a theatrical space in which he diverts, reworks, and authors the commands of his three masters—Leontes, Polixenes, and Florizel. At the same time, Camillo generates theater to advance his own interests. Thus, he introduces a counterplot to expose Florizel and Perdita's flight to Polixenes so that he will pursue the lovers. Camillo's motive is that he wants to "re-view Sicilia, for whose sight/I have a woman's longing" (4.4.649–50). Camillo is both loyal, to a fault, and willing to betray; he serves his masters' interests and his own; he is honest and deceptive, even tricky. The effectiveness of the transformations he works depend on his deployment of these contradictory, socially discrepant qualities. Camillo turns the ethical quandaries of courtiership into aesthetic performances that draw from different discourses of service.

If Camillo is so effective, why doesn't Shakespeare have him reform Leontes directly? In Shakespeare's main source, Robert Greene's *Pandosto* (1588), there are no equivalents to Paulina and two to Camillo. Franion, the first, refuses to kill Pandosto's friend Egistus and flees with him, but he disappears from the narrative thereafter. He is replaced by Capnio, described as "an old servant" of Dorastus's (Florizel), who aids the lovers in their escape.[24] Greene has Pandosto realize his tragic error without the help of a loyal servant. Greene's text thus does not make it necessary for a second figure to take over Camillo's role as the king's most trusted counselor. Shakespeare could have kept Camillo in Sicilia for the duration of the dramatic action (after all, Paulina is also threatened with death by Leontes and remains at his court) or, following Greene's precedent, he could have had Leontes repent on his own. Shakespeare's decision to replace Camillo with Paulina raises the question of what she adds to the play's formulation of service. Paulina herself announces: "The office/Becomes a woman best. I'll take't upon me" (2.2.34–35). Indeed, the play positions Paulina as a woman and servant to create a particular kind of aesthetic space. She becomes Hermione's representative, standing in and speaking for her mistress in a way that Hermione herself could not.[25] Paulina thereby exploits the ambiguity that resides between acting for one's master and acting as one's master. With the queen apparently dead, Paulina is free to create the image of the mistress she serves. This representational space also becomes the space she manufactures between Leontes's desire and its fruition, as she gradually reworks his authority into healthier familial and political modes.

Paulina has a dual role as Leontes's wife and servant, echoing analogies in the didactic literature of service between marriage and service. But Paulina rebuts the patriarchal expectation that wives and servants should be deferent and obedient. She reprimands an attendant: " 'Tis such as you,/That creep like shadows by him, and do sigh/At each his needless heavings, such as you/Nourish the cause of his awaking" (2.3.33–36). Paulina does not act in subordinate fashion, either, toward her husband, Antigonus. Her unorthodoxy emerges in contrast to his more conventional response to the king's orders. In pledging to obey Leontes's unjustifiable command to abandon the infant Perdita, Antigonus fails to recognize a potential space for interpretation and action.[26] The last embodiment of a tragic ending, Autolycus illustrates the destructive ethical consequences of what we might see as a servant's lack of aesthetic imagination.

Paulina's service reverses the perception, so common in the didactic literature of service, that aesthetics primarily or solely shroud a self-interested will. Rather, the play follows Castiglione in endorsing her self-representation as a "physician" (2.3.54) giving Leontes a powerful antidote to his poisoned state. The cure that she follows is to withhold the objects of Leontes's desire—Hermione's death and later Hermione's living body—and then to subject her master to a withering course of moral correction. She acknowledges the harshness of the cure, pointing to the discrepancy between her seeming insubordination and her faithful intent:

> And I beseech you hear me, who professes
> Myself your loyal servant, your physician,
> Your most obedient counsellor; yet that dares
> Less appear so in comforting your evils
> Than such as most seem yours. (2.3.53–57)

The complex version of obedient service that she articulates marks it as willing to "appear" that which it is not. Paulina generates an aesthetics, in other words, that strives to bring dis-"comfort" to the king. We might understand this aesthetically produced discomfort as teaching Leontes that self-reproductions are a malignant form of self-deception. Paulina's defiance instructs Leontes in the virtues of representational difference, which she instantiates by acting for Hermione and ultimately by resurrecting her.

While Camillo stages a drama to unite his two masters, Paulina mounts a virtuosic performance of Hermione that lasts for sixteen years. Even after all that time, the image that Paulina creates for Leontes is of a wronged, vengeful specter, which she conjures graphically to prevent Leontes from choosing a new wife:

> Were I the ghost that walked I'd bid you mark
> Her eye, and tell me for what dull part in't
> You chose her. Then I'd shriek, that even your ears
> Should rift to hear me, and the words that followed
> Should be, "Remember mine." (5.1.63–67)

Like Camillo, Paulina scripts, directs, and acts in the performance. Her scene derives straight from Jacobean revenge tragedy. In chapter 2 I discussed a similar scene staged by Jack Wilton and the Earl of Surrey in Nashe's *The Unfortunate Traveller*. There, servant and master play melodramatic versions of each other. In *The Winter's Tale*, Paulina plays the roles of both servant and mistress. Her theatrical piece works on Leontes by using the servant's body to impersonate and ventriloquize the absent mistress. Like any actor playing a role, Paulina interprets Hermione in the act of impersonating her. And just as the actor sometimes shows through the character, so this version of Hermione is refracted through Paulina's violent tongue and "red-looked anger" (2.2.37). Paulina's performance both projects her into the mistress's role and reconstructs the mistress in her image.[27]

The statue scene of act 5, which completes the transformation of tragedy into comedy, is the product of Paulina's aesthetic choices. While earlier Paulina assimilates Hermione, in the final scene she disjoins herself from her mistress and unveils her in the form of the living "statue." Whether or not Paulina is actually the "artist"—allegedly Julio Romano, who "makes her/As she lived now" (5.3.31–32)—it is Paulina who stages the altered representation of Hermione. Her manipulation of the statue recalls an instruction from *The Book of the Courtier* on how the male courtier should mold the prince. The courtier should remember "the example of those famous captains and other outstanding men of whom it was customary in the ancient world to make statues of bronze and marble, and sometimes of gold, and to erect them in public places, both to honour the great and to inspire others to work to achieve the same glory through worthy emulation" (*BC*, 288). Paulina adapts this use of the statue as a secondhand exemplar; while the statue of Hermione makes a mimetic appeal to Leontes, it is also transmuted into a living example and becomes thereby a second kind of mimetic model. In rehearsals, Paulina has prepared Leontes to react appropriately to Hermione's reappearance, and as she uncovers the tableau vivant, she puts the finishing touches on her transformation of the king. Observing that he is "almost so far transported that/He'll think anon it lives" (5.3.69–70), she promises or threatens to "afflict [him] farther" (5.3.75), to which he responds with the eagerness of a trained spectator: "Do, Paulina,/For this affliction has a taste as sweet/As any cordial comfort" (5.3.75–77). She has "stirred" Leontes (5.3.74) and then orders Hermione literally to "Stir" (5.3.101).[28] The royal couple is thus reanimated through and in the theatrical space that Paulina's service creates. Shakespeare implies that playing and spectating collude to return Hermione and Leontes to familial and political life.

There is little precedent in the courtesy book tradition for a female courtier to take the active role that Paulina does.[29] *The Book of the Courtier* sends a mixed message about the degree of agency that women of the court possess. The magnifico Giuliano initially describes the ideal woman as "neither proud, envious or evil-tongued," displaying "serene and modest behaviour" (*BC*, 211, 212), precepts that hardly apply to Paulina, who unashamedly "use[s] that tongue I have" (2.2.55). Moreover, the text's examples of great women rarely depict them as servants, courtiers, or counselors. The absence of a tradition of female courtiership may, in part, explain why Paulina's role seems to draw from multiple traditions of female service, from midwifery to nursing to witchcraft.[30] In this sense, Shakespeare represents Paulina as a high-ranking member of the court who nevertheless participates in folkloric, marginal, and even socially disreputable discourses. Prominent among these are discourses associated with the female rouge, which, as Harman describes it, could be a kind of umbrella term for suspect female figures such as the witch, the shrew, and other controversial female characters. Harman situates female rogues within familiar cultural narratives of transgressive women. Shakespeare, in turn, puts Paulina's aesthetic manipulations of service in proximity to an expansive realm of illicit female behavior.

Comparing Paulina's deceptions directly to Autolycus's illuminates her affinities with the rogue. Whereas Autolycus steals purses, foists off ballads on the country folk, and then schemes to put the shepherd and his son together with Florizel, Paulina pulls off an even more audacious string of hoaxes: She fakes Hermione's death, hides her from her master for years on end, brings Leontes to repentance on false premises, and finally stages a fraudulent resurrection of the queen to effect the reconciliation of the royal family and of two kingdoms. Paulina outdoes the rogue at his own game. Indeed, her early display of outrage brings her dangerously close to losing the respectability and protection afforded by her position within the inner court circle. Leontes unleashes a series of violent epithets and threats against her. She is "A mankind witch!" "A most intelligencing bawd, a "crone," "A callat/of boundless tongue," and "A gross hag!" (2.3.68, 69, 77, 91–92, 108). He orders his attendants to drag her away, tells Antigonus to shut her up, and commands her to be burned. The crass rhetoric that Leontes uses to accuse Paulina is more appropriate to Harman's world than to Sicilia's court, and beyond indicating a near total breakdown of civility, it shows how close Paulina comes rhetorically to the descent from service into roguery that Harman depicts. Only the disobedience of the other courtly servants prevents Leontes's orders against Paulina from being carried out.

The Winter's Tale explores how a female courtier turns vulnerability into strength, constraint into opportunity. Paulina accomplishes these reversals of fortune by maintaining enough of the rogue's critical distance to avoid the fate that Antigonus suffers. From a grave liability, her "boundless tongue" becomes one of Paulina's greatest assets in building her reputation as a loyal servant who practices a distinctly roguelike agency. Shakespeare's stress on the feminized components of Paulina's service that intersect with roguery—the magic that verges on witchcraft, her shrew's tongue, the trickery straight out of rogue literature—magnifies the porousness between high and low in the courtier's role.[31]

At the other end of the social spectrum, the rogue Autolycus betrays serviceable tendencies. Service defines itself initially in relation to Autolycus by its absence; however, Autolycus's self-accounting represents the progression (or regression) from courtier to rogue as a slippery continuum rather than as a rigid divide. His entrance, celebrating in song and thieves' cant the pleasures of spring, sex, and the itinerant life, establishes Autolycus as a variation on the "merry beggar," a stock figure familiar to early modern audiences.[32] As if to complete the picture of his freedom from conventional cares, the first thing he reveals about himself is that "I have served Prince Florizel, and in my time wore three-pile, but now I am out of service" (4.3.13–14). Immediately, then, Autolycus puts himself in opposition to service, defining himself as having escaped its clutches; at the same time, by announcing himself as a former courtly servant, he raises the possibility of a return to service. To defraud the hapless Clown, he claims to have been robbed of his clothes and money by a courtly ex-servant, whose description happens to match his own. It is a trick that comes straight from the rogue literature. Yet his story is not devoid of truth, for he has lost the wages, status, and livery of his service position. Autolycus performs a version of his story that, even as it celebrates the rogue's release from service, exposes that release as a loss.

If at first Autolycus traces the route from courtier to rogue, by the end of act 4 he begins to stage the reverse narrative. Camillo's order for Autolycus to exchange garments with Florizel puts him back in courtly apparel. During the long pastoral interlude of the sheep-shearing festival, he had played the rogue to the hilt, singing and telling fantastic stories, selling and stealing simultaneously. In his multiple connections to the ballad, Autolycus emerges as a figure for the flourishing print culture: inventive, openly commercial, self-promoting, socially suspect. But whereas in the guise of a ballad seller Autolycus authors and directs a production in which he is also a principal actor, upon his reentrance he is swept into Camillo's production. He reflects: "The Prince himself is about a piece of iniquity. . . . If I thought it were a piece of honesty to acquaint the King withal, I would not do't. I hold it the more knavery to conceal it, and therein am I constant to my profession" (4.4.659–64). Shakespeare lays the groundwork for Autolycus's absorption into service, for although Autolycus pledges constancy to his roguish "profession," he has already taken the first step toward serving Florizel by staying quiet on his behalf. Indeed, his incorporation into courtly service exceeds his agency and control. He is Camillo's "instrument" (4.4.609) in a plot of which he has only partial knowledge. Later, Autolycus says, "Here comes those I have done good to against my will" (5.2.111), a recognition of the limitations of his will in regard to faithful service. When he is most the rogue, unbeknownst to him he is also most the servant.[33] Autolycus resists the loss of self-determination entailed by taking a service role. But once enlisted, he recognizes the opportunities, too: "I am courted now with a double occasion: gold, and a means to do the Prince my master good, which who knows how that may turn back to my advancement?" (4.4.802–5). Autolycus's rhetoric stresses gold and the possibility of promotion, making profit the uppermost consideration and the chance to aid his master secondary. He thus reverses the order of priorities that holds for Camillo and Paulina, but like them, his aesthetic service is driven by competing impulses. All three servants do "good" for their masters in reforming the abuse of royal power, even as they seek profit or at least self-preservation.

While the didactic literature of service maintains that aesthetic service is both cause and symptom of a disintegrating moral and social order, Shakespeare suggests that it can be a profoundly ethical act. The true servant in *The Winter's Tale* is one who acts with a consciousness that all service requires interpretive performances. In chapter 1, I argued that *Two Gentlemen* develops a concept of subjectivity in which the roles of master and servant coexist. *The Winter's Tale* in its turn posits a subjectivity that is based on aesthetic acts rather than fixed social positions. The courtiers and the rogue realize the potential of such subject positions in the theatrical space of service.

This theatrical space generates not only subjective possibilities but also the dramatic form of tragicomedy. Jonson's "servant-monster" gets its sprawling, hybrid shape from the diverse discourses and genres of service that collaborate to transform tragedy into comedy. The servants accomplish this generic transformation by interpreting and representing their masters' desires, a duplicative process that becomes a creative one. This space is ultimately Shakespeare's theater, too, one increasingly structured by capitalist service relations, as I discussed in chapters 3 and 4. *The Winter's Tale* is mostly preoccupied with courtly and aristocratic service rather than with capitalist modes. Yet by this point in the early seventeenth century, the influence of capitalism on service had been absorbed to the extent that Shakespeare did not need to explicitly render it thematically to make its presence felt. In the play, servants and categories of service exchange identities according to the logic of capitalist economic circulation in which people and things substitute for and replace one another. In the London theaters, *The Winter's Tale* circulated among audiences that included rogues and courtiers, along with those whom the play does not represent: tradesmen, merchants, artisans, apprentices, and others. The theatrical space of service was their space as well. Just as rogue literature inflects Shakespeare's portrayal of Paulina and Camillo, so the play's multiple public receptions infiltrate and alter its portrayal of a closed court culture.

Leontes's theatrical language in the play's closing speech suggests that the space crafted by servants is still open:

> Good Paulina,
> Lead us from hence, where we may leisurely
> Each one demand and answer to his part
> Performed in this wide gap of time since first
> We were dissevered. Hastily lead away. (5.3.152–56)

The disseverance and the "wide gap of time"—the sixteen years during which Paulina sustained the fiction of Hermione's death and represented Hermione by proxy—remind the audience of the space between master's will and servant's execution. By looking forward to the narration of each person's "part" in this "performance," Leontes articulates his right to know but also evinces his changed attitude toward other people, seeing them now as coparticipants in a theatrical community rather than as static reproductive images.[34] He tells Paulina twice to "lead" the company offstage, implicitly acknowledging that the rest of the court, himself included, will follow.

Aesthetic Slavery: *The Tempest*

In *The Tempest,* Shakespeare exposes courtly service to the new category of inter-Atlantic slavery. In chapter 1, I discussed Shakespeare's engagement with classical slavery in one of his earliest plays, *The Comedy of Errors,* where the guarantee for the Antipholuses that mastery ensures self-possession is threatened by the imitations of their slaves, the Dromios. Shakespeare renews this point in *The Tempest,* but he does so by exploring not only the self-possession of the master, now imagined in domestic *and* colonial terms, but also the drastic implications for the servant who is literally owned by his master.

This book has argued that service was being transformed in a capitalist economy in ways that signaled new opportunities for mobility but also the potential for increased stratification and vulnerability. Slavery represents a radical, but logical, extension of the latter point. Practices of slavery were precipitated in the early seventeenth century by increased global commerce and the development of labor markets and eventually colonies for European nations. *The Tempest* suggests the worst of what the transition to capitalism could mean for servants: they might become commodities and objects of exchange rather than controlling, profiting from, or simply participating in exchanges.[35] Even under the conditions of extreme oppression and objectification enforced upon Ariel and Caliban, however, they emerge as imitative servants, who, like the servants in *The Winter's Tale,* produce tragicomic space that in turn defines their subject positions.

Like many of the servants I have discussed, slaves were difficult to assimilate to traditional taxonomies. As aliens who were owned, they did not fit anywhere in domestic social hierarchies.[36] But there was also continuity and confusion in representations of servitude and slavery, with the result that, rhetorically, slaves often served as a limit case for service. Just as early modern apprenticeship, for example, challenged social distinctions, so the slave trade in Spanish and other colonies was putting new pressure on metropolitan discourses of service.[37] By staunchly denying the existence of slaves in England, many commentators tried to avoid classifying slaves. Slaveholding went against the prevailing religious and moral ideologies of service. Thomas Becon makes this point explicit in his *New Catechism*, advising masters on how *not* to treat their servants: "Christian men may not handle their servants as the unfaithful Turks do, which entreat their servants as bond-slaves, yea, as beasts, without any respect of manhood."[38] Here, slaveholding is attributed to the Turkish infidels and made a mark of their unenlightened religion and culture.[39] Slavery and servitude are in oppositional relation to one another, and the absence of slavery is a condition of the humane servitude that ostensibly was the standard in England.

Such rhetoric belied the fact that slaves from Africa were gradually entering the nation's consciousness, both at home and in the colonies. Because practices of slavery had not yet been fully codified in domestic or imperial social structures, there was a fungibility between service and slavery, as expressed for example in the intermediary condition of indentured servitude or in the custom of freeing African slaves imported to serve English aristocrats.[40] Becon's admonition against masters treating their servants as slaves hints that transition from the first category to the second was possible. We have only to think of Othello and his account of having been "taken by the insolent foe/And sold to slavery," and "my redemption hence" (1.3.136–37), to catch a glimpse of the narrative modes of passage from slavery to service that were available in the early modern period.

The rhetorical lack of distinction between servitude and slavery also makes itself felt in the use of "slave" as a term of moral opprobrium or as an indication of self-dispossession. In *King Lear*, Kent accuses Oswald of being "one-trunk-inheriting slave; one that wouldst be a bawd, in way of good service" (2.2.16–17). Kent insults both Oswald's social status and his moral behavior. Although "slave" was not a behavioral identity limited to servants, the association between low social and moral standing was commonplace. Ferdinand uses the continuum between service and slavery differently, to persuade Miranda of the intensity of his emotions: "The very instant that I saw you did/My heart fly to your service; there resides,/To make me slave to it. And for your sake/Am I this patient log-man" (3.1.64–67). In this case, Ferdinand's indentured servitude to Prospero precipitates his love for Miranda, a love which in turn enslaves him. In this chain of servitude, service, and slavery, enforced labor leads to a metaphoric slavery, and in turn the pleasure of this enslavement reconciles Ferdinand to a servitude that borders on slavery. Still, this usage betrays a sense that the individual has subordinated his higher faculties to passions like greed, jealousy, anger, or love, as "one who is completely under the domination of, or subject to, a specified influence."[41] Because slavery represented cognitive and moral defects, it was at times implied to be the sign that the servant was ordained to play a subordinate role. Jonson inveighed against the figure of the "servant-monster" for precisely this transgression of lower faculties against higher ones. This violation registers on the level of dramatic form as the enslavement of tragicomedy to base instincts. Jonson's criticisms suggest that Shakespeare has improperly allowed the slave not only to usurp his master's place but to distort dramatic decorum as well.

Shakespeare challenges this definition of tragicomedy by depicting slave characters in *The Tempest* as self-possessed and aesthetically powerful.[42] Despite their abject status, Ariel and Caliban are very much like Shakespeare's other servants, and in particular the servants of *The Winter's Tale*. The permeability between service and slavery in *The Tempest* recalls the permeability between the practices of courtier and rogue. Prospero usually uses "servant" for Ariel and "slave" for Caliban, a division enacted not only by the distinction in their labors but also by the fact that freedom is repeatedly promised to Ariel while Caliban is permanently subject to Prospero's authority. But there is one instance in which Prospero calls Ariel a slave, when he relates Ariel's treatment at the hands of Sycorax: "Thou, my slave,/As thou report'st thyself, was then her servant" (1.2.272–73). Ariel "report[s]" himself Prospero's slave, although it was Sycorax who imprisoned Ariel "Into a cloven pine" (1.2.279). But while Prospero intends to remind Ariel that he is better off with him than with Sycorax, his use of the word "slave" can point in the opposite direction: toward Ariel's lack of self-ownership.

Part servant, part slave, Ariel nevertheless displays agency through his aesthetic service. In doing so, he generates tragicomic space between Prospero's command and its fulfillment. It may not at first seem that way, for Prospero has only to say his name and Ariel appears instantaneously. "Thy thoughts I cleave to" (4.1.164), he says to Prospero, gesturing to a master's fantasy in which the servant provides instant gratification of his desires; the servant is folded into the very recesses of his master's mind. There is no space between servant and master here, no "wide gap of time." However, the emphasis on Ariel's aesthetics reveals his independent agency in generically productive terms. He narrates how he created the tempest with an attention to process, detail, and the effects created:

> Sometime I'd divide,
> And burn in many places; on the top-mast,
> The yards, and the bowsprit, would I flame distinctly;
> Then meet and join. (1.2.199–202)

Although the tempest belongs to Prospero, Ariel not only brings it into being but also produces its tragicomic effect, which, like the genre as a whole, divides and then rejoins. Prospero calls it "The direful spectacle" (1.2.26), an apt description of the mixed affect that Ariel's destructive yet creative theater piece produces. Again, in the episode where Prospero orders first the materialization and then the sudden withdrawal of the banquet from his enemies, it is Ariel, in the guise of a harpy, who delivers the words that make such an impression on Alonso and company: "Thee of thy son, Alonso,/They have bereft, and do pronounce by me/Ling'ring perdition" (3.3.75–77). Officially, Ariel ventriloquizes his master here, but the doubleness of "pronounce," signifying both utterance and the authority behind it, implies that the servant might assume ownership of his master's assertions. Afterward, Prospero tries to restore the hierarchy of representation by describing Ariel's enunciation of power as a theatrical device that he controls: "Bravely the figure of this harpy hast thou/Performed, my Ariel" (3.3.84–85). But "performed," with its evocations of transformation, surrogation, and replacement, undercuts his intention. Ariel's interventions follow but also supplement Prospero's agenda.

Ariel's excessive representations of Prospero evoke Valerie Forman's point that for tragicomedies to work, an initial loss must be redeemed as profit. It is Ariel's art which extracts profit from unpromising scenes of anger, treachery, grief, and mourning. It is Ariel who represents Prospero to himself in a way that converts him from the desire to wreak revenge to a disposition for mercy and reconciliation. In a crucial bit of dialogue, Ariel becomes the model for his master's imitation by exploiting his license to act for his master. He persuades Prospero to forgive his captives, assuring him that "if you now beheld them your affections/Would become tender./. . ./Mine would, sir, were I human" (5.1.18–19, 20). Here, Ariel writes a script for Prospero to follow, notwithstanding his use of the conditional to distance himself from the appearance of authority. The intensity of Prospero's need to match and surpass his servant is betrayed in his response: "And mine shall. . . . shall not myself,/One of their kind, that relish all as sharply/Passion as they, be kindlier moved than thou art?" (5.1.20, 22–24). In a play absorbed with the rhetoric of "humane" mastery, it poses a significant challenge when a nonhuman servant exhibits a more human emotion and a more ethical response than his master. Prospero hastily emulates Ariel's example. The servant-slave's aesthetic agency effects the play's metamorphosis from tragedy to comedy. When a few lines later Prospero announces, "Yet with my nobler reason 'gainst my fury/Do I take part" (5.1.26–27), Shakespeare intimates not only that it is Ariel who stands for the elevated faculty of reason but also that the tragicomedy models itself on his service.

Whereas Ariel floridly represents Prospero's interests, Caliban flagrantly opposes them. In keeping with early modern definitions of slavery, his opposition to the patriarchal ideology of service marks him as an appropriate object of enslavement. Jonathan Goldberg has argued that Shakespeare affirms Caliban's fitness for slavery. He uses as principal evidence Prospero's damning reflection: "A devil, a born devil, on whose nature/Nurture can never stick; on whom my pains,/Humanely taken, all, all lost, quite lost" (4.1.188–90), coupled with Miranda's: "Abhorrèd slave,/Which any print of goodness wilt not take,/Being capable of all ill!" (1.2.354–56). The notion of "imprinting" the student with instruction was, as Goldberg points out, a staple metaphor for the practice of *imitatio*. Caliban's failure to absorb "any print of goodness" or to let nurture "stick" confirms his refusal in multiple registers to imitate in the approved manner, a refusal that puts him beyond hope of education or reform.[43] Thus, "he is fundamentally incapable of the movement that is foundationally human," the movement from the animalistic to the reasonable and, finally transcendentally, human.[44] On the basis of his incapacity, argues Goldberg, Caliban's enslavement is given a rationale that accords with Renaissance humanism and anticipates Enlightenment criteria for the subject. In short, the servant who will not imitate deserves to become a slave, registering a transition from a servant-master relationship based on patriarchal hierarchy to an imperial relation constructed around the dichotomy of subject and object.

Caliban may not take the "print" that Prospero and Miranda wish to put on him, but *The Tempest* portrays him as skilled at imitating the role of the courtly servant. His aesthetic capabilities manifest Caliban's agency and belie his status as an enslaved object. In the same speech in which Miranda accuses Caliban of rebuffing "any print of goodness," she adds, "But thy vile race,/Though thou didst learn, had that in't which good natures/Could not abide to be with" (1.2.361–64). Her statement acknowledges that Caliban learned something and leaves open the question of what, precisely, that is. Caliban himself has an answer:

"You taught me language, and my profit on't/Is I know how to curse" (1.2.366–67). "Profit" evokes the capitalist transactions that suffuse the island's global context but that are mostly invisible on the island; the word in Caliban's mouth is ironic, since his enslavement precludes his access to capital and profit. But just as Ariel creates tragicomic profit out of Prospero's thirst for revenge, so Caliban's curses produce a profitable dissent that is equally integral to tragicomedy.

Caliban articulates dissent by redirecting humanist *imitatio* toward alternative modes of imitation, most notably in the scenes he shares with Trinculo, the jester to the king of Naples, and Stefano, the king's butler. As Paul Brown suggests, the king's servants are temporarily "masterless men." Not coincidentally, they come across Caliban when he is at a remove from his own master.[45] In the company of these other marginal servants, Caliban imitates the loyal courtly servant he has refused to embody. He parodies courtly service with utterances directed to his new "masters": "That's a brave god, and bears celestial liquor./I will kneel to him," "I'll swear upon that bottle to be thy true subject," and "I'll show thee every fertile inch o'th'island,/And I will kiss thy foot. I prithee, be my god" (2.2.109–10, 116, 140–41). The physical gestures of kneeling and kissing the lord's foot enact an exaggerated theater of the sacred oath that irrevocably binds servant to master. But of course, Caliban proves that loyalty and fealty do not bind him to any particular master, a point that he underscores in his last lines of the scene: "'Ban, 'ban, Cacaliban/Has a new master.—Get a new man!" (2.2.175–76). The servant's allegiance reveals itself in this construction to be easily transferable from one master to another, a portability that Caliban also manifests in his offer to show Stefano the island, a direct repetition of his initial willingness to show Prospero "all the qualities o'th' isle" (1.2.340). We may suspect that Caliban played the servant's part convincingly in his original encounters with Prospero. In imitating an exemplary servant in the patriarchal mold, Caliban both shows his mastery over the discourse and empties it of its guarantees. Later, Caliban amplifies his appeal to Stefano, promising him sovereignty over the island as well as over his new servant: "Thou shalt be lord of it, and I'll serve thee" (3.2.55). Caliban's performance of service is the basis for Stefano's aspirations to the wider scope of colonial authority, revealing, first, how dependent the master is on the servant even when he is defined as a slave, and, second, how dependent the colonizing relationship is on the personalized bond of servant and master.

Shakespeare exposes the fragility of colonial subjugation, which stakes its claim on mastery of an enslaved person. Despite the dispossession that slavery entails, the slave is still required to represent his master as other servants do. Therein lie the seeds of Caliban's aesthetic agency. Like deceitful servants in the didactic literature of service, the slave can conceal a dissenting will behind a dutiful performance of service. The fact that Caliban stages scenes of service for a pair of low-ranking servants who impersonate masters and sovereigns only magnifies the sense that colonial settings, where hierarchies are temporarily displaced, are especially susceptible to the workings of aesthetic service.

Whereas *imitatio* is embedded in a humanist context that supplies approved models for the student to imitate and excludes inappropriate models, the mimesis that Caliban undertakes obeys no such sense of decorum. Describing colonial mimesis, Michael Taussig proposes that what occurs is "the magical power of replication, the image affecting what it is an image of, wherein the representation shares in or takes power from the represented—testimony to the power of the mimetic faculty."[46] While Prospero's mastery requires that he remain the originary source of representations on the island, Caliban's mimetic representations, like Ariel's, produce a refracted, often broken image of his authority in which Prospero is obliged to see himself reflected. In this way, Caliban's "copy" of service reflects back on Prospero's mastery a vacuous, parodic version of itself. "To mime means a chameleon-like capacity to copy any and everything in a riot of mergers and copies posing as originals," writes Taussig, evoking the distorted images of authority that Prospero glimpses in the confederacy of disenfranchised servants and slave.[47] Prospero is thrown into a "passion" (4.1.143), forced to call off the wedding masque that Ariel is in the middle of staging, to cope with the "foul conspiracy" (4.1.139). Caliban's performance of service has inserted a space not only between Prospero's commands and their fulfillment but also between Prospero and his identity as master. Caliban is clearly the "anti-masque" and in this sense a force which threatens tragicomic transformation. Yet in unsettling Prospero's absolute authority, he joins with Ariel in creating the conditions for a comic redemption. When Caliban makes Prospero an object of dissenting representation, he enforces the value of representational difference, the same lesson that servants in *The Winter's Tale* enforce upon their masters.

Caliban's insurrection is short-lived, but it destroys Prospero's attempt to fix Caliban in the emerging category of the subhuman, those creatures that cannot learn. Caliban not only learns, he makes Prospero learn, too. Precisely because he can and does imitate familiar discourses of service, Caliban claims a place within them, even as he recognizes that he has been thrust out of them. In other words, Caliban's aesthetic service is a powerful form of resistance that marks him as an agent. While it is Ariel who is usually associated with creativity and art, Caliban, too, stages an aesthetically shaped performance, one that follows in a long line of early modern literary servants. The aesthetics of service augur the development of modern subjectivity, and Shakespeare makes the fascinating choice in *The Tempest* to invest the emerging category of the slave with an equally emergent subjectivity.

In making characters such as Autolycus, Caliban, and Ariel the bearers of aesthetic subjectivity, Shakespeare defines his authorial identity in unexpected ways. Alongside more sanctioned images of the playwright as a courtier who provides sponsored entertainment to the court, Shakespeare presents images of the playwright as a roguish purveyor of a popular commodity and, even more subversively, as an enslaved servant struggling against his bonds and the threat of dispossession. This may seem an odd self-image for a playwright who had achieved substantial prosperity and who was already recognized as the best of his generation, but the mix of constriction and resourcefulness that Ariel and Caliban display helps us remember that even the most successful playwrights still operated as servants beholden to several masters, including the playing company, James I and his court, and ticket-buying audiences. Each of these masters had demands that the playwright was required to satisfy. Like Jonson, Shakespeare is all too aware of the hard labor that drives theatrical illusion.[48]

Along with the demands placed on the servant come representational opportunities, and Shakespeare's tragicomedies self-servingly demonstrate that the author is the servant best equipped to profit from these chances. Shakespeare suggests throughout his career, and nowhere with more boldness than in the tragicomedies, that in framing dramatic authorship as service, the playwright can manufacture not only the demands but also the desires of his audiences. The more diversified the servant personae the playwright can inhabit and the categories of service he can perform, the more effectively he can define the desires of his various audiences and the larger his profit base grows. In this way, the heterogeneity of the tragicomedies is the condition for a theater that strives to define itself as a space for public interaction and engagement. Self-serving though the author's motives are, they also have an ethical quality. The public space of theater enjoins playgoers to see themselves and others in the audience as servants and masters who are always capable of changing places. Prospero's famous line—"This thing of darkness I/Acknowledge mine" (5.1.278–79)—balances an assertion of mastery with a powerful identification with the servant.

The Epilogue

As *The Tempest* draws to a close, Prospero gives Ariel one last "charge" (5.1.321) and then a final promise of freedom and a farewell. He also gives Caliban his last duty—to "trim" Prospero's cell—and a conditional promise, not of manumission but of "pardon" (5.1.297). Ariel is released from indenture back to the indefinitely described "elements," while Caliban will at best escape his master's wrath if he performs the slave's part more diligently. The diverging potential futures of these two servant-slaves exemplify the polarizing possibilities that capitalism stands poised to offer servants in the early seventeenth century. This transitional period gave rise to new performances of service in which the sanctioned substitution of the servant for the master merges with the servant's replacement of the master. The aesthetics of service I have traced across dramas by Shakespeare, Jonson, and Dekker and prose fictions by Nashe and Deloney signify deteriorating patriarchal hierarchies and the widening potential for social mobility and economic agency. "Then to the elements/Be free" (5.1.321–22), says Prospero to Ariel, gesturing at an expansion of opportunity that fictions of early modern service envision, an expansion both limitless and elusive precisely because it had not yet been defined. Performances of service could thus tantalize with the prospect of a release from service into "freedom," a word that conjures a germinating republican subjectivity.

Performances of service could also produce the need to continue performing service. The intransigence of early modern service has been a recurrent theme in this book. It is a theme that often appears in the same texts that attach economic and social power to service. Although the representational power afforded to the servant can be considerable, it relies on remaining subordinate. In fact, the socioeconomic changes in early modern England created new forms of subjection for servants. In a capitalist economy, servants replace their masters, but servants too become fungible and replaceable—objects, rather than agents, of exchange. Caliban represents one extension of the possibility that capitalism constricts, rather than expands, the range of material and social opportunities for servants. The servant's oppression does not imply an absence of subjectivity, however. Caliban's subjectivity emerges as an effect of his resistant yet imitative performances of service. In portraying abject forms of service, *The Tempest* suggests that even the most stringent constraints cannot deny—and may even foster—servant subjectivities that are increasingly autonomous and "free." The aesthetics of service that Ariel and Caliban each practice mediate dispossession and self-possession, dependence and autonomy. The emphasis on aesthetics in early modern service reflects the qualities of a transitional historical moment, when resolutions are deferred and contradictory possibilities coexist and interact.

The Tempest's epilogue, in which Prospero appears unattended by his servants, contains his most candid assessment of his servants' constitutive roles in compensating for, and supplementing, his insufficiency: "What strength I have's mine own,/Which is most faint" (2–3). Tellingly, he turns to the audience to stand in for his servants: only its favorable response can substitute for "spirits to enforce, art to enchant" (14). "With the help of your good hands" (10), the audience can free Prospero from the island. But Shakespeare's language also reverses the servant-master relationship, so that the audience is revealed to itself as the master and Prospero as the servant who pleads: "release me from my bands," and "Let your indulgence set me free" (20). The rhetorical shift reminds us that authors increasingly projected audiences and readers into positions of mastery. The epilogue suggests that the vitality of drama and fiction derives from the same mimetic, collaborative principle that allows servants and masters to exchange identities. Servants' impersonations, transformations, and displacements of their masters continue indefinitely, and they continue to produce new identifications and new arrangements. While Prospero's desire to be liberated from his "bands" resonates with Gonzalo's imagining of a commonwealth where there is no "use of service" (2.1.151), the absence of service would have been a dystopian, not a utopian, premise for early modern drama and prose fiction. These literary forms used service to invent new places for themselves.

All references to Shakespeare's works are from William Shakespeare, *The Norton Shakespeare*, 2nd ed., ed. Stephen Greenblatt et al. (New York: W. W. Norton, 2008). References are to act, scene, and line.

Introduction

1. Jean-Christophe Agnew, *Worlds Apart: The Market and the Theater in Anglo-American Thought* (Cambridge: Cambridge University Press, 1986), 102.

2. Joseph Roach, *Cities of the Dead: Circum-Atlantic Performances* (New York: Columbia University Press, 1996), xiii.

3. Ibid., ix.

4. Ibid., 3.

5. Terry Eagleton, *The Ideology of the Aesthetic* (Oxford: Blackwell, 1990), 16–17, 19. See also George Levine, "Introduction: Reclaiming the Aesthetic," in *Aesthetics and Ideology,* ed. George Levine (New Brunswick, N.J.: Rutgers University Press, 1994), 1–28.

6. Eagleton emphasizes the ways in which the aesthetic regulates the bourgeois state from within the individual but can also undermine that control by providing a space for dissenting thought and action. My point is that the aesthetic can have a disruptive effect on subjects as well as, or along with, a consolidating one (ibid., 3).

7. Philip Sidney, *The Defence of Poesy* (1580–85), in *Sir Philip Sidney: The Major Works,* ed. Katherine Duncan-Jones (Oxford: Oxford University Press, 2002), 217.

8. Aristotle, *Poetics,* in *The Complete Works of Aristotle: The Revised Oxford Translation,* vol. 2, ed. Jonathan Barnes (Princeton, N.J.: Princeton University Press, 1984), 2318.

9. Sidney, *Defence of Poesy,* 218.

10. Sidney is explicit that the aim of instilling delight is to "move men to take that goodness in hand, which without delight they would fly as from a stranger" and "to make them know that goodness whereunto they are moved" (*Defence of Poesy,* 218). "Move" implies a purifying ascent on which Sidney elaborates in a subsequent passage: "The final end is to lead and draw us to as high a perfection as our degenerate souls, made worse by their clayey lodgings, can be capable of" (219).

11. Aristotle, *Poetics,* 2323.

12. Henry S. Turner, *The English Renaissance Stage: Geometry, Poetics, and the Practical Spatial Arts 1580–1630* (Oxford: Oxford University Press, 2006), 84–89.

13. Sidney, *Defence of Poesy,* 232.

14. Turner, *English Renaissance Stage,* 104, 110.

15. Roger Ascham, *The Schoolmaster* (1570), ed. Lawrence V. Ryan, Folger Shakespeare Library (Ithaca, N.Y.: Cornell University Press, 1967), 82–83.

16. Ibid., 43–44.

17. Ibid., 46.

18. Ascham renders his prototypical servant as male, a gender bias shared by many early modern commentators on service. I use the male pronoun to reflect this pattern, although I discuss female servants in particular later in the introduction and elsewhere in the book.

19. Richard Halpern has shown that *imitatio* could be deployed to challenge structures of authority as much as to reinforce them. Richard Halpern, *The Poetics of Primitive Accumulation: English Renaissance Culture and the Genealogy of Capital* (Ithaca, N.Y.: Cornell University Press, 1991), 44.

20. Ascham, *Schoolmaster,* 92, 115. See Erich Auerbach, *Mimesis: The Representation of Reality in Western Literature,* trans. Willard Trask (Princeton, N.J.: Princeton University Press, 1953), for a narrative of the evolution of aesthetic decorum in Western literary history. For Auerbach, servants remain outside the province of tragedy, which only much later becomes associated with what Auerbach calls the "everyday" as instantiated in the common people. When members of the lower class appear, "it is always in the low style" (328).

21. As Rosalie Colie suggests, "The breaking of decorum, in this case, has to do with social as well as aesthetic premises." Rosalie Colie, *The Resources of Kind: Genre-Theory in the Renaissance,* ed. Barbara Lewalski (Berkeley: University of California Press, 1973), 8.

22. George Puttenham, *The Art of English Poesy by George Puttenham: A Critical Edition,* ed. Frank Whigham and Wayne A. Rebhorn (Ithaca, N.Y.: Cornell University Press, 2007), 234.

23. Ibid., 237.

24. Sidney, *Defence of Poesy,* 244.

25. Colie, *Resources of Kind,* 8.

26. I define form in the expansive sense for which Caroline Levine advocates in "Strategic Formalism: Toward a New Method in Cultural Studies," *Victorian Studies* 48 (2006): 625–57. She argues that literary forms "have force in the social world and are capable of shaping political arrangements" and also that "social hierarchies and institutions can themselves be understood as *forms*" (626). Form, for Levine, refers "to shaping patterns, to identifiable interlacings of repetitions and differences, to dense networks of structuring principles and categories" (632). See also Derek Attridge, "Literary Form and the Demands of Politics," in G. Levine, *Aesthetics and Ideology,* 243–63.

27. Gunter Gebauer and Christoph Wulf, *Mimesis: Culture—Art—Society,* trans. Don Reneau (Berkeley: University of California Press, 1992), 22.

28. Michael Taussig, *Mimesis and Alterity* (New York: Routledge, 1993), 2.

29. An important exception to the earlier neglect of servants is Jonas A. Barish and Marshall Waingrow, "'Service' in *King Lear,*" *Shakespeare Quarterly* 9 (1958): 347–55.

30. H. B. Charlton, *Shakespearian Comedy*, 4th ed. (1938; repr., London: Methuen, 1949), 41.

31. Mark Thornton Burnett, *Masters and Servants in English Renaissance Drama and Culture: Authority and Obedience* (London: Macmillan, 1997); Richard Strier, *Resistant Structures: Particularity, Radicalism, and Renaissance Texts* (Berkeley: University of California Press, 1995), 165–202; and Michael Neill, "Servant Obedience and Master Sins: Shakespeare and the Bonds of Service," in *Putting History to the Question: Power, Politics, and Society in English Renaissance Drama* (New York: Columbia University Press, 2000), 13–48.

32. Judith Weil, *Service and Dependency in Shakespeare's Plays* (Cambridge: Cambridge University Press, 2005); David Schalkwyk, *Shakespeare, Love and Service* (Cambridge: Cambridge University Press, 2008); Linda Anderson, *A Place in the Story: Servants and Service in Shakespeare's Plays* (Newark: University of Delaware Press, 2005); and David Evett, *Discourses of Service in Shakespeare's England* (New York: Palgrave Macmillan, 2005). See also Michael Neill, ed., "Special Section: Shakespeare and the Bonds of Service," *Shakespearean International Yearbook* 5 (2005): 3–144, which includes essays by Schalkwyk, Evett, Burnett, Weil, Neill, and Michelle Dowd.

33. Evett, who is most openly critical of a materialist approach, accuses it of imposing post-Marxist critical desires on early modern servants and misreading the bond of service as a symptom of false consciousness. Evett, *Discourses of Service*, esp. 151.

34. On the rise of wage labor, see Ralph A. Houlbrooke, *The English Family 1450–1700* (London: Longman, 1984), 173; A. L. Beier, *Masterless Men: The Vagrancy Problem in England 1560–1640* (London: Methuen, 1985), 23; and Keith Wrightson, *Earthly Necessities: Economic Lives in Early Modern Britain* (New Haven, Conn.: Yale University Press, 2000), 194–98. Although domestic servants often stayed with one master for a substantial period, Ilana Krausman Ben-Amos has noted that it was becoming more and more common, especially in London, for them to change their positions on a yearly or biyearly basis, a trend that gathered momentum in the later seventeenth and eighteenth centuries. Ilana Krausman Ben-Amos, *Adolescence and Youth in Early Modern England* (New Haven, Conn.: Yale University Press, 1994), 152.

35. Wrightson, *Earthly Necessities*, 197.

36. Ben-Amos, *Adolescence and Youth*, 217.

37. Weil writes that "social practice and dramatic form are mutually illuminating" (*Service and Dependency*, 1), and Schalkwyk notes that the aesthetics of service are not reducible to material practices or moral ideology (*Shakespeare, Love and Service*, 26).

38. Evett justifies his decision to exclude nondramatic genres by stating that "in no other genre are master-servant relationships so fully and variously explored," and then to exclude non-Shakespearean drama by asserting that "no one explores the ethical as well as the social and economic aspects of these relationships with such subtlety, complexity, tenacity, and vigor" (*Discourses of Service*, 30, 31).

39. On the relationship between genres and form, see Heather Dubrow, "The Politics of Aesthetics: Recuperating Formalism and the Country House Poem," in *Renaissance Literature and Its Formal Engagements,* ed. Mark David Rasmussen (New York: Palgrave, 2002), 72. Following Dubrow, I use "genres" to refer to particular instantiations of form.

40. Bruce Robbins, *The Servant's Hand: English Fiction from Below* (New York: Columbia University Press, 1986), 125, 160.

41. Kristina Straub, *Domestic Affairs: Intimacy, Eroticism, and Violence Between Servants and Masters in Eighteenth-Century Britain* (Baltimore: Johns Hopkins University Press, 2009), 4.

42. Ibid., 5.

43. In most parishes of England, Ann Kussmaul has reported, around 60 percent of people between the ages of fifteen and twenty-four were in service at any given time. Ann Kussmaul, *Servants in Husbandry in Early Modern England* (Cambridge: Cambridge University Press, 1981), 3. For related definitions of "servant" and "service," see Burnett, *Masters and Servants,* 2–3; Weil, *Service and Dependency,* 2; and Schalkwyk, *Shakespeare, Love and Service,* 23–24. While my book discusses many servant characters, my primary term is "service," a word that connotes a capacious, variable set of practices rather than a person of any particular social rank.

44. A number of long-term factors contributed to the decline of neofeudal service. See Felicity Heal, "Reciprocity and Exchange in the Late Medieval Household," in *Bodies and Disciplines: Intersections of Literature and History in Fifteenth-Century England,* ed. Barbara A. Hanawalt and David Wallace (Minneapolis: University of Minnesota Press, 1996), 194–95. The dissolution of monasteries in the sixteenth century, and lack of provision for their servants, played a part. Arthur Kinney, introduction to *Rogues, Vagabonds, and Sturdy Beggars: A New Gallery of Tudor and Early Stuart Rogue Literature,* 2nd ed., ed. Arthur Kinney (Amherst: University of Massachusetts Press, 1990), 11–57, at 24.

45. *The Epistle of Paul to the Ephesians,* 6.5–7, in *The Geneva Bible,* facsimile of the 1560 edition, intro. Lloyd E. Berry (Madison: University of Wisconsin Press, 1969).

46. Thomas Becon, *A New Catechism, Set Forth Dialogue-Wise in Familiar Talk Between the Father and the Son* (London, c. 1560), in *The Catechism of Thomas Becon,* ed. Rev. John Ayre, Parker Society (Cambridge: Cambridge University Press, 1844), 362.

47. Studies that explore intimacy and inequality in service include Mario DiGangi, *The Homoerotics of Early Modern Drama* (Cambridge: Cambridge University Press, 1997); Laurie Shannon, *Sovereign Amity: Figures of Friendship in Shakespearean Contexts* (Chicago: University of Chicago Press, 2002); and Bruce R. Smith, *Homosexual Desire in Shakespeare's England: A Cultural Poetics* (Chicago: University of Chicago Press, 1991).

48. Thomas Fosset, *The Servants Dutie; or, the Calling and Condition of Servants* (London, 1613), 22.

49. William Gouge, *Of Domesticall Duties: Eight Treatises* (London, 1622), 617.

50. Richard Brathwait, *The English Gentleman* (London, 1630), 160.

51. Walter Darell, *A Short Discourse of the Life of Serving-Men* (London, 1578), B.

52. [Markham Gervase], "I. M.," *A Health to the Gentlemanly Profession of Servingmen* (1598), Shakespeare Association Facsimiles No. 3 (London: Oxford University Press, 1931), E3, F2.

53. Fosset, *Servants Dutie*, 42, 44.

54. Kinney, introduction to *Rogues, Vagabonds, and Sturdy Beggars*, 11–57.

55. Peter Clark and Paul Slack, *English Towns in Transition 1500–1700* (London: Oxford University Press 1976), 67. See also Ian Archer, "Material Londoners?," in *Material London, ca. 1600*, ed. Lena Cowen Orlin (Philadelphia: University of Pennsylvania Press, 2000), 175–76.

56. Thirsk stresses the comprehensive social effects of new patterns of production and consumption: "In broader terms these industrial by-employments heralded the development of a consumer society that embraced not only the nobility and gentry and the substantial English yeomen, but included humble peasants, labourers, and servants as well." Joan Thirsk, *Economic Policy and Projects: The Development of a Consumer Society in Early Modern England* (Oxford: Clarendon Press, 1978), 8.

57. Clark and Slack, *English Towns in Transition*, 67. Later, they discuss the less savory side of the commercial economy, an "underemployed" urban population that "could only be supported by an unhealthy expansion of marginal, service activities" (78).

58. As Thirsk details, many of the large-scale economic "projects" of the late sixteenth century were undertaken by courtiers and actively encouraged by the Crown (*Economic Policy and Projects*, see esp. 57–60).

59. Service in a commercial, capitalist economy was continuous with paternalistic service in some important respects. Both meet the basic criteria of this twentieth-century definition of occupations in the service sector: "their product is typically an immediate one, often continuously provided and often of a personal (tailored) nature, with an output hard to measure in conventional accounting terms." J. I. Gershuny and I. D. Miles, *The New Service Economy: The Transformation of Employment in Industrial Societies* (London: Frances Pinter, 1983), 11.

60. "I. M.," *Health to the Gentlemanly Profession*, C2.

61. Natasha Korda, "Women's Theatrical Properties," in *Staged Properties in Early Modern English Drama*, ed. Jonathan Gil Harris and Natasha Korda (Cambridge: Cambridge University Press, 2002), 205, 204. On the marginality of many women servants, see Fiona McNeill, *Poor Women in Shakespeare* (Cambridge: Cambridge University Press, 2007).

62. McNeill, *Poor Women in Shakespeare*, 59–60.

63. Michelle Dowd has detailed other narrative possibilities, from the domestic servant who could not save enough money for a dowry to the female

servants who cultivated marketable skills, including the ability to read and write. Michelle Dowd, *Women's Work in Early Modern English Literature and Culture* (New York: Palgrave Macmillan, 2009), 14.

64. William Ingram, *The Business of Playing: The Beginnings of the Adult Professional Theater in Elizabethan London* (Ithaca, N.Y.: Cornell University Press, 1992), 89.

65. Adrian Johns discusses the book as traditional instrument of patronage. Adrian Johns, *The Nature of the Book: Print and Knowledge in the Making* (Chicago: University of Chicago Press, 1998), 15.

66. Kathleen McLuskie and Felicity Dunsworth point out that patronage was posited on social relations, with the economic terms often defined murkily. Kathleen McLuskie and Felicity Dunsworth, "Patronage and the Economics of Theater," in *A New History of Early English Drama*, ed. John D. Cox and David Scott Kastan (New York: Columbia University Press, 1997), 428.

67. Andrew Gurr, *The Shakespeare Company, 1594–1642* (Cambridge: Cambridge University Press, 2004), 87–89.

68. Alexandra Halasz, *The Marketplace of Print: Pamphlets and the Public Sphere in Early Modern England* (Cambridge: Cambridge University Press, 1997), 23–26; Michael D. Bristol and Arthur F. Marotti, introduction to *Print, Manuscript, and Performance: The Changing Relations of the Media in Early Modern England*, ed. Bristol and Marotti (Columbus, Ohio: Ohio State University Press, 2000), 8.

69. Roslyn Lander Knutson, *Playing Companies and Commerce in Shakespeare's Time* (Cambridge: Cambridge University Press, 2001), 10; David Kathman, "Grocers, Goldsmiths, and Drapers: Freemen and Apprentices in the Elizabethan Theater," *Shakespeare Quarterly* 55 (2004): 4; and Stephen Orgel, *Impersonations: The Performance of Gender in Shakespeare's England* (Cambridge: Cambridge University Press, 1996), 64–74.

70. On the changing structure of patronage in an evolving print culture, see Arthur F. Marotti, "Patronage, Poetry, and Print," chap. 5 in *Manuscript, Print, and the English Renaissance Lyric* (Ithaca, N.Y.: Cornell University Press, 1995).

71. John Cocke, "Description of a Common Player, 1615," in *English Professional Theatre, 1530–1660*, ed. Glynne Wickham, Herbert Berry, and William Ingram (Cambridge: Cambridge University Press, 2000), 179–80.

72. All references to *The Alchemist* are from New Mermaids, 2nd ed., ed. Elizabeth Cook (London: A and C Black; New York: W. W. Norton, 1991).

73. David Margolies, *Novel and Society in Elizabethan England* (London: Croom Helm, 1985), 24–25. The development of authorial voices that spoke to a variety of possible readerships shows the other side of the jealous prerogative that Lori Humphrey Newcomb argues elite writers were defending against lower fictions and readers. Lori Humphrey Newcomb, *Reading Popular Romance in Early Modern England* (New York: Columbia University Press, 2002), 78.

74. John Lyly, *Euphues: The Anatomy of Wit*, in *An Anthology of Elizabethan Prose Fiction*, ed. Paul Salzman (Oxford: Oxford University Press, 1987),

88; Thomas Lodge, *Rosalynde*, ed. W. W. Greg (New York: Duffield, 1907), xxix.

75. Steve Mentz, *Romance for Sale in Early Modern England: The Rise of Prose Fiction* (Aldershot, UK: Ashgate, 2006); Derek B. Alwes, *Sons and Authors in Elizabethan England* (Newark: University of Delaware Press, 2004); Constance Relihan and Goran V. Stanivukovic, eds., *Prose Fiction and Early Modern Sexualities in England, 1570–1640* (New York: Palgrave Macmillan, 2003); Naomi Conn Liebler, ed., *Early Modern Prose Fiction: The Cultural Politics of Reading* (New York: Routledge, 2007); Constance Relihan, ed., *Framing Elizabethan Fictions: Contemporary Approaches to Early Modern Narrative Prose* (Kent, Ohio: Kent State University Press, 1996); *Fashioning Authority: The Development of Elizabethan Novelistic Discourse*, ed. Relihan (Kent, Ohio: Kent State University Press, 1994).

76. Douglas Bruster, "The Structural Transformation of Print in Late Elizabethan England," in Bristol and Marotti, *Print, Manuscript and Performance*, 63.

77. Bristol and Marotti argue that "the theater linked up with new social constituencies and new forms of public space created by the culture of the printed book" (introduction to *Print, Manuscript and Performance*, 20).

78. The tide has turned against the once standard argument that print entailed fixed authority and stable meaning. In addition to Bruster, see Johns, who asserts that "those faced with using the press to create and sustain knowledge thus found themselves confronting a culture characterized by nothing so much as indeterminacy" (*Nature of the Book*, 36).

79. See Jonathan Goldberg, "The Print of Goodness," in *The Culture of Capital: Property, Cities, and Knowledge in Early Modern England*, ed. Henry S. Turner (New York: Routledge, 2002), 231–54.

Chapter One

1. Stanley Wells, "The Failure of *The Two Gentlemen of Verona*," in *Shakespeare: Early Comedies*, ed. Pamela Mason (London: Macmillan, 1995), 169.

2. James Darmesteter, quoted in the introduction to *The Works of William Shakespeare*, ed. Sir Henry Irving, Frank A. Marshall, and Edward Dowden (New York: Scribner and Welford, 1888–90), xlv; David Daiches, *A Critical History of English Literature*, rev. ed., vol. 2 (New York: Donald Press, 1979), 248.

3. Alexander Pope, writing in 1725, helped instigate the tradition of doubting that Shakespeare could be fully responsible for "the lowest and most trifling conceits" expressed in the play. See Pope's *Preface to Shakespear's Work* (1725), excerpted in Mason, *Shakespeare: Early Comedies*, 141. Pope excuses Shakespeare from full responsibility for less desirable scenes in the play by asserting that several were "interpolated by the Players." Arthur Quiller-Couch's introduction to the Cambridge New Shakespeare edition of *Two Gentlemen* (1921) pronounces the final scene to be "vitiated . . . by a flaw too unnatural to be charged upon Shakespeare" (Mason, *Shakespeare: Early Comedies*, 144–45).

4. Robert Y. Turner, *Shakespeare's Apprenticeship* (Chicago: University of Chicago Press, 1974), 5.

5. Ibid., 5–6.

6. David Kathman notes that the usual age range for theatrical apprentices was from thirteen to twenty-two. David Kathman, "Players, Livery Companies, and Apprentices," in *The Oxford Handbook of Early Modern Theatre*, ed. Richard Dutton (Oxford: Oxford University Press, 2009), 427.

7. See Kathman, "Grocers, Goldsmiths, and Drapers," 4. Kathman also speculates that playwrights who held apprentices through their nontheatrical livery companies might have used those apprentices in the theater (16).

8. Katherine Duncan-Jones, *Ungentle Shakespeare: Scenes from his Life*, Arden Shakespeare (London: Thomson Learning, 2001), 56–57.

9. Ibid., 43; and Scott McMillin and Sally-Beth McLean, *The Queen's Men and Their Plays* (Cambridge: Cambridge University Press, 1998). For cautions about the limits of knowledge about Shakespeare's pre-1594 career, see Terence G. Schoone-Jongen, *Shakespeare's Companies: William Shakespeare's Early Career and the Acting Companies, 1577–1594* (Farnham, UK: Ashgate, 2009).

10. See Schoone-Jongen, *Shakespeare's Companies*, 197.

11. Charles Hallett complains about act 1, scene 1, for instance, that "an audience will be far more aware of Speed's wit than of Proteus's purpose and, further, that the less important character, Speed, seems to dominate to the point of obscuring the love plot." Charles Hallett, "'Metamorphising' Proteus: Reversal Strategies in *The Two Gentlemen of Verona*," in *"Two Gentlemen of Verona": Critical Essays*, ed. June Schlueter (New York: Garland, 1996), 160.

12. The twinning of Dromio is indebted to moments in the *Amphitruo* where the slave Sosia encounters Mercury disguised as him. On the intertextuality between Shakespeare's slaves and Plautus's, see Wolfgang Riehle, *Shakespeare, Plautus and the Humanist Tradition* (Cambridge: D.S. Brewer, 1990), 37–38, 127–28.

13. See David Cressy, *Literacy and the Social Order: Reading and Writing in Tudor and Stuart England* (Cambridge: Cambridge University Press, 1980), 118, for foundational research on early modern literacy, based primarily on signatures. Much subsequent scholarship has argued for a broader, more inclusive concept of early modern literacy. See Margaret Ferguson, "A Room Not Their Own: Renaissance Women as Readers and Writers," in *The Comparative Perspective on Literature: Approaches to Theory and Practice*, ed. Clayton Koelb and Susan Noakes (Ithaca, N.Y.: Cornell University Press, 1988), 93–116; Eve Sanders, *Gender and Literacy on Stage in Early Modern England* (Cambridge: Cambridge University Press, 1998); Sasha Roberts, "Reading in Early Modern England: Contexts and Problems," *Critical Survey* 12 (2000): 1–16; and Heidi Brayman Hackel, "The 'Great Variety' of Readers and Early Modern Reading Practices," in *A Companion to Shakespeare*, ed. David Scott Kastan (Oxford: Blackwell, 1999), 139–57.

14. Douglas Lanier, "'Stigmatical in Making': The Material Character of *The Comedy of Errors*," *English Literary Renaissance* 23 (1993): 83. Lanier's essay has fundamentally shaped my ideas about literacy and character.

15. "Bond" or "bondsman" occurs seven times, "band" four, and "bound" seventeen. "Band" and "bond" are often used interchangeably, as the *OED* confirms was common in the period. On the affective dimension of service bonds, see Schalkwyk, *Shakespeare, Love and Service*, 81–85.

16. *Oxford English Dictionary*, 2nd ed., s.vv. "bond" *n.*², 3, and "bondman" 2: "A man in bondage; a villein; a serf, slave," accessed November 23, 2010, http://dictionary.oed.com.

17. For the first kind of suffering, see Antipholus of Syracuse's soliloquy that begins "I to the world am like a drop of water/That in the ocean seeks another drop," (1.2.35); for the second, see Luciana's articulation of divine hierarchy: "There's nothing situate under heaven's eye/But hath his bound in earth, in sea, in sky" (2.1.16–17), an ideology that Antipholus of Ephesus resists.

18. See Lanier, "'Stigmatical in Making,'" 93, for a related reading of this line.

19. A. W. B. Simpson, *A History of the Common Law of Contract: The Rise of the Action of Assumpsit* (Oxford: Clarendon Press, 1975), 90.

20. *OED*, s.v. "bond" *n.*¹, II.8.c., accessed November 23, 2010.

21. Simpson notes that people who entered into bonds could be illiterate, "and if so would have to rely upon having the terms of the bond read over to them by the scrivener or attorney" (*History of Common Law*, 98). Nevertheless, such people could evidently take an active role in legal and literate affairs, thus reinforcing the complexity of defining early modern literacy.

22. Curtis Perry, "Commerce, Community, and Nostalgia in *The Comedy of Errors*," in *Money and the Age of Shakespeare*, ed. Linda Woodbridge (New York: Macmillan, 2003), 44, 48. Shankar Raman argues that the "doubling, exchange, and possession" which characterize the market threaten originary identity. Shankar Raman, "Marking Time: Memory and Market in *The Comedy of Errors*," *Shakespeare Quarterly* 56 (2005): 193. On the play's tentative engagement with a global economic system, see Jonathan Gil Harris, *Sick Economies: Drama, Mercantilism, and Disease in Shakespeare's England* (Philadelphia: University of Pennsylvania Press, 2004), 49.

23. D. S. Bland, ed., *Gesta Grayorum*, English Reprints Series, no. 22 (Liverpool, UK: Liverpool University Press, 1968). Text references are to page numbers of this edition. Only five Inns of Court revels survive in written accounts. More context can be found in D. S. Bland, "The 'Night of Errors' at Gray's Inn, 1594," *Notes and Queries* 13 (1966): 127–28.

24. Lanier, "'Stigmatical in Making,'" 104.

25. Bland persuasively argues against the notion that the events described in *Gesta Grayorum* were scripted elements in the revels ("'Night of Errors,'" 127).

26. See Ann Jennalie Cook, *The Privileged Playgoers of Shakespeare's London, 1576–1642* (Princeton, N.J.: Princeton University Press, 1981), 37; and Wilfrid R. Prest, *The Inns of Court Under Elizabeth I and the Early Stuarts 1590–1640* (London: Longman, 1972), 23–24.

27. On the theatrical space, see Margaret Knapp and Michal Kobialka, "Shakespeare and the Prince of Purpoole: The 1594 Production of *The*

Comedy of Errors at Gray's Inn Hall," *Theatre History Studies* 4 (1984): 77. The authors speculate that "entrances and exits through the hall would have brought the audience in the scaffolds into the action of the play."

28. Using the *Gesta Grayorum* as an example, William N. West argues that the early modern theater deliberately cultivated confusion as a commentary on theatrical representation. William N. West, "'But this will be a mere confusion': Real and Represented Confusions on the Elizabethan Stage," *Theatre Journal* 60 (2008): 217–33.

29. Lanier ("'Stigmatical in Making,'" 108) notes that the scapegoating of a "sorcerer" figure resonates with Antipholus of S.'s (false) attribution of the confusions that befall him in Ephesus to "Dark-working sorcerers" and "Soul-killing witches" (1.2.99, 1.2.100).

30. Riehle, *Shakespeare, Plautus*, 8.

31. Sanders, *Gender and Literacy*, 55.

32. Jeffrey Masten, *Textual Intercourse: Collaboration, Authorship, and Sexualities in Renaissance Drama* (Cambridge: Cambridge University Press, 1997), 37–48, and "*The Two Gentlemen of Verona*: A Modern Perspective," in *The Two Gentlemen of Verona*, ed. Barbara Mowat and Paul Werstine, Folger Shakespeare Library Series (New York: Washington Square Press, 1990), 199–221. For a more recent discussion of how the play "produces" heterosexuality, see Stephen Guy-Bray, "Shakespeare and the Invention of the Heterosexual," special issue, *Early Modern Literary Studies* 16 (2007): 12.1–28, http://purl.oclc.org/emls/si-16/brayshks.htm.

33. Hallett, "'Metamorphising' Proteus,'" 162.

34. See note 4 to 1.2.96.

35. For a reading of Lucetta as "table," see Frederick Kiefer, "Love Letters in *The Two Gentlemen of Verona*," in Schlueter, "*Two Gentlemen of Verona*": *Critical Essays*, 133–52; and Jonathan Goldberg, "Shakespearean Characters: The Generation of Silvia," in *Shakespeare's Hand* (Minneapolis: University of Minnesota Press, 2003), 10–45.

36. The *OED* defines "character" as (1) "to engrave, imprint; to inscribe, write" (with this example from *Two Gentlemen* cited); (2) "to represent, symbolize, portray"; and (3) "to describe the qualities of." The first use of definition 3 is listed as 1618. *OED*, s.v. "character," v., accessed November 30, 2010.

37. Goldberg, "Shakespearean Characters," 24. See also Richard Rambuss, "The Secretary's Study: The Secret Designs of the *Shepheardes Calender*," *English Literary History* 59 (1992): 319.

38. Frank Whigham, *Ambition and Privilege: The Social Tropes of Elizabethan Courtesy Theory* (Berkeley: University of California Press, 1984), 5.

39. Camille Wells Slights reads *Two Gentlemen* as critiquing Proteus and Valentine's corruption of the courtly ideal. Camille Wells Slights, "Common Courtesy in *The Two Gentlemen of Verona*," *Shakespeare's Comic Commonwealths* (Toronto: University of Toronto Press, 1993), 57–73.

40. Proteus appears in book 4 of Homer's *Odyssey* as well as in Virgil's *Georgics*. In the *Odyssey*, Proteus is a wily old sea god who will not yield his knowledge until he is forcibly prevented from changing shapes. There is a

compulsive quality to his shape-shifting that resonates with Shakespeare's Proteus, who continually reconstitutes himself in the image of whoever is closest to him, a form of mimesis that seems to trap both him and his objects.

41. Masten argues that *Two Gentlemen* features "a homosocial circuit of writing" in which women act as pretexts and texts, but not as agents of circulation (*Textual Intercourse*, 42–43). Lorna Hutson makes the case that the English humanist program trafficked in women to propagate a male line of property and capital. Lorna Hutson, *The Usurer's Daughter: Male Friendship and Fictions of Women in Sixteenth-Century England* (London: Routledge, 1994), 64–76.

42. Girard is not, however, very attentive to moments where this symmetrical mirroring fractures and allows an asymmetrical dynamic to take shape. René Girard, "Love Delights in Praises: A Reading of *The Two Gentlemen of Verona*," *Philosophy and Literature* 13 (1989): 231–47.

43. Marc Norman and Tom Stoppard, *Shakespeare in Love: A Screenplay* (New York: Hyperion/Miramax Books, 1998), 20.

44. See, for example, Harold Brooks, "Two Clowns in a Comedy (To Say Nothing of the Dog): Speed, Launce (and Crab) in *The Two Gentlemen of Verona*," in Mason, *Shakespeare: Early Comedies*, 153.

45. As John Timpane suggests, there is comic potential in performance both in the use of a live dog and in the substitution of a stuffed animal. John Timpane, "'I Am But a Foole, Looke You': Launce and the Social Functions of Humor," in Schlueter, *"Two Gentlemen of Verona": Critical Essays*, 209.

46. "Knave" could refer to "a boy or lad employed as a servant; hence, a male servant or menial in general; one of low condition" (*OED*, s.v. "knave," n. 2) or to "an unprincipled man, given to dishonourable and deceitful practices; a base and crafty rogue" (*OED*, s.v. "knave," n. 3, accessed November 30, 2010).

47. Ruth Nevo reads Launce as a "foil for Julia, his unconquerable good nature acting not to undercut but to underwrite Julia's 'folly.'" Ruth Nevo, *Comic Transformations in Shakespeare* (New York: Methuen, 1980), 62.

48. Orgel, *Impersonations*, 70. See also Lisa Jardine, *Still Harping on Daughters: Women and Drama in the Age of Shakespeare* (Sussex, UK: Harvester Press, 1983), 9–36.

49. Orgel, *Impersonations*, 81.

50. Critics have begun to look to play texts for evidence of how apprentice actors were trained on female roles. Richard Madeline's speculation that "apprentices in their early years might have been given roles that allowed or encouraged self-conscious imitation of theatrical female gait and gesture" has an intriguing application to act 4, scene 4, in which gender is performed with an unusually keen awareness of its artifice. Richard Madeline, "Material Boys: Apprenticeship and the Boy Actors' Shakespearean Roles," in *Shakespeare Matters: History, Teaching, Performance*, ed. Lloyd Davis (Newark: University of Delaware Press, 2003), 229. See also Scott McMillin, "The Sharer and His Boy: Rehearsing Shakespeare's Women," in *From Script to Stage in Early Modern England*, ed. Peter Holland and Stephen Orgel (Houndmills,

UK: Palgrave Macmillan, 2004), 231–45; and Evelyn Tribble, "Marlowe's Boy Actors," *Shakespeare Bulletin* 27 (2009): 5–17.

51. See Masten, *Textual Intercourse*, 45–48, for a synopsis of critical attitudes toward the play's controversial final scene.

52. Ibid., 48.

53. *Groats-worth of Witte, bought with a million of Repentance, and The Repentance of Robert Greene* (1592), ed. G. B. Harrison, Elizabethan and Jacobean Quartos (New York: Barnes and Noble, 1966), 46.

54. Ibid. One of the most satisfying recent readings of the passage is Duncan-Jones, *Ungentle Shakespeare*, 43–48.

55. Stephen Greenblatt, *Will in the World: How Shakespeare Became Shakespeare* (New York: Norton, 2004), 213.

56. *OED*, s.v. "groom," n.¹, 1, accessed November 30, 2010.

57. Duncan-Jones, *Ungentle Shakespeare*, 47.

58. Ibid.

59. *OED*, s.v. "factotum," 1.a., 1.b, accessed November 30, 2010.

Chapter Two

1. See Duncan-Jones, *Ungentle Shakespeare*, 43–48.

2. Thomas Nashe, *The Unfortunate Traveller*, in *The Works of Thomas Nashe*, vol. 2, ed. Ronald B. McKerrow and F. P. Wilson (Oxford: Basil Blackwell, 1958), 187–328. Text references are to page numbers of this edition.

3. Marotti, *Manuscript, Print, and the English Renaissance Lyric*, 293. See also Julian Yates, *Error Misuse Failure: Object Lessons from the English Renaissance* (Minneapolis: University of Minnesota Press, 2003), 101–37. Yates explores the ways in which print constructs authorial and textual agency for Nashe. Nashe's engagement with print underlies his innovations in fiction, but my emphasis in this chapter is more on the subject positions enabled by prose fiction than on those enabled by print technology more generally.

4. The ambiguity of the page's social status is reflected in the *OED*'s definitions, which include a highborn youth placed in service during his education (n¹, 2.a), and "a youth or man of low status" (n¹, 4).

5. A number of critics have written about the unsettling and generative effects of Nashe's punning on "page." See Margaret Ferguson, "Nashe's *The Unfortunate Traveller*: The 'Newes of the Maker' Game, *English Literary Renaissance* 11 (1981): 165–82; and Mihoko Suzuki, "'Signorie ouer the Pages': The Crisis of Authority in Nashe's *The Unfortunate Traveller*," *Studies in Philology* 81 (1984): 348–71. Until the draft revision of September 2010, the *OED* credited Nashe's preface to Robert Greene's *Menaphon* (1589) with the first use of "page" as "One side of a leaf of a book, manuscript, letter, etc.," (n², I.1.a). Now the *OED* cites two prior examples, both from the late fifteenth century. Accessed December 2, 2010.

6. Jonathan Crewe provides an important precedent for my discussion of the page's representational doubleness: the page "affirms itself . . . when it discovers in a moment of sophistication that it possesses a capacity for diverting mimicry and play in addition to, and as opposed to, its assigned role in

representing another (person, thing)." Jonathan Crewe, *Unredeemed Rhetoric: Thomas Nashe and the Scandal of Authorship* (Baltimore: Johns Hopkins University Press, 1982), 71.

7. Steve Mentz makes the crucial point that for Nashe, "print publication, not noble patronage, conveys value" (*Romance for Sale*, 1–2). He argues that prose authors, including Nashe, were engaged in the important project of conceptualizing the emerging relation of author, book, and readership in a print economy.

8. Margaret Spufford, *Small Books and Pleasant Histories: Popular Fiction and Its Readership in Seventeenth-Century England* (Athens: University of Georgia Press, 1981), 48–49.

9. Mentz discusses the mixed message, both hostile and supplicatory, of the dedication to Southampton (*Romance for Sale*, 187). On the front matter, see also Suzuki, "'Signorie ouer the Pages,'" 350–52, and Ferguson, "Nashe's *Unfortunate Traveller*," 167–68.

10. According to G. R. Hibbard, Nashe's patrons included Ferdinando Stanley, Lord Strange, probably for a period in 1592, Archbishop Whitgift in later 1592, and Sir George Carey in 1593–94. G. R. Hibbard, *Thomas Nashe: A Critical Introduction* (London: Routledge and Kegan Paul, 1962), 87–90, 135–41, 21. Near the end of his career, Nashe composed parodic dedications to individuals such as Richard Lichfield, the barber of Trinity College.

11. On Nashe's complex attitude toward patronage, see Margolies, *Novel and Society*, 87–90; and Charles Nicholl, *A Cup of News: The Life of Thomas Nashe* (London: Routledge and Kegan Paul, 1984), 160.

12. Hibbard, *Thomas Nashe*, 21.

13. Anthony Arthur, *The Tailor-King: The Rise and Fall of the Anabaptist Kingdom of Münster* (New York: Thomas Donne/St. Martin's Press, 1999).

14. *Geneva Bible*, Acts 2:40: "Saue your selues from this forwarde generation" and John 13:16: "Verely, verely, I say vnto you, The servuant is not greater then his master, neither the ambassadour greater then he that sent him," reiterated at 15:20.

15. Crewe's comment on Nashe's erotic poem "The Choice of Valentines" applies to *The Unfortunate Traveller* as well: "Paradoxically, the low imitation supplants the deficient original, of which it becomes a mockingly substantial and superior image" (*Unredeemed Rhetoric*, 53).

16. McKerrow suggests that Nashe may have borrowed the name "Brunquell" from Anthony Munday's *Palmendos* (1589), a translation of continental romances (Nashe, *Works of Thomas Nashe*, 4:277, n6). In *Palmendos*, Brunquell is a Pigmy, so the choice on Jack's part intimates that he has chosen a particularly demeaning type of servant for the earl to play.

17. The definition of "shadows" as players, as for example in Puck's epilogue to *A Midsummer Night's Dream*, also bears on Nashe's use of the word.

18. Crewe, *Unredeemed Rhetoric*, 81.

19. Mentz suggests that Nashe represents Diamante's unscrupulous tactics, especially her forays into prostitution, as images of his own authorship (*Romance for Sale*, 195–96).

20. Yates, *Error Misuse Failure*, 136.

21. My reading of these anticlosural elements counters the argument some critics have made for Jack's moral renewal, including Madelon Gohlke, "Wits Wantonness: *The Unfortunate Traveller* as Picaresque," *Studies in Philology* 73 (1976): 411; and Louise Simons, "Rerouting *The Unfortunate Traveller*: Strategies for Coherence and Direction," *Studies in English Literature* 28 (1988): 35. By contrast, Philip Schwyzer defends the narrative's lack of resolution as one of its defining marks. Philip Schwyzer, "Summer Fruit and Autumn Leaves: Thomas Nashe in 1593," *English Literary Renaissance* 24 (1994): 604, 617.

22. Suzuki, "'Signorie ouer the Pages,'" 369.

23. W. A. Sessions, *Henry Howard, the Poet Earl of Surrey: A Life* (Oxford: Oxford University Press, 1999), 4–5.

24. Sessions quotes a poem by Sir John Checke, which glorifies Surrey's "dual genealogy," as well as the works of Foxe, both of which participated in his posthumous glorification (ibid., 1, 5).

25. Stephen Guy-Bray argues that Surrey becomes less admirable as the narrative progresses, allowing Nashe to advance the claims of English prose fiction over classically and continentally influenced poetry of the kind that Surrey represented. Stephen Guy-Bray, "How to Turn Prose into Literature: The Case of Thomas Nashe," in Liebler, *Early Modern Prose Fiction*, 33–45. Jonathan Bate points out that Surrey represents an anachronistic poetic ideal. Jonathan Bate, "The Elizabethans in Italy," in *Travel and Drama in Shakespeare's Time*, ed. Jean-Pierre Maquerlot and Michèle Willems (Cambridge: Cambridge University Press, 1996), 66.

26. Quoted in Katherine Duncan-Jones, *Sir Philip Sidney: Courtier Poet* (New Haven, Conn.: Yale University Press, 1991), 189–90.

27. See Edward Berry, *The Making of Sir Philip Sidney* (Toronto: University of Toronto Press, 1998), 13. On the outpouring of eulogies for Sidney, see Roger Howell, *Sir Philip Sidney: The Shepherd Knight* (London: Hutchinson, 1968), 263–67.

28. Nashe also praised Sidney in the epistle to *The Anatomie of Abuse*: "England afforded many mediocrities, but never saw any thing more singular than worthy Sir Phillip Sidney" (Nashe, *Works of Thomas Nashe*, 1:7).

29. Preface to *Astrophil and Stella*, in Nashe, *Works of Thomas Nashe*, 3:329. On Nashe's preface, see Nicholl, *Cup of News*, 82–85.

30. Sidney, *Defence of Poesy*, 244.

31. Ibid., 218.

32. Preface to *Astrophil and Stella*, in Nashe, *Works of Thomas Nashe*, 3:333.

33. The house echoes the historical Earl of Surrey's controversial construction of Surrey House on a hill overlooking Norwich. The property included three sumptuous, towerlike "banquetting houses" which were interpreted by some observers as evidence of Surrey's overweening ambition (Sessions, *Poet Earl of Surrey*, 170). During much of Nashe's childhood, his father was the rector in a village within the Howard family's jurisdiction in Norfolk, so

Nashe would likely have been familiar with the story of Surrey's scandalous architecture (Nicholl, *Cup of News,* 16).

34. Nashe, *Works of Thomas Nashe,* 3:329.

35. Simons writes that "Nashe . . . cannot allow himself to become a chained bird piping the official tune" ("Rerouting *The Unfortunate Traveller,*" 32).

36. See Joan Pong Linton, "Counterfeiting Sovereignty, Mocking Mastery: Trickster Poetics and the Critique of Romance in Nashe's *Unfortunate Traveller,*" in Liebler, *Early Modern Prose Fiction,* 130–47, for a similar reading of Nashe's form, in this case as manifested through Jack's trickster identity.

37. Yates reads the mechanical birds as an autonomous machine, part of the house's "economy of fixed quantity and perfect equilibrium" (*Error Misuse Failure,* 127). The machinery seems to me less ordered and symmetrical than it appears in Yates's description.

38. Sidney, *Defence of Poesy,* 241.

Chapter Three

1. *The Anatomie of Absurditie,* in Nashe, *Works of Thomas Nashe,* 1:24.

2. Deloney's most frequent subject, not surprising given his occupational background, was clothiers, as treated in *Jack of Newbury* (1597) and *Thomas of Reading* (1598–1600). On the relation between textile and textual production in Deloney's work, see Roze Hentschell, *The Culture of Cloth in Early Modern England: Textual Constructions of a National Identity* (Aldershot, UK: Ashgate, 2008), 51–71.

3. Steve Mentz has highlighted the competition between prose fiction and drama in his recent essay "'A Note Beyond Your Reach': Prose Romance's Rivalry with Elizabethan Drama," in *Staging Early Modern Romance: Prose Fiction, Dramatic Romance, and Shakespeare,* ed. Mary Ellen Lamb and Valerie Wayne (New York: Routledge, 2009), 75–90. Mentz's argument usefully corrects the persistent critical tendency to privilege early modern drama over prose. It seems to me, however, that there is less a sense of rivalry between Deloney's prose and Dekker's fiction than of cooperative, often overlapping strategies.

4. Stevenson writes, "The 'history' of the gentle craft was not history; it was nostalgia. While the gentle craftsman looked forward to the world of capitalism, he looked backward to an idealized medieval economy." Laura Caroline Stevenson, *Praise and Paradox: Merchants and Craftsmen in Elizabethan Popular Literature* (Cambridge: Cambridge University Press, 1984), 198–99.

5. Deloney's shoemakers mediate between what Raymond Williams designated as residual, dominant, and emergent cultural elements. Discussing the difficulty of recognizing genuinely emergent aspects, as opposed to new or assimilated aspects *within* the dominant order, Williams asserts that "elements of emergence may indeed be incorporated, but just as often the incorporated forms are merely facsimiles of the genuinely emergent cultural practice." Raymond Williams, *Marxism and Literature* (Oxford: Oxford University Press, 1977), 121–27, at 126.

6. As many of Deloney's critics have suggested, he "gentles" shoemakers by layering an aristocratic framework of class privilege and a protocapitalist framework with its own criteria for gentility. See, for example, Stevenson, *Praise and Paradox*; Eugene P. Wright, *Thomas Deloney* (Boston: Twayne, 1981); Margolies, *Novel and Society*; and Mihoko Suzuki, *Subordinate Subjects: Gender, the Political Nation, and Literary Form in England, 1588–1688* (Burlington, Vt.: Ashgate, 2003).

7. Halasz, *Marketplace of Print*, 119. My line of inquiry in this chapter is influenced by Halasz's argument that early modern English literature participates crucially in the formation of a public sphere, although she focuses more on the discursive positions enabled by the technology of print than on projects of aesthetic definition.

8. Halasz's emphasis is on Deloney's alignment of his form with gossip, initiating "a circulation of discourse that is contingent rather than controlled" (ibid., 148).

9. At least eight editions of *The Gentle Craft* are extant from the second half of the seventeenth century, in addition to a modified chapbook version and an unknown number of earlier editions (all but one now lost) that must have followed its original registration with the Stationers in 1597. By the middle of the eighteenth century, twenty-four complete editions of *The Gentle Craft* had appeared in print.

10. A recently discovered edition of the text may shed new light on the relationship of *The Gentle Craft* to the Cordwainers' Guild: a volume located at the Biblioteka Gadańska in Poland, which has a date of 1599, prefaces the usual dedication in other known editions of part 1 with one addressed almost identically to the dedication in part 2: "To the Masters and Wardens . . ." If the 1599 date is correct, this is the earliest extant edition of part 1 by some twenty-eight years. Simon Barker generously shared with me a copy of the 1599 text in advance of its publication. His recently published edition includes this dedication as well as two chapters that appear only in the Gdańsk text. Thomas Deloney, *The Gentle Craft*, ed. Simon Barker (Aldershot, UK: Ashgate, 2007).

11. Neither Relihan and Stanivukovic's *Prose Fiction and Early Modern Sexualities* nor Liebler's *Early Modern Prose Fiction* nor Relihan's earlier anthology *Framing Elizabethan Fictions* contains essays on Deloney, though Relihan's *Fashioning Authority* does consider a few examples from his works. Deloney is not featured, either, by Mentz in *Romance for Sale*, by Alwes in *Sons and Authors*, or by Richard Helgerson in his still important *The Elizabethan Prodigals* (Berkeley: University of California Press, 1976).

12. All references to *The Gentle Craft*, part 1, and *Jack of Newbury*, except for that cited in n. 13, are from Thomas Deloney, *The Novels of Thomas Deloney*, ed. Merritt Lawlis (Bloomington: Indiana University Press, 1961). Line numbers are indicated when verse appears in the text. On the cultural history of shoemakers, see E. J. Hobsbawm and Joan Wallach Scott, "Political Shoemakers," *Past and Present* 89 (1980): 99; and Joan Lane, *Apprenticeship in England, 1600–1914* (Boulder, Colo.: Westview Press, 1996), 139. Details on the pre-1800 history of the Cordwainers' Guild are scarce, however, since

most of the guild's early records, along with its hall, perished in London's Great Fire of 1666.

13. Barker, *The Gentle Craft*, 2.

14. Sidney, *Defence of Poesy*, 216.

15. Ibid. See also Paul Yachnin, *Stage-Wrights: Shakespeare, Jonson, Middleton, and the Making of Theatrical Value* (Philadelphia: University of Pennsylvania Press, 1997), xii; and H. Turner, *English Renaissance Stage*, 53–55.

16. Deloney's editor Francis Oscar Mann posited what used to be the conventional view of his readership: because Deloney's subject matter involved common trades and he drew on traditional English folklore, his readers must have been correspondingly humble. See Thomas Deloney, *The Works of Thomas Deloney*, ed. Francis Oscar Mann (Oxford: Clarendon Press, 1912), xxix. This belief has now been debunked, as for instance by Tessa Watt, who says of printed material far more ephemeral than *The Gentle Craft*, "The audience presupposed within the cheap print itself appears to be inclusive rather than exclusive, addressed both as 'readers' and as 'hearers'; as substantial householders expected to employ labourers, and as couples 'whose whole stocke' could hardly purchase a wedding ring." Tessa Watt, *Cheap Print and Popular Piety, 1550–1640* (Cambridge: Cambridge University Press, 1991). See also Spufford, who notes that Samuel Pepys owned two late seventeenth-century editions of *The Gentle Craft*: a quarto edition and a chapbook (*Small Books and Pleasant Histories*, 111–28).

17. Editor Mann thoroughly catalogued sources for *The Gentle Craft*, part 1 (Deloney, *Works*, 522–23).

18. Mentz suggests what may seem to modern readers alien or even "unreadable" in early modern fictions is actually "a function of historical distance, and that Elizabethan fictions assume coherence once we assimilate their generic codes and intertextual patterns" (*Romance for Sale*, 11). See also Hentschell, *Culture of Cloth*, 60.

19. Watt, *Cheap Print and Popular Piety*, 268.

20. Ibid., 257, 270–77. Watt lists *Guy of Warwick* and *Bevis of Hampton* among the ten works that were most often cited as "favourite titles" in commentaries, libraries, and collections. Although *Long Meg of Westminster* does not appear, others that do, such as *Robin Hood* and *100 Merry Tales,* represent a similar genre.

21. The guild context for service was itself unstable in the period. See Steve Rappaport, *Worlds Within Worlds: Structures of Life in Sixteenth-Century London* (Cambridge: Cambridge University Press, 1989), 376; Ian W. Archer, *The Pursuit of Stability: Social Relations in Elizabethan London* (Cambridge: Cambridge University Press, 1991), 102; and Ian Gadd and Patrick Wallis, eds. *Guilds, Society and Economy in London 1450–1800* (London: Centre for Metropolitan History, 2002).

22. *OED,* s.v. "business," III.11.a, accessed December 4, 2010.

23. *OED,* s.v. "business," III.12.a: "Stated occupation, profession, or trade," accessed December 4, 2010. Ben-Amos says that it was typical for apprentices to use the skills acquired in their training for their own purposes rather than

their masters', as witnessed by the relatively low completion rate of apprenticeships in larger towns and cities (*Adolescence and Youth*, 129–30).

24. Tracing the history of shoemaking across Europe from the early modern period through the nineteenth century, Hobsbawm and Scott, in "Political Shoemakers," concluded that it constituted the single largest trade in several countries, Britain among them, and also that it was one of the least profitable of trades and thus the cheapest in which to invest, so that it represented a realistic choice for families of humble means. It was not an occupation in which the wealthier strata of yeomen, gentlemen, or merchants were likely to apprentice their sons.

25. Deloney's text has become so closely identified with "the gentle craft" that most later definitions steer the reader back to Deloney's text. But the phrase certainly predated the fiction. The first traceable references occur in the late sixteenth century, just before the publication of *The Gentle Craft*, suggesting that a proverbial label was just then being consolidated in print.

26. Although Robert Greene is no longer believed to have written it, *George a Greene, the Pinner of Wakefield* is included in *The Plays and Poems of Robert Greene*, vol. 2, ed. J. Churton Collins (Oxford: Clarendon Press, 1905).

27. See, for example, Nashe's *Pierce Penilesse his Supplication to the Diuell* (1592), in Nashe, *Works of Thomas Nashe*, 1:201; and Robert Greene, *A Quip for an Upstart Courtier* (1592), ed. Charles Hindley (London: Reeves and Turner, 1871).

28. Hobsbawm and Scott, "Political Shoemakers," 95–97.

29. *King Henry the VIII and a Cobler*, in Samuel Pepys, *Samuel Pepys' Penny Merriments*, ed. Roger Thompson (New York: Columbia University Press, 1977), 28.

30. *The famous Hystory off George a Greene*, in Greene, *Plays and Poems*, 177. The prose narrative, like the similarly titled play, is unlikely to be by Greene. The date of composition is likewise unknown. The first surviving printed copy is from 1706, although the volume editor Collins asserted with confidence that the surviving manuscript dates from the late sixteenth or seventeenth century.

31. Watt, *Cheap Print and Popular Piety*, 30, 34.

32. There are records of a 1613 guild pageant that featured the Wells Cordwainers' Company mounting a production titled "Krispie and Krispianie," which was attended by Queen Anne. James Stokes, ed., *Records for Early English Drama: Somerset*, vol. 1 (Toronto: University of Toronto Press, 1996), 377.

33. Neill, "Servant Obedience and Master Sins," 21.

34. Merritt Lawlis, introduction to Deloney, *Novels*, xxvii.

35. The assimilative qualities of Deloney's fiction anticipate novelistic heteroglossia as defined by Mikhail Bakhtin in *Dialogic Imagination: Four Essays*, ed. Michael Holquist, trans. Caryl Emerson and Michael Holquist (Austin: University of Texas Press, 1981), especially the observation that "extraliterary genres (the everyday genres, for example) are incorporated into the novel not in order to 'ennoble' them, to 'literarize' them, but for the sake of

their extraliterariness, for the sake of their potential for introducing nonliterary language (or even dialects) into the novel. It is precisely this very multiplicity of the era's languages that must be represented in the novel" (411).

36. Like the first episode, the second is built on the scaffolding of a saint's tale, this time *The Lives of Saints Crispin and Crispinian.* Caxton details how the noble-born brothers, persecuted in their native Rome for their profession of Christianity, move to the city of Soissons in France and become shoemakers before their martyrdom. William Caxton, *The Golden Legend or Lives of the Saints,* vol. 6, ed. F. S. Ellis (London: J. M. Dent and Sons, 1900), 69–71.

37. On representations of Christian enslavement, see Nabil Matar, *Turks, Moors, and Englishmen in the Age of Discovery* (New York: Columbia University Press, 1999); 43–82; and Daniel Vitkus, introduction to *Piracy, Slavery, and Redemption: Barbary Captivity Narratives from Early Modern England,* ed. Daniel Vitkus (New York: Columbia University Press, 2001), 1–54.

38. The Epistle of Paul to the Ephesians, 6.5–7, in *Geneva Bible.*

39. Paul Griffiths, *Youth and Authority: Formative Experiences in England 1560–1640* (Oxford: Clarendon Press, 1996), 286.

40. See Suzuki, *Subordinate Subjects,* 41.

41. Linda Ann Hutjens, "The Renaissance Cobbler: The Significance of Shoemaker and Cobbler Characters in Renaissance Drama" (PhD diss., University of Toronto, 2004).

42. Unlike *The Gentle Craft,* the anonymous texts do not feature a prince in disguise as an apprentice but rather a provincial youth born, at least in one version, to "wealthy" parents who bind him to a merchant. The emphasis is firmly on the London apprentice as conversionary agent of Christian Britain. See, for example, *The honour of an Apprentice* (London, 1664).

43. See Naomi Conn Liebler, "Bully St. George: Richard Johnson's *Seven Champions of Christendom* and the Creation of the Bourgeois National Hero," in Liebler, *Early Modern Prose Fiction,* 115. Guild ideology encouraged the notion that shoemakers might act as heroes for the English nation during a period when, Antony Black argues, the corporate makeup of guilds generated a model for the transition between feudalism and the rise of the nation-state. Antony Black, *Guild and State: European Political Thought from the Twelfth Century to the Present,* 2nd ed. (New Brunswick, N.J.: Rutgers University Press, 2003), 149.

44. That the brothers gain dignity and honor through service does not necessarily mean, as Burnett would have it, that "members of the aristocracy in Deloney's fiction are invariably victims of financial and sexual profligacy who descend the social scale, and present, therefore, perilous role models" (*Masters and Servants,* 66). Like Sir Hugh, Crispine and Crispianus are explicitly represented as victims of religious persecution, which is in turn linked to their native English identities. It is difficult to find in them traces of aristocratic degeneracy, and their exemplarity—as defined through the convergence of shoemaking and the nobility—is never in question.

45. Although there is no certain information about the origin of "A Shoomakers son is a Prince borne," I would suggest, following Deloney's editor

Lange, that Deloney adapted it from classical sources to provide a motto for the Cordwainers' Guild. Lange wrote that one of Deloney's sources for the character of the Persian general Iphicrates in the Crispianus story is Plutarch's *Regum et Imperatorum Apophthegmata*, where Iphicrates retorts (as he does in Deloney's version) to an accusation of his low birth, "Meum a me incipit genus, tuum in te definit," that is, "My ancestry originates with me; yours reaches its limit in you." Thomas Deloney, *The Gentle Craft*, ed. Alexis F. Lange (Berlin: Mayer und Muller, 1903), xxxiii. My thanks to Matthew Stratton for the translation.

46. According to James Robertson, the first extant version of the Dick Whittington story is Richard Johnson's ballad from 1612. He notes that although a play and ballad were both entered into the Stationers' Register in 1605, their texts are lost. James Robertson, "The Adventures of Dick Whittington and the Social Construction of Elizabethan London," in Gadd and Wallis, *Guilds, Society and Economy*, 51–66. It is likely that the story circulated still earlier in oral and print forms.

47. Rappaport, *Worlds Within Worlds*, 368.

48. Deloney may have read Stow's book before its publication, or else he drew on Stow's sources on Eyre. John Stow, *A Survey of London*, vol. 1, ed. Charles Lethbridge Kingsford (Oxford: Clarendon Press, 1908).

49. Ibid., 110.

50. In 1603, Dekker made major contributions to the Royal Entry of James I, an event informed by a series of struggles for control between the City and the new king. And the *Troia-Noua Triumphans*, his script for the Lord Mayor's Show in 1612, adapts many of the techniques and features of a royal entertainment to glorify civic structures and the mayor in particular. See James D. Mardock, *Our Scene Is London: Ben Jonson's City and the Space of the Author* (New York: Routledge, 2008), 23–44.

51. E. K. Chambers, *The Elizabethan Stage* (Oxford: Clarendon Press, 1923), 4:112; and Andrew Gurr, *The Shakespearean Stage 1574–1642* (Cambridge: Cambridge University Press, 1992), 241.

52. Thomas Dekker, *The Shoemaker's Holiday*, New Mermaids ed., ed. Anthony Parr (London: A and C Black; New York: W. W. Norton, 1990). Text references are to line number of prologue and dedication and to scene and line number of the rest of the play.

53. In this assertion, I differ from Peter Stallybrass, who assigns the shoemaker a powerful role and yet a disempowered position: "The shoemaker is thus materially and symbolically the maker of the social (she or he is the foundation of social *movement* in its most literal sense); at the same time, she or he is the person most trodden upon by a hierarchical society that imagines itself in terms of an elite who put their foot upon whom they subordinate." Peter Stallybrass, "Footnotes," in *The Body in Parts: Fantasies of Corporeality in Early Modern Europe*, ed. David Hillman and Carla Mazzio (New York: Routledge, 1997), 320.

54. For discussions of how shoemaking "ennobles" Lacy, see Jean Howard, "Material Shakespeare/Materialist Shakespeare," in Davis, *Shakespeare*

Matters, 37; Alison Chapman, "Whose Saint Crispin's Day Is It? Shoemaking, Holiday Making, and the Politics of Memory in Early Modern England," *Renaissance Quarterly* 54 (2001): 1477; and Julia Gasper, *The Dragon and the Dove: The Plays of Thomas Dekker* (Oxford: Clarendon Press, 1990), 28.

55. Ronda Arab argues that the play coalesces emerging national values of "work, productivity, and patriotism" in the laboring bodies of male artisans. Ronda Arab, "Work, Bodies, and Gender," *Medieval and Renaissance Drama in England* 13 (2000): 182.

56. Thirsk, *Economic Policy and Projects,* 1.

57. On the representation of the Dutch in the play, see Andrew Fleck, "Marking Difference and National Identity in Dekker's *The Shoemaker's Holiday,*" *Studies in English Literature* 46 (2006): 349–70.

58. Brian Walsh, "Performing Historicity in Dekker's *The Shoemaker's Holiday,*" *Studies in English Literature* 46 (2006): 342; and Jonathan Gil Harris, "Ludgate Time: Simon Eyre's Oath and the Temporal Economies of *The Shoemaker's Holiday,*" *Huntington Library Quarterly* 71 (2008): 32.

59. Peter Stallybrass, "Worn Worlds: Clothes and Identity on the Renaissance Stage," in *Subject and Object in Renaissance Culture,* ed. Margreta de Grazia, Maureen Quilligan, and Peter Stallybrass (Cambridge: Cambridge University Press, 1996), 312.

60. Rappaport cites a contemporary reference to "divers journeymen and other servants in the company" (*Worlds Within Worlds,* 240), a phrasing that suggests that journeymen were perceived as servants in some key respects.

61. Ibid., 333.

62. A number of critics have been sensitive to the fantasy of community, and its internal tensions, in *The Shoemaker's Holiday.* See Kate McLuskie, *Dekker and Heywood: Professional Dramatists* (London: St. Martin's, 1994), 57, 71; David Scott Kastan, "Workshop and/as Playhouse: Comedy and Commerce in *The Shoemaker's Holiday,*" *Studies in Philology* 84 (1987): 324–37; Thomas Worden, "Idols in the Early Modern Material World (1599): Deloney's *The Gentle Craft,* Dekker's *The Shoemaker's Holiday,* and Shakespeare's *Henry V,*" *Exemplaria* 11 (1999): 431–71; and Jean Howard, "Material Shakespeare/Materialist Shakespeare," 29–45. None of these critics have addressed the ways in which service drove urban community and revealed its failures.

63. Fiona McNeill, "Gynocentric London Spaces: (Re)Locating Masterless Women in Early Stuart Drama," *Renaissance Drama* 28 (1997): 200.

64. It is also true, as Ronda Arab points out, that Hammon's courtship puts Jane in a traditionally gendered position of vulnerability that mitigates against her independence ("Work, Bodies, and Gender," 202–3).

65. Hobsbawm and Scott note that "the lame cobbler is recorded as early as the Latin dramatist *Plautus*" ("Political Shoemakers," 97), while Lane writes that because it was not physically demanding, "shoemaking was a suitable skill for a physically small or even disabled boy" (*Apprenticeship in England,* 34).

66. On similar moments of exchange, see Michael LeMahieu, "Gift Exchange and Social Hierarchy in Thomas Deloney's *Jack of Newbury,*" in Woodbridge, *Money and the Age of Shakespeare,* 129–41.

67. Kathman discusses examples such as James Tunstall/Dunstone, who formally identified as both a saddler and a player ("Goldsmiths, Grocers, and Drapers," 39–40).

68. Ibid., 10.

69. See Carol Chillington Rutter, *Documents of the Rose Playhouse* (Manchester, UK: Manchester University Press, 1984), 127; and Kathman, "Goldsmiths, Grocers, and Drapers," 10.

70. Chambers, *Elizabethan Stage*, 2:153.

71. Rutter, *Documents of the Rose Playhouse*, 119. See also Kathman, "Goldsmiths, Grocers, and Drapers," 4–5, on the frequency of players signing bonds with playhouse owners. The backstory of Henslowe's 1597–98 bonds involves the defection of some members of the Admiral's Men to a new venture by Pembroke's Men at the Swan Playhouse, a venture that notably failed and from which these bonds resecured players for the Admiral's Men.

72. McLuskie and Dunsworth observe that by 1613, when players of Lady Elizabeth's Men filed a grievance against Henslowe for taking too much control over the company, "he had also so exploited the changing relationship between bound servants and wage labor among the nonsharer members of the company as to transfer their allegiance from the company to himself" ("Patronage and the Economics of Theater," 436).

73. R. L. Smallwood and Stanley Wells, introduction to *The Shoemaker's Holiday* (Manchester, UK: Manchester University Press; Baltimore: Johns Hopkins University Press, 1979), 3.

74. Dekker's money problems worsened later; he was in debtors' prison for the years 1612–19 and seems never to have gotten entirely free of debt thereafter. Ibid., 4.

Chapter Four

1. Laurie Ellinghausen, *Labor and Writing in Early Modern England, 1567–1667* (Aldershot, UK: Ashgate, 2008), 63–92.

2. Richard Helgerson argued that Jonson was instrumental in inventing the category of the professional author. In Helgerson's view, the professional author saw himself as a serious public servant, whose "poetry was itself a means of making a contribution to the order and improvement of the state." Elements of this argument are still powerful, but in this chapter I pursue a more expansive definition of authorial service. Richard Helgerson, *Self-Crowned Laureates: Spenser, Jonson, Milton, and the Literary System* (Berkeley: University of California Press, 1983), 29.

3. On Jonson's relations with the court, see Leah S. Marcus, "Jonson and the Court," in *The Cambridge Companion to Ben Jonson*, ed. Richard Harp and Stanley Stewart (Cambridge: Cambridge University Press, 2000), 30–42; Robert Evans, *Ben Jonson and the Poetics of Patronage* (Lewisburg, Pa.: Bucknell University Press, 1989), 250; and David Riggs, *Ben Jonson: A Life* (Cambridge, Mass.: Harvard University Press, 1989), 179.

4. Joseph Loewenstein, *Ben Jonson and Possessive Authorship* (Cambridge: Cambridge University Press, 2002), 2.

5. Bruce Boehrer, "The Poet of Labor: Authorship and Property in the Work of Ben Jonson," *Philological Quarterly* 72 (1993): 296.

6. Ibid., 294.

7. Ben Jonson, *The Alchemist*, New Mermaids, 2nd ed., ed. Elizabeth Cook (London: A and C Black; New York: W. W. Norton, 1991). Text references are to act, scene, and line numbers of this edition (or line numbers only in the case of the front matter).

8. On criminality and its negotiations with "legitimate" society in *The Alchemist*, see Jonathan Haynes, "Representing the Underworld: *The Alchemist*," *Studies in Philology* 86 (1989): 18–41.

9. *OED*, s.v. "work," n., I. 4, accessed December 7, 2010.

10. Kussmaul gives two definitions of the servant: "The first, specific use was to denote all those who worked for one master, and were maintained by that master," while "the second . . . extended still further to include all those who worked for others. Used in this general sense, 'servant' comprised both servants, in the specific sense of the word, and day-labourers" (*Servants in Husbandry*, 5, 6.)

11. In discussing the new capitalist inequities springing up in the late sixteenth century, Wrightson emphasizes that apprenticeships, which required paying an increasingly expensive premium, were essential to advancement in an urban economy (*Earthly Necessities*, 193).

12. Jonson and Dekker worked together on plays, but they also took shots at each other during the theatrical disputes at the turn of the seventeenth century. Jonson attacked Dekker in *Poetaster* (1601), and Dekker countered in *Satiromastix* (1601) with a deflationary portrayal of Jonson as a writer for hire. See Riggs, *Ben Jonson*, 72–84.

13. It has been commonplace for critics to discuss the inflationary (and deflationary) implications of alchemy in the play. See, for example, John Mebane, "Renaissance Magic and the Return of the Golden Age: Utopianism and Religious Enthusiasm in *The Alchemist*," *Renaissance Drama* 8 (1977): 128.

14. Thirsk, *Economic Policy and Projects*, 1.

15. In discussing the growth of industrial capitalism, Marx describes the English East India Company as dispensing contracts to investors "under conditions whereby they, cleverer than the alchemists, made gold out of nothing." Karl Marx, *Capital: A Critique of Political Economy*, vol. 1, trans. Ben Fowkes (New York: Vintage, 1977), 917. Eric Wilson highlights the fetishistic value of the desired products of alchemy in Jonson's play, resulting in "a symptomatic confusion of persons and things." Eric Wilson, "Abel Drugger's Sign and the Fetishes of Material Culture," in *Historicism, Psychoanalysis, and Early Modern Culture*, ed. Carla Mazzio and Douglas Trevor (New York: Routledge, 2000), 119. A similar reification exists in the transformation of the activities of work into "a work," a process that Theodore Leinwand discusses in *Theatre, Finance and Society in Early Modern England* (Cambridge: Cambridge University Press, 1999), 134. Leinwand makes the point that the capitalist venture, contrary to its fantasy presentation, demands extraordinary amounts of labor.

16. For a contrasting perspective, see Andrew Gurr, "Prologue: Who Is Lovewit? What Is He?," in *Ben Jonson and Theatre: Performance, Practice and Theory*, ed. Richard Cave, Elizabeth Schafer, and Brian Woolland (London: Routledge, 1999), 14.

17. On the expansion of marginal service activities, see Clark and Slack, *English Towns in Transition*, 78. Natasha Korda discusses women's subsistence labor in "Labors Lost: Women's Work and Early Modern Theatrical Commerce," in *From Script to Stage in Early Modern England*, ed. Peter Holland and Stephen Orgel (Houndmills, UK: Palgrave, 2004), 195–230.

18. See William Carroll, *Fat King, Lean Beggar: Representations of Poverty in the Age of Shakespeare* (Ithaca, N.Y.: Cornell University Press, 1996); and Linda Woodbridge, *Vagrancy, Homelessness, and English Renaissance Literature* (Urbana: University of Illinois Press, 2001).

19. Patricia Fumerton, *Unsettled: The Culture of Mobility and the Working Poor in Early Modern England* (Chicago: University of Chicago Press, 2006), 11.

20. Wrightson argues that the economic crisis attending labor resulted in a condition of "structural poverty" (*Earthly Necessities*, 197).

21. Thomas Harman, *A Caveat for Common Cursitors, Vulgarly Called Vagabonds* (1566), in Kinney, *Rogues, Vagabonds, and Sturdy Beggars*, 115.

22. From a 1596 letter by Edward Hext, Somerset J. P., to Lord Burghley, quoted in Christopher Hill, *Liberty Against the Law: Some Seventeenth-Century Controversies* (London: Allen Lane/Penguin Press, 1996), 52.

23. Quoted in Wrightson, *Earthly Necessities*, 219.

24. Catherine Gimelli Martin makes a similar point in "Angels, Alchemists and Exchange: Commercial Ideology in Court and City Comedy, 1596–1610," in *The Witness of Times: Manifestations of Ideology in Seventeenth Century England*, ed. Katherine Z. Keller and Gerald J. Schiffhorst (Pittsburgh: Duquesne University Press, 1993), 128.

25. Craig Dionne, "Fashioning Outlaws: The Early Modern Rogue and Urban Culture," in *Rogues and Early Modern English Culture*, ed. Craig Dionne and Steve Mentz (Ann Arbor: University of Michigan Press, 2004), 55.

26. As a noun in the play, "work" functions most often as "an act, deed, proceeding, business," in place of the definition cited in note 9 of this chapter. *OED* n., I.1, accessed December 7, 2010.

27. As Leinwand puts it, "A Blackfriars house is transmuted not only into an alchemical workshop and a dream machine but into a sweatshop" (*Theatre, Finance and Society*, 131).

28. Jean Howard, "Sex and the Early Modern City: Staging the Bawdy Houses of London," in *The Impact of Feminism in English Renaissance Studies*, ed. Dympna Callaghan (Basingstoke, UK: Palgrave Macmillan, 2007), 123.

29. Korda addresses how the "networks of commerce" through which many women sustained themselves with a combination of regulated and unregulated work were intertwined with the early modern stage. See Korda, "Labors Lost" and "Women's Theatrical Properties."

30. Howard makes the point that "whore" city comedies depict fluid conversions between prostitutes and respectable wives ("Sex and the Early Modern

City," 131). Jonson teases at, but does not carry through with, a conversion narrative of this sort in *The Alchemist*, not only by stressing the similarities between Dol and elite women but also through Face and Subtle's plot to prostitute the widow Dame Pliant when they find themselves with one too many clients on their hands.

31. Michelle Dowd, "Labours of Love: Women, Marriage and Service in *Twelfth Night* and *The Compleat Servant-Maid*," *Shakespearean International Yearbook* 5 (2005): 118, 112.

32. It may be true, as Karen Newman writes, that in Jonson, "the relations of all the women to commodification are represented as the same, which tends to level class differences," but in *The Alchemist*, the (dis)possession of capital becomes the crucial marker of class difference between women. Karen Newman, "Women and Commodification in Jonson's *Epicoene*," *English Literary History* 56 (1989): 512.

33. Hill, *Liberty Against the Law*, 60.

34. As Gurr explains, housekeeping shares were not necessarily controlled by active participants in the company; they could be sold or passed on by inheritance, and many shares in the first decades of the seventeenth century became dissociated from the King's Men in that fashion (*Shakespeare Company*, 118).

35. Ibid., 89. Out of a company of fifteen at the turn of the century, almost half the members were hired labor rather than shareholders.

36. Korda, "Women's Theatrical Properties," 204.

37. Gurr, *Shakespeare Company*, 116–17; Theodore Leinwand, *Theatre, Finance and Society*, 137–38; Melissa D. Aaron, "'Beware at what hands thou receiv'st thy commodity': *The Alchemist* and the King's Men Fleece the Customers, 1610," in *Inside Shakespeare: Essays on the Blackfriars Stage*, ed. Paul Menzer (Selinsgrove, Pa.: Susquehanna University Press, 2006), 72–79; and Anthony J. Ouellette, "*The Alchemist* and the Emerging Adult Private Playhouse," *Studies in English Literature* 45 (2005): 375–99.

38. Gurr, *Shakespeare Company*, 89.

39. Ibid., 112.

40. Ingram, *Business of Playing*, 49. David Kathman has shown that even some prominent people in the theater were aligned with nontheatrical trades and crafts ("Grocers, Goldsmiths, and Drapers," 18, 38–39).

41. Gurr, *Shakespeare Company*, 220, 227, 243. More details on early casts of *The Alchemist* are provided by James A. Riddell, "Some Actors in Jonson's Plays," *Shakespeare Studies* 5 (1969): 285–98.

42. Ben Jonson, *Conversations with Drummond, Ben Jonson*, 11 vols., ed. C. H. Herford, Percy Simpson, and Evelyn Simpson (Oxford: Clarendon Press, 1925–52), 1:242 (hereafter cited in text as *BJ* with volume and page number, and, when applicable, line number).

43. Kathman, "Grocers, Goldsmiths, and Drapers," 31–32.

44. Loewenstein, *Ben Jonson and Possessive Authorship*, 165.

45. See Sanders, *Gender and Literacy*, 61.

46. George E. Rowe, *Distinguishing Jonson: Imitation, Rivalry, and the Direction of a Dramatic Career* (Lincoln: University of Nebraska Press, 1988), 12.

47. Sidney, *Defence of Poesy*, 240.

48. See also the passage in which Jonson asserts that poverty is his "domestick" and that "no great worke, or worthy of praise, or memory, but came out of poor cradles" (*BJ* 8:605).

49. Jonathan Goldberg notes that in the *Discoveries*, Jonson draws analogies between royal and self-representation. Thus, the state provided Jonson with metaphors for more local and subjective concerns. Jonathan Goldberg, *James I and the Politics of Literature: Jonson, Shakespeare, Donne, and Their Contemporaries* (Stanford, Calif.: Stanford University Press, 1989), 224.

50. Loewenstein, *Ben Jonson and Possessive Authorship*, 147.

51. Hugh Maclean, ed., *Ben Jonson and the Cavalier Poets* (New York: W. W. Norton, 1974), 1 (hereafter cited as *CP*). The induction to *Bartholomew Fair* (1614) mentions Jonson's "man, Master Brome," who was in this earlier period presumably still learning the trade from Jonson. Ben Jonson, *Bartholomew Fair*, New Mermaids, ed. G. R. Hibbard (London: A and C Black; New York: W. W. Norton, 1977), 8 (hereafter cited as *BF*).

52. On Jonson's redefinition of authorship through an engagement with space and architecture, see H. Turner, *English Renaissance Stage*, 244–78; Ian Donaldson, "Jonson's Magic Houses," in *Jonson's Magic Houses: Essays in Interpretation* (Oxford: Clarendon Press, 1997), 66–88; and Mardock, *Our Scene Is London*.

53. "Bilbo" also appears in Jonson's "An Execration upon Vulcan," in which the poet wishes that Vulcan had stayed away from him and instead simply "maintain'd the trade at Bilbo, or else-where" (*BJ* 8:199). Bilbo is the northern city, Bilbao, in Spain, a center for the production of blades. A "bilbo-smith" is a highly skilled practitioner of sword or blade making.

54. Helgerson, *Self-Crowned Laureates*, 181.

Chapter Five

1. Duncan-Jones, *Ungentle Shakespeare*, 256.

2. Sidney, *Defence of Poesy*, 244; *BF*, induction, 122–23.

3. Zachary Lesser, "Tragical-Comical-Pastoral-Colonial," *English Literary History* 74 (2007): 882. Lesser focuses on plays from the 1620s, but his observations resonate with Shakespeare's tragicomedies.

4. Chambers, *Elizabethan Stage*, 4:127.

5. Andrew Gurr, "The *Tempest's Tempest* at Blackfriars," *Shakespeare Survey* 41 (1989): 91–102.

6. Valerie Forman, *Tragicomic Redemptions: Global Economics and the Early Modern Stage* (Philadelphia: University of Pennsylvania Press, 2008), 7. See Lesser, "Tragical-Comical-Pastoral-Colonial," 881–908, for the complementary argument that tragicomedy enacts a delay and distance between cause and effect, action and reaction, that characterize global economic transactions.

7. Strier, *Resistant Structures*, 200–201.

8. On Paulina, see Janet Adelman, *Suffocating Mothers: Fantasies of Maternal Origin in Shakespeare's Plays, "Hamlet" to "The Tempest"* (New York: Routledge, 1992), 228; Gail Kern Paster, *The Body Embarrassed: Drama*

and the Disciplines of Shame in Early Modern England (Ithaca, N.Y.: Cornell University Press, 1993), 271; Frances Dolan, *Dangerous Familiars: Representations of Domestic Crime in England, 1550–1700* (Ithaca, N.Y.: Cornell University Press, 1994), 182; Mary Ellen Lamb, "Engendering the Narrative Act: Old Wives' Tales in *The Winter's Tale, Macbeth,* and *The Tempest,*" *Criticism* 40 (1998): 536. In recent discussions of Autolycus, he often becomes synonymous with Robert Greene, thus representing the popular "old tales" that *The Winter's Tale* both suppresses and reinvokes. See Newcomb, *Reading Popular Romance,* 81; Aaron Kitch, "Bastards and Broadsides in *The Winter's Tale,*" *Renaissance Drama* 30 (1999–2001): 43–71; and Steve Mentz, "Wearing Greene: Autolycus, Robert Greene, and the Structure of Romance in *The Winter's Tale,*" *Renaissance Drama* 30 (1999–2001): 73–92. On Autolycus, see also Joan Hartwig, "Cloten, Autolycus, and Caliban: Bearers of Parodic Burdens," in *Shakespeare's Romances Reconsidered,* ed. Carol McGinnis Kay and Henry E. Jacobs (Lincoln: University of Nebraska Press, 1978), 91–103, 100–101; Stephen Orgel, introduction to *The Winter's Tale,* ed. Stephen Orgel (Oxford: Clarendon Press, 1996), 52–53; and Ronald W. Cooley, "Speech Versus Spectacle: Autolycus, Class and Containment in *The Winter's Tale,*" *Renaissance and Reformation* 21 (1997): 5–23.

9. Analyses of Camillo include David Schalkwyk, *Shakespeare, Love and Service,* 263–66; James Siemon, "'But It Appears She Lives': Iteration in *The Winter's Tale,*" in *William Shakespeare's "The Winter's Tale,"* ed. Harold Bloom (New York: Chelsea House, 1987), 47–58; and B. J. Sokol, *Art and Illusion in "The Winter's Tale"* (Manchester: Manchester University Press, 1994).

10. Forman discusses the ways in which Autolycus represents a kind of surplus value in the capitalist and generic economy of the play (*Tragicomic Redemptions,* 98–103).

11. Baldesar Castiglione, *The Book of the Courtier,* trans. George Bull (London: Penguin, 1967) (hereafter cited as *BC*). On how Castiglione, among other courtesy book writers, shaped the rhetoric and social identities of courtiers, see Whigham, *Ambition and Privilege,* 15, 26; and Peter Burke, *The Fortunes of the "Courtier": The European Reception of Castiglione's Cortegiano* (University Park: Pennsylvania State University Press, 1995), 64.

12. Wayne Rebhorn, *Courtly Performances: Masking and Festivity in Castiglione's "Book of the Courtier"* (Detroit: Wayne State University Press, 1978), 18, 29; and Daniel Javitch, preface to *The Book of the Courtier,* by Baldesar Castiglione, trans. Charles Singleton (New York: W. W. Norton, 2002), xiii.

13. Javitch and Joseph D. Falvo each suggest that the subtleties of sprezzatura separate real courtiers from pretenders. Javitch, preface to *Book of the Courtier,* xi; and Joseph D. Falvo, *The Economy of Human Relations: Castiglione's "Libro Del Cortegiano"* (New York: Peter Lang, 1992), 45. On the other hand, Harry Berger notes that "the representational techniques associated with sprezzatura ... subject physiognomic norms of authenticity and truth to the pressure of continuous mimicry." Harry Berger, *The Absence of Grace: Sprezzatura and Suspicion in Two Renaissance Courtesy Books* (Stanford, Calif.: Stanford University Press, 2000), 15.

14. On the legal and cultural definitions of "rogue," see Woodbridge, *Vagrancy, Homelessness, and English Renaissance Literature,* 3, 28–29, 41; and Barbara Mowat, "Rogues, Shepherds, and the Counterfeit Distressed: Texts and Infracontexts of *The Winter's Tale* 4.3," *Shakespeare Studies* 22 (1994): 65.

15. Thomas Harman, *A Caveat for Common Cursitors Vulgarly Called Vagabonds,* in Kinney, *Rogues, Vagabonds, and Sturdy Beggars,* 105–53, at 115 (hereafter cited as CC).

16. See Woodbridge, *Vagrancy, Homelessness, and English Renaissance Literature,* on Harman's determination to uncover the disguises of rogues, based on his assumption that "vagrants were constantly acting" (54), which, as she notes, puts actors in the same category as rogues.

17. Kinney, *Rogues, Vagabonds, and Sturdy Beggars,* 297–98n23.

18. "I. M.," *Health to the Gentlemanly Profession,* C4.

19. Orgel, introduction to *Winter's Tale,* 17. See also Paster, *Body Embarrassed,* 264, and Adelman, *Suffocating Mothers,* 224.

20. Shakespeare evokes a conventional analogy between servant and child: "For in these dayes what greater loue could almost be found, then betwixt the Maister and the Seruant: it was in maner equall with the Husbandes to the Wyfe, and the Childes to the Parent." "I. M.," *Health to the Gentlemanly Profession,* C2ᵛ.

21. See Kitch, "Bastards and Broadsides," 46.

22. "I. M.," *Health to the Gentlemanly Profession,* C2ᵛ.

23. Schalkwyk, *Shakespeare, Love and Service,* 265.

24. Robert Greene, *Pandosto,* in Salzman, *Anthology of Elizabethan Prose Fiction,* 191.

25. See Schalkwyk, *Shakespeare, Love and Service,* 268.

26. Strier interprets Antigonus as attempting unsuccessfully to adopt "a middle position" between resistant and obsequious service (*Resistant Structures,* 201).

27. On the multiple aspects of Hermione's role which Paulina takes on in her absence, see Janet Wolf, "'Like an Old Tale Still': Paulina, 'Triple Hecate,' and the Persephone Myth in *The Winter's Tale,*" in *Images of Persephone: Feminist Readings in Western Literature,* ed. Elizabeth T. Hayes (Gainesville: University Press of Florida, 1994), 36.

28. See Lynn Enterline, "'You speak a language that I understand not': The Rhetoric of Animation in *The Winter's Tale,*" *Shakespeare Quarterly* 48 (1997): 17–44.

29. Carolyn Asp, "Shakespeare's Paulina and the Consolatio Tradition," *Shakespeare Studies* 11 (1978): 152.

30. Dolan points out that many accused witches were servants (*Dangerous Familiars,* 181–82).

31. Woodbridge observes the close connection between Harman's stories and anecdotes and the jestbook tradition, which itself evolved from continental novella and fabliaux (*Vagrancy, Homelessness, and English Renaissance Literature,* 46–51).

32. See Carroll, *Fat King, Lean Beggar,* 168–69, on Autolycus's debt to the "merry beggar" tradition.

33. Orgel makes a similar point about Autolycus (introduction to *Winter's Tale,* 53).

34. For a provocative discussion about how the play moves from "iconic surrogation" to "figural representation," see Lowell Gallagher, "'This seal'd-up Oracle': Ambivalent Nostalgia in *The Winter's Tale,*" *Exemplaria* 7 (1995): 466.

35. On the distinction between slavery and other forms of labor, see Kim Hall, *Things of Darkness: Economies of Race and Gender in Early Modern England* (Ithaca, N.Y.: Cornell University Press, 1995), 212–13.

36. Slaves must be considered somewhat tentatively because English involvement with the African slave trade was still in its infancy. However, as Hall has argued in *Things of Darkness,* slaves were already present in the art and literature of the period and were known as well from the ancient world. The early seventeenth-century conception of inter-Atlantic slavery was heavily influenced by these traditions.

37. Andrew Gurr has shown that Ariel and Caliban have attributes of both the apprentice and the slave. Andrew Gurr, "Industrious Ariel and Idle Caliban," in Maquerlot and Willems, *Travel and Drama in Shakespeare's Time,* 193–208.

38. Becon, *New Catechism,* 362.

39. On narratives of Christians enslaved by Turks, see Daniel Vitkus, *Turning Turk: English Theater and the Multicultural Mediterranean, 1570–1630* (New York: Palgrave Macmillan, 2003).

40. See Hall, *Things of Darkness,* 121, on the increase in slaves in seventeenth-century English colonies, and 211–53, on the rare but salient practice of importing Africans to England to serve as slaves to the nobility.

41. *OED,* s.v. "slave," n¹, I.2.b, accessed December 10, 2010. See Weil, *Service and Dependency,* 129–45, on the opposition between service and slavery in *Macbeth,* a counterpoint to the conflation of service and slavery that I examine in *The Tempest.*

42. My argument departs from Dolan's point in *Dangerous Familiars* that in *The Tempest,* "aesthetic order reinforces a social order that depends on hierarchy" (70).

43. See Goldberg, "The Print of Goodness." Stephen Greenblatt makes the related point that European travelers often assumed that language was transparent to universalist truths and ideas. Stephen Greenblatt, "Learning to Curse: Aspects of Linguistic Colonialism in the Sixteenth Century," in *Learning to Curse: Essays in Early Modern Culture* (New York: Routledge, 1990), 28.

44. Goldberg, "Print of Goodness," 241.

45. Paul Brown's influential thesis is that discourses of mastery and colonialism merge in the doubled inside/outside threat of masterless and savage men. Paul Brown, "'This thing of darkness I acknowledge mine': *The Tempest* and the Discourse of Colonialism," in *Political Shakespeare: New Essays*

in Cultural Materialism, ed. Jonathan Dollimore and Alan Sinfield, 48–71 (Ithaca, N.Y.: Cornell University Press, 1985). More recently, Mark Netzloff has connected domestic and colonial service by showing that England's marginal servants, laborers, and masterless men, like Trinculo and Stefano, were exported from the domestic service economy in which they were considered surplus labor to burgeoning colonial economies. Mark Netzloff, *England's Internal Colonies: Class, Capital, and the Literature of Early Modern Colonialism* (New York: Palgrave Macmillan, 2003), 91–134.

46. Taussig, *Mimesis and Alterity,* 2.

47. Ibid., 42.

48. For a different reading of how *The Tempest* represents working conditions in the theater, see Douglas Bruster, "Local *Tempest:* Shakespeare and the Work of the Early Modern Playhouse," *Journal of Medieval and Renaissance Studies* 25 (1995): 33–53.

BIBLIOGRAPHY

Aaron, Melissa D. "'Beware at what hands thou receiv'st thy commodity': *The Alchemist* and the King's Men Fleece the Customers, 1610." In *Inside Shakespeare: Essays on the Blackfriars Stage,* edited by Paul Menzer, 72–79. Selinsgrove, Pa.: Susquehanna University Press, 2006.

Adelman, Janet. *Suffocating Mothers: Fantasies of Maternal Origin in Shakespeare's Plays, "Hamlet" to "The Tempest."* New York: Routledge, 1992.

Agnew, Jean-Christophe. *Worlds Apart: The Market and the Theater in Anglo-American Thought.* Cambridge: Cambridge University Press, 1986.

Alwes, Derek B. *Sons and Authors in Elizabethan England.* Newark: University of Delaware Press, 2004.

Anderson, Linda. *A Place in the Story: Servants and Service in Shakespeare's Plays.* Newark: University of Delaware Press, 2005.

Arab, Ronda. "Work, Bodies, and Gender." *Medieval and Renaissance Drama in England* 13 (2000): 182–212.

Archer, Ian W. "Material Londoners?" In *Material London, ca. 1600,* edited by Lena Cowen Orlin, 174–92. Philadelphia: University of Pennsylvania Press, 2000.

———. *The Pursuit of Stability: Social Relations in Elizabethan London.* Cambridge: Cambridge University Press, 1991.

Aristotle. *Poetics.* In *The Complete Works of Aristotle: The Revised Oxford Translation.* Vol. 2. Edited by Jonathan Barnes, 2316–40. Princeton, N.J.: Princeton University Press, 1984.

Arthur, Anthony. *The Tailor-King: The Rise and Fall of the Anabaptist Kingdom of Münster.* New York: Thomas Donne / St. Martin's Press, 1999.

Ascham, Roger. *The Schoolmaster.* Edited by Lawrence V. Ryan. Folger Shakespeare Library. Ithaca, N.Y.: Cornell University Press, 1967.

Asp, Carolyn. "Shakespeare's Paulina and the Consolatio Tradition." *Shakespeare Studies* 11 (1978): 145–58.

Attridge, Derek. "Literary Form and the Demands of Politics." In G. Levine, *Aesthetics and Ideology,* 243–63.

Auerbach, Erich. *Mimesis: The Representation of Reality in Western Literature.* Translated by Willard Trask. Princeton, N.J.: Princeton University Press, 1953.

Bakhtin, Mikhail. *Dialogic Imagination: Four Essays.* Edited by Michael Holquist. Translated by Caryl Emerson and Michael Holquist. Austin: University of Texas Press, 1981.

Barish, Jonas A., and Marshall Waingrow. "'Service' in *King Lear.*" *Shakespeare Quarterly* 9 (1958): 347–55.

Bate, Jonathan. "The Elizabethans in Italy." In Maquerlot and Willems, *Travel and Drama in Shakespeare's Time*, 55–74.

Becon, Thomas. *A New Catechism, Set Forth Dialogue-Wise in Familiar Talk between the Father and the Son* (London, c. 1560). In *The Catechism of Thomas Becon*. Edited by Rev. John Ayre. Parker Society. Cambridge: Cambridge University Press, 1844.

Beier, A. L. *Masterless Men: The Vagrancy Problem in England 1560–1640*. London: Methuen, 1985.

Ben-Amos, Ilana Krausman. *Adolescence and Youth in Early Modern England*. New Haven, Conn.: Yale University Press, 1994.

Berger, Harry. *The Absence of Grace: Sprezzatura and Suspicion in Two Renaissance Courtesy Books*. Stanford, Calif.: Stanford University Press, 2000.

Berry, Edward. *The Making of Sir Philip Sidney*. Toronto: University of Toronto Press, 1998.

Black, Antony. *Guild and State: European Political Thought from the Twelfth Century to the Present*. 2nd ed. New Brunswick, N.J.: Rutgers University Press, 2003.

Bland, D. S. "The 'Night of Errors' at Gray's Inn, 1594." *Notes and Queries* 13 (1966): 127–28.

———, ed. *Gesta Grayorum*. English Reprint Series, 22. Liverpool: Liverpool University Press, 1968.

Boehrer, Bruce. "The Poet of Labor: Authorship and Property in the Work of Ben Jonson." *Philological Quarterly* 72 (1993): 289–312.

Brathwait, Richard. *The English Gentleman*. London, 1630.

Bristol, Michael, and Arthur Marotti, eds. *Print, Manuscript, and Performance: The Changing Relations of the Media in Early Modern England*. Columbus: Ohio State University Press, 2000.

Brooks, Harold. "Two Clowns in a Comedy (To Say Nothing of the Dog): Speed, Launce (and Crab) in *The Two Gentlemen of Verona*." In Mason, *Shakespeare: Early Comedies*, 149–59. First published in *Essays and Studies* 14 (1963): 91–100.

Brown, Paul. "'This thing of darkness I acknowledge mine': *The Tempest* and the Discourse of Colonialism." In *Political Shakespeare: New Essays in Cultural Materialism*, edited by Jonathan Dollimore and Alan Sinfield, 48–71. Ithaca, N.Y.: Cornell University Press, 1985.

Bruster, Douglas. "Local *Tempest*: Shakespeare and the Work of the Early Modern Playhouse." *Journal of Medieval and Renaissance Studies* 25 (1995): 33–53.

———. "The Structural Transformation of Print in Late Elizabethan England." In Bristol and Marotti, *Print, Manuscript and Performance*, 49–89.

Burke, Peter. *The Fortunes of the "Courtier": The European Reception of Castiglione's Cortegiano*. University Park: Pennsylvania State University Press, 1995.

Burnett, Mark Thornton. *Masters and Servants in English Renaissance Drama and Culture: Authority and Obedience*. London: Macmillan, 1997.

Carroll, William. *Fat King, Lean Beggar: Representations of Poverty in the Age of Shakespeare*. Ithaca, N.Y.: Cornell University Press, 1996.

Castiglione, Baldesar. *The Book of the Courtier*. Translated by George Bull. London: Penguin, 1967.

Caxton, William. *The Golden Legend or Lives of the Saints*. Vol. 6. Ed. F. S. Ellis. London: J. M. Dent and Sons, 1900.

Chambers, E. K. *The Elizabethan Stage*. 4 vols. Oxford: Clarendon, 1923.

Chapman, Alison. "Whose Saint Crispin's Day Is It? Shoemaking, Holiday Making, and the Politics of Memory in Early Modern England." *Renaissance Quarterly* 54 (2001): 1467–94.

Charlton, H. B. *Shakespearian Comedy* (1938). 4th ed. Reprint, London: Methuen, 1949.

Clark, Peter, and Paul Slack. *English Towns in Transition 1500–1700*. London: Oxford University Press, 1976.

Cocke, John. "Description of a Common Player, 1615." In *English Professional Theatre, 1530–1660*, edited by Glynne Wickham, Herbert Berry, and William Ingram, 179–80. Cambridge: Cambridge University Press, 2000.

Colie, Rosalie. *The Resources of Kind: Genre-Theory in the Renaissance*. Edited by Barbara Lewalski. Berkeley: University of California Press, 1973.

Cook, Ann Jennalie. *The Privileged Playgoers of Shakespeare's London, 1576–1642*. Princeton, N.J.: Princeton University Press, 1981.

Cooley, Ronald W. "Speech Versus Spectacle: Autolycus, Class and Containment in *The Winter's Tale*." *Renaissance and Reformation* 21 (1997): 5–23.

Cressy, David. *Literacy and the Social Order: Reading and Writing in Tudor and Stuart England*. Cambridge: Cambridge University Press, 1980.

Crewe, Jonathan D. *Unredeemed Rhetoric: Thomas Nashe and the Scandal of Authorship*. Baltimore: Johns Hopkins University Press, 1982.

Daiches, David. *A Critical History of English Literature*. Rev ed. Vol. 2. New York: Donald Press, 1979.

Darell, Walter. *A Short Discourse of the Life of Serving-Men*. London, 1578.

Davis, Lloyd, ed. *Shakespeare Matters: History, Teaching, Performance*. Newark: University of Delaware Press, 2003.

Dekker, Thomas. *The Shoemaker's Holiday*. New Mermaids. Edited by Anthony Parr. London: A and C Black; New York: W. W. Norton, 1990.

Deloney, Thomas. *The Gentle Craft*. Edited by Simon Barker. Aldershot, UK: Ashgate, 2007.

———. *The Gentle Craft*. Edited by Alexis F. Lange. Berlin: Mayer und Müller, 1903.

———. *The Novels of Thomas Deloney*. Edited by Merritt Lawlis. Bloomington: Indiana University Press, 1961.

———. *The Works of Thomas Deloney*. Edited by Francis Oscar Mann. Oxford: Clarendon Press, 1912.

DiGangi, Mario. *The Homoerotics of Early Modern Drama*. Cambridge: Cambridge University Press, 1997.

Dionne, Craig. "Fashioning Outlaws: The Early Modern Rogue and Urban Culture." In *Rogues and Early Modern English Culture,* edited by Craig Dionne and Steve Mentz, 33–61. Ann Arbor: University of Michigan Press, 2004.

Dolan, Frances. *Dangerous Familiars: Representations of Domestic Crime in England, 1550–1700.* Ithaca, N.Y.: Cornell University Press, 1994.

Donaldson, Ian. "Jonson's Magic Houses." In *Jonson's Magic Houses: Essays in Interpretation,* 66–88. Oxford: Clarendon Press, 1997.

Dowd, Michelle. "Labours of Love: Women, Marriage and Service in *Twelfth Night* and *The Compleat Servant-Maid.*" *Shakespearean International Yearbook* 5 (2005): 103–26.

———. *Women's Work in Early Modern English Literature and Culture.* New York: Palgrave Macmillan, 2009.

Dubrow, Heather. "The Politics of Aesthetics: Recuperating Formalism and the Country House Poem." In *Renaissance Literature and Its Formal Engagements,* edited by Mark David Rasmussen, 67–88. New York: Palgrave, 2002.

Duncan-Jones, Katherine. *Sir Philip Sidney: Courtier Poet.* New Haven, Conn.: Yale University Press, 1991.

———. *Ungentle Shakespeare: Scenes from His Life.* Arden Shakespeare. London: Thomson Learning, 2001.

Eagleton, Terry. *The Ideology of the Aesthetic.* Oxford: Blackwell, 1990.

Ellinghausen, Laurie. *Labor and Writing in Early Modern England, 1567–1667.* Aldershot, UK: Ashgate, 2008.

Enterline, Lynn. "'You speak a language that I understand not': The Rhetoric of Animation in *The Winter's Tale.*" *Shakespeare Quarterly* 48 (1997): 17–44.

Evans, Robert. *Ben Jonson and the Poetics of Patronage.* Lewisburg, Pa.: Bucknell University Press, 1989.

Evett, David. *Discourses of Service in Shakespeare's England.* New York: Palgrave Macmillan, 2005.

Falvo, Joseph D. *The Economy of Human Relations: Castiglione's "Libro Del Cortegiano."* New York: Peter Lang, 1992.

Ferguson, Margaret. "Nashe's *The Unfortunate Traveller:* The 'Newes of the Maker' Game." *English Literary Renaissance* 11 (1981): 165–82.

———. "A Room Not Their Own: Renaissance Women as Readers and Writers." In *The Comparative Perspective on Literature: Approaches to Theory and Practice,* edited by Clayton Koelb and Susan Noakes, 93–116. Ithaca, N.Y.: Cornell University Press, 1988.

Fleck, Andrew. "Marking Difference and National Identity in Dekker's *The Shoemaker's Holiday.*" *Studies in English Literature* 46 (2006): 349–70.

Forman, Valerie. *Tragicomic Redemptions: Global Economics and the Early Modern Stage.* Philadelphia: University of Pennsylvania Press, 2008.

Fosset, Thomas. *The Servants Dutie; or, the Calling and Condition of Servants.* London, 1613.

Fumerton, Patricia. *Unsettled: The Culture of Mobility and the Working Poor in Early Modern England*. Chicago: University of Chicago Press, 2006.

Gadd, Ian, and Patrick Wallis, eds. *Guilds, Society and Economy in London 1450–1800*. London: Centre for Metropolitan History, 2002.

Gallagher, Lowell. "'This seal'd-up Oracle': Ambivalent Nostalgia in *The Winter's Tale*." *Exemplaria* 7 (1995): 465–98.

Gasper, Julia. *The Dragon and the Dove: The Plays of Thomas Dekker*. Oxford: Clarendon Press, 1990.

Gebauer, Gunter, and Christoph Wulf. *Mimesis: Culture—Art—Society*. Translated by Don Reneau. Berkeley: University of California Press, 1992.

The Geneva Bible. A facsimile of the 1560 edition. Introduced by Lloyd E. Berry. Madison: University of Wisconsin Press, 1969.

Gershuny, J. I., and I. D. Miles. *The New Service Economy: The Transformation of Employment in Industrial Societies*. London: Frances Pinter, 1983.

[Gervase, Markham.] "I. M." *A Health to the Gentlemanly Profession of Servingmen*. 1598. Shakespeare Association Facsimiles No. 3. London: Oxford University Press, 1931.

Girard, René. "Love Delights in Praises: A Reading of *The Two Gentlemen of Verona*." *Philosophy and Literature* 13 (1989): 231–47.

Gohlke, Madelon. "Wits Wantonness: *The Unfortunate Traveller* as Picaresque." *Studies in Philology* 73 (1976): 397–413.

Goldberg, Jonathan. *James I and the Politics of Literature: Jonson, Shakespeare, Donne, and Their Contemporaries*. Stanford, Calif.: Stanford University Press, 1989.

———. "The Print of Goodness." In *The Culture of Capital: Property, Cities, and Knowledge in Early Modern England*, edited by Henry S. Turner, 231–54. New York: Routledge, 2002.

———. "Shakespearean Characters: The Generation of Silvia." In *Shakespeare's Hand*, 10–45. Minneapolis: University of Minnesota Press, 2003. First published in *Voice Terminal Echo: Postmodernism and English Renaissance Texts*. London: Methuen, 1986.

Gouge, William. *Of Domesticall Duties: Eight Treatises*. London, 1622.

Greenblatt, Stephen. *Learning to Curse: Essays in Early Modern Culture*. New York: Routledge, 1990.

———. *Will in the World: How Shakespeare Became Shakespeare*. New York: W. W. Norton, 2004.

Greene, Robert. *Pandosto*. 1588. In Salzman, *An Anthology of Elizabethan Prose Fiction*, 151–204.

———. *The Plays and Poems of Robert Greene*. Edited by J. Churton Collins. Oxford: Clarendon, 1905.

———. *A Quip for an Upstart Courtier*. 1592. Edited by Charles Hindley. London: Reeves and Turner, 1871.

Griffiths, Paul. *Youth and Authority: Formative Experiences in England 1560–1640*. Oxford: Clarendon Press, 1996.

Groats-worth of Witte, bought with a million of Repentance, and The Repentance of Robert Greene (1592). Edited by G. B. Harrison. Elizabethan and

Jacobean Quartos. New York: Barnes and Noble, 1966. Reissue of Bodley Head Quartos edition. London: John Lane/The Bodley Head, 1922–26.

Gurr, Andrew. "Industrious Ariel and Idle Caliban." In Maquerlot and Willems, *Travel and Drama in Shakespeare's Time*, 193–208.

———. "Prologue: Who Is Lovewit? What Is He?" In *Ben Jonson and Theatre: Performance, Practice and Theory*, edited by Richard Cave, Elizabeth Schafer, and Brian Woolland, 5–19. London: Routledge, 1999.

———. *The Shakespeare Company, 1594–1642*. Cambridge: Cambridge University Press, 2004.

———. *The Shakespearean Stage 1574–1642*. 3rd ed. Cambridge: Cambridge University Press, 1992.

———. "The Tempest's *Tempest* at Blackfriars." *Shakespeare Survey* 41 (1989): 91–102.

Guy-Bray, Stephen. "How to Turn Prose into Literature: The Case of Thomas Nashe." In Liebler, *Early Modern Prose Fiction*, 33–45.

———. "Shakespeare and the Invention of the Heterosexual." Special issue, *Early Modern Literary Studies* 16 (2007): 12.1–28. http://purl.oclc.org/emls/si-16/brayshks.htm.

Hackel, Heidi Brayman. "The 'Great Variety' of Readers and Early Modern Reading Practices." In *A Companion to Shakespeare*, edited by David Scott Kastan, 139–57. Oxford: Blackwell, 1999.

Halasz, Alexandra. *The Marketplace of Print: Pamphlets and the Public Sphere in Early Modern England*. Cambridge: Cambridge University Press, 1997.

Hall, Kim. *Things of Darkness: Economies of Race and Gender in Early Modern England*. Ithaca, N.Y.: Cornell University Press, 1995.

Hallett, Charles. "'Metamorphising' Proteus: Reversal Strategies in *The Two Gentlemen of Verona*." In Schlueter, *"Two Gentlemen of Verona": Critical Essays*, 153–77.

Halpern, Richard. *The Poetics of Primitive Accumulation: English Renaissance Culture and the Genealogy of Capital*. Ithaca, N.Y.: Cornell University Press, 1991.

Harman, Thomas. *A Caveat for Common Cursitors Vulgarly Called Vagabonds*. 1566. In Kinney, *Rogues, Vagabonds, and Sturdy Beggars*, 105–53.

Harris, Jonathan Gil. "Ludgate Time: Simon Eyre's Oath and the Temporal Economies of *The Shoemaker's Holiday*." *Huntington Library Quarterly* 71 (2008): 11–32.

———. *Sick Economies: Drama, Mercantilism, and Disease in Shakespeare's England*. Philadelphia: University of Pennsylvania Press, 2004.

Hartwig, Joan. "Cloten, Autolycus, and Caliban: Bearers of Parodic Burdens." In *Shakespeare's Romances Reconsidered*, edited by Carol McGinnis Kay and Henry E. Jacobs, 91–103. Lincoln: University of Nebraska Press, 1978.

Haynes, Jonathan. "Representing the Underworld: *The Alchemist*," *Studies in Philology* 86 (1989): 18–41.

Heal, Felicity. "Reciprocity and Exchange in the Late Medieval Household." In *Bodies and Disciplines: Intersections of Literature and History in*

Fifteenth-Century England, edited by Barbara A. Hanawalt and David Wallace, 179–98. Minneapolis: University of Minnesota Press, 1996.

Helgerson, Richard. *The Elizabethan Prodigals.* Berkeley: University of California Press, 1976.

———. *Self-Crowned Laureates: Spenser, Jonson, Milton, and the Literary System.* Berkeley: University of California Press, 1983.

Hentschell, Roze. *The Culture of Cloth in Early Modern England: Textual Constructions of a National Identity.* Aldershot, UK: Ashgate, 2008.

Hibbard, G. R. *Thomas Nashe: A Critical Introduction.* London: Routledge and Kegan Paul, 1962.

Hill, Christopher. *Liberty Against the Law: Some Seventeenth-Century Controversies.* London: Allen Lane/Penguin Press, 1996.

Hobsbawm, E. J., and Joan Wallach Scott. "Political Shoemakers." *Past and Present* 89 (1980): 86–114.

Houlbrooke, Ralph A. *The English Family 1450–1700.* London: Longman, 1984.

Howard, Jean. "Material Shakespeare/Materialist Shakespeare." In Davis, *Shakespeare Matters,* 29–45.

———. "Sex and the Early Modern City: Staging the Bawdy Houses of London." In *The Impact of Feminism in English Renaissance Studies,* edited by Dympna Callaghan, 117–36. Basingstoke, UK: Palgrave Macmillan, 2007.

Howell, Roger. *Sir Philip Sidney: The Shepherd Knight.* London: Hutchinson, 1968.

Hutjens, Linda Ann. "The Renaissance Cobbler: The Significance of Shoemaker and Cobbler Characters in Elizabethan Drama." PhD diss., University of Toronto, 2004.

Hutson, Lorna. *The Usurer's Daughter: Male Friendship and Fictions of Women in Sixteenth-Century England.* London: Routledge, 1994.

Ingram, William. *The Business of Playing: The Beginnings of the Adult Professional Theater in Elizabethan London.* Ithaca, N.Y.: Cornell University Press, 1992.

Irving, Henry, Frank A. Marshall, and Edward Dowden, eds. *The Works of William Shakespeare.* New York: Scribner and Welford, 1888–90.

Jardine, Lisa. *Still Harping on Daughters: Women and Drama in the Age of Shakespeare.* Sussex, UK: Harvester Press, 1983.

Javitch, Daniel. Preface to *The Book of the Courtier,* by Baldesar Castiglione, translated by Charles Singleton, vii–xvi. New York: W. W. Norton, 2002.

Johns, Adrian. *The Nature of the Book: Print and Knowledge in the Making.* Chicago: University of Chicago Press, 1998.

Jonson, Ben. *The Alchemist.* New Mermaids. 2nd ed. Edited by Elizabeth Cook. London: A and C Black; New York: W. W. Norton, 1991.

———. *Bartholomew Fair.* New Mermaids. Edited by G. R. Hibbard. London: A and C Black; New York: W. W. Norton, 1977.

———. *Ben Jonson.* 11 vols. Edited by C. H. Herford, Percy Simpson, and Evelyn Simpson. Oxford: Clarendon Press, 1925–52.

———. *Ben Jonson and the Cavalier Poets.* Edited by Hugh Maclean. New York: W. W. Norton, 1974.

Kastan, David Scott. "Workshop and/as Playhouse: Comedy and Commerce in *The Shoemaker's Holiday.*" *Studies in Philology* 84 (1987): 324–37.

Kathman, David. "Grocers, Goldsmiths, and Drapers: Freemen and Apprentices in the Elizabethan Theater." *Shakespeare Quarterly* 55 (2004): 1–49.

———. "Players, Livery Companies, and Apprentices." In *The Oxford Handbook of Early Modern Theatre*, edited by Richard Dutton, 413–28. Oxford: Oxford University Press, 2009.

Kiefer, Frederick. "Love Letters in *The Two Gentlemen of Verona.*" In Schlueter, *"Two Gentlemen of Verona": Critical Essays*, 133–52. First published in *Shakespeare Studies* 18 (1986): 65–85.

Kinney, Arthur, ed. *Rogues, Vagabonds, and Sturdy Beggars: A New Gallery of Tudor and Early Stuart Rogue Literature.* 2nd ed. Amherst: University of Massachusetts Press, 1990.

Kitch, Aaron. "Bastards and Broadsides in *The Winter's Tale.*" *Renaissance Drama* 30 (1999–2001): 43–71.

Knapp, Margaret, and Michal Kobialka. "Shakespeare and the Prince of Purpoole: The 1594 Production of *The Comedy of Errors* at Gray's Inn Hall." *Theatre History Studies* 4 (1984): 71–81.

Knutson, Roslyn Lander. *Playing Companies and Commerce in Shakespeare's Time.* Cambridge: Cambridge University Press, 2001.

Korda, Natasha. "Labors Lost: Women's Work and Early Modern Theatrical Commerce." In *From Script to Stage in Early Modern England*, edited by Peter Holland and Stephen Orgel, 195–230. Houndmills, UK: Palgrave, 2004.

———. "Women's Theatrical Properties." In *Staged Properties in Early Modern English Drama*, edited by Jonathan Gil Harris and Natasha Korda, 202–29. Cambridge: Cambridge University Press, 2002.

Kussmaul, Ann. *Servants in Husbandry in Early Modern England.* Cambridge: Cambridge University Press, 1981.

Lamb, Mary Ellen. "Engendering the Narrative Act: Old Wives' Tales in *The Winter's Tale*, *Macbeth*, and *The Tempest.*" *Criticism* 40 (1998): 529–53.

Lane, Joan. *Apprenticeship in England, 1600–1914.* Boulder, Colo.: Westview Press, 1996.

Lanier, Douglas. "'Stigmatical in Making': The Material Character of *The Comedy of Errors.*" *English Literary Renaissance* 23 (1993): 81–112.

Lawlis, Merritt. Introduction to *The Novels of Thomas Deloney.* Edited by Merritt Lawlis. Bloomington: Indiana University Press, 1961.

Leinwand, Theodore. *Theatre, Finance and Society in Early Modern England.* Cambridge: Cambridge University Press, 1999.

LeMahieu, Michael. "Gift Exchange and Social Hierarchy in Thomas Deloney's *Jack of Newbury.*" In Woodbridge, *Money and the Age of Shakespeare*, 129–41.

Lesser, Zachary. "Tragical-Comical-Pastoral-Colonial: Economic Sovereignty, Globalization, and the Form of Tragicomedy." *English Literary History* 74 (2007): 881–908.

Levine, Caroline. "Strategic Formalism: Toward a New Method in Cultural Studies." *Victorian Studies* 48 (2006): 625–57.

Levine, George, ed. *Aesthetics and Ideology.* New Brunswick, N.J.: Rutgers University Press, 1994.

———. "Introduction: Reclaiming the Aesthetic." In G. Levine, *Aesthetics and Ideology*, 1–28.

Liebler, Naomi Conn, ed. *Early Modern Prose Fiction: The Cultural Politics of Reading.* New York: Routledge, 2007.

Linton, Joan Pong. "Counterfeiting Sovereignty, Mocking Mastery: Trickster Poetics and the Critique of Romance in Nashe's *Unfortunate Traveller.*" In Liebler, *Early Modern Prose Fiction*, 130–47.

Lodge, Thomas. 1590. *Rosalynde.* Edited by W. W. Greg. New York: Duffield, 1907.

Loewenstein, Joseph. *Ben Jonson and Possessive Authorship.* Cambridge: Cambridge University Press, 2002.

Lyly, John. *Euphues: The Anatomy of Wit.* 1578. In Salzman, *Anthology of Elizabethan Prose Fiction*, 83–150.

Madelaine, Richard. "Material Boys: Apprenticeship and the Boy Actors' Shakespearean Roles." In Davis, *Shakespeare Matters*, 225–38.

Maquerlot, Jean-Pierre, and Michèle Willems, eds. *Travel and Drama in Shakespeare's Time.* Cambridge: Cambridge University Press, 1996.

Marcus, Leah S. "Jonson and the Court." In *The Cambridge Companion to Ben Jonson*, edited by Richard Harp and Stanley Stewart, 30–42. Cambridge: Cambridge University Press, 2000.

Mardock, James D. *Our Scene Is London: Ben Jonson's City and the Space of the Author.* New York: Routledge, 2008.

Margolies, David. *Novel and Society in Elizabethan England.* London: Croom Helm, 1985.

Marotti, Arthur F. *Manuscript, Print, and the English Renaissance Lyric.* Ithaca, N.Y.: Cornell University Press, 1995.

Martin, Catherine Gimelli. "Angels, Alchemists and Exchange: Commercial Ideology in Court and City Comedy, 1596–1610." In *The Witness of Times: Manifestations of Ideology in Seventeenth Century England*, edited by Katherine Z. Keller and Gerald J. Schiffhorst, 121–47. Pittsburgh: Duquesne University Press, 1993.

Marx, Karl. *Capital: A Critique of Political Economy.* Vol. 1. Translated by Ben Fowkes. New York: Vintage, 1977.

Mason, Pamela, ed. *Shakespeare: Early Comedies.* London: Macmillan, 1995.

Masten, Jeffrey. *Textual Intercourse: Collaboration, Authorship, and Sexualities in Renaissance Drama.* Cambridge: Cambridge University Press, 1997.

———. "*The Two Gentlemen of Verona*: A Modern Perspective." In *The Two Gentlemen of Verona*, edited by Barbara Mowat and Paul Werstine, 199–221. Folger Shakespeare Library. New York: Washington Square Press, 1990.

Matar, Nabil. *Turks, Moors, and Englishmen in the Age of Discovery.* New York: Columbia University Press, 1999.

McLuskie, Kathleen. *Dekker and Heywood: Professional Dramatists.* London: St. Martin's, 1994.

McLuskie, Kathleen, and Felicity Dunsworth. "Patronage and the Economics of Theater." In *A New History of Early English Drama,* edited by John D. Cox and David Scott Kastan, 423–40. New York: Columbia University Press, 1997.

McMillin, Scott. "The Sharer and His Boy: Rehearsing Shakespeare's Women." In *From Script to Stage in Early Modern England,* ed. Peter Holland and Stephen Orgel, 231–45. Houndmills, UK: Palgrave Macmillan, 2004.

McMillin, Scott, and Sally-Beth McLean. *The Queen's Men and Their Plays.* Cambridge: Cambridge University Press, 1998.

McNeill, Fiona. "Gynocentric London Spaces: (Re)Locating Masterless Women in Early Stuart Drama." *Renaissance Drama* 28 (1997): 195–244.

———. *Poor Women in Shakespeare.* Cambridge: Cambridge University Press, 2007.

Mebane, John. "Renaissance Magic and the Return of the Golden Age: Utopianism and Religious Enthusiasm in *The Alchemist.*" *Renaissance Drama* 8 (1977): 117–39.

Mentz, Steve. "'A Note Beyond Your Reach': Prose Romance's Rivalry with Elizabethan Drama." In *Staging Early Modern Romance: Prose Fiction, Dramatic Romance, and Shakespeare,* edited by Mary Ellen Lamb and Valerie Wayne, 75–90. New York: Routledge, 2009.

———. *Romance for Sale in Early Modern England: The Rise of Prose Fiction.* Aldershot, UK: Ashgate, 2006.

———. "Wearing Greene: Autolycus, Robert Greene, and the Structure of Romance in *The Winter's Tale.*" *Renaissance Drama* 30 (1999–2001): 73–92.

Mowat, Barbara. "Rogues, Shepherds, and the Counterfeit Distressed: Texts and Infracontexts of *The Winter's Tale* 4.3." *Shakespeare Studies* 22 (1994): 58–76.

Nashe, Thomas. *The Works of Thomas Nashe.* 5 vols. 1904–10. Edited by Ronald B. McKerrow and F. P. Wilson. Reprint, Oxford: Basil Blackwell, 1958.

Neill, Michael. "Servant Obedience and Master Sins: Shakespeare and the Bonds of Service." In *Putting History to the Question: Power, Politics, and Society in English Renaissance Drama,* 13–48. New York: Columbia University Press, 2000.

———, ed. "Special Section: Shakespeare and the Bonds of Service." *Shakespearean International Yearbook* 5 (2005): 3–144.

Netzloff, Mark. *England's Internal Colonies: Class, Capital, and the Literature of Early Modern Colonialism.* New York: Palgrave Macmillan, 2003.

Nevo, Ruth. *Comic Transformations in Shakespeare.* New York: Methuen, 1980.

Newcomb, Lori Humphrey. *Reading Popular Romance in Early Modern England*. New York: Columbia University Press, 2002.

Newman, Karen. "Women and Commodification in Jonson's *Epicoene*." *English Literary History* 56 (1989): 503–18.

Nicholl, Charles. *A Cup of News: The Life of Thomas Nashe*. London: Routledge and Kegan Paul, 1984.

Norman, Marc, and Tom Stoppard. *Shakespeare in Love: A Screenplay*. New York: Hyperion/Miramax Books, 1998.

Orgel, Stephen. *Impersonations: The Performance of Gender in Shakespeare's England*. Cambridge: Cambridge University Press, 1996.

———. Introduction to *The Winter's Tale*, by William Shakespeare, edited by Stephen Orgel, 1–83. Oxford: Clarendon Press, 1996.

Ouellette, Anthony J. "*The Alchemist* and the Emerging Adult Private Playhouse." *Studies in English Literature* 45 (2005): 375–99.

Paster, Gail Kern. *The Body Embarrassed: Drama and the Disciplines of Shame in Early Modern England*. Ithaca, N.Y.: Cornell University Press, 1993.

Pepys, Samuel. *Samuel Pepys' Penny Merriments*. Edited by Roger Thompson. New York: Columbia University Press, 1977.

Perry, Curtis. "Commerce, Community, and Nostalgia in *The Comedy of Errors*." In Woodbridge, *Money and the Age of Shakespeare*, 39–52.

Prest, Wilfrid R. *The Inns of Court Under Elizabeth I and the Early Stuarts 1590–1640*. London: Longman, 1972.

Puttenham, George. *The Art of English Poesy*. 1589. Edited by Frank Whigham and Wayne A. Rebhorn. Ithaca, N.Y.: Cornell University Press, 2007.

Raman, Shankar. "Marking Time: Memory and Market in *The Comedy of Errors*." *Shakespeare Quarterly* 56 (2005): 176–205.

Rambuss, Richard. "The Secretary's Study: The Secret Designs of the *Shepheardes Calender*." *English Literary History* 59 (1992): 313–35.

Rappaport, Steve. *Worlds Within Worlds: Structures of Life in Sixteenth-Century London*. Cambridge: Cambridge University Press, 1989.

Rebhorn, Wayne. *Courtly Performances: Masking and Festivity in Castiglione's "Book of the Courtier."* Detroit: Wayne State University Press, 1978.

Relihan, Constance. *Fashioning Authority: The Development of Elizabethan Novelistic Discourse*. Kent, Ohio: Kent State University Press, 1994.

———, ed. *Framing Elizabethan Fictions: Contemporary Approaches to Early Modern Narrative Prose*. Kent, Ohio: Kent State University Press, 1996.

Relihan, Constance, and Goran V. Stanivukovic, eds. *Prose Fiction and Early Modern Sexualities in England, 1570–1640*. New York: Palgrave Macmillan, 2003.

Riddell, James A. "Some Actors in Jonson's Plays." *Shakespeare Studies* 5 (1969): 285–98.

Riehle, Wolfgang. *Shakespeare, Plautus and the Humanist Tradition*. Cambridge: D. S. Brewer, 1990.

Riggs, David. *Ben Jonson: A Life*. Cambridge, Mass.: Harvard University Press, 1989.

Roach, Joseph. *Cities of the Dead: Circum-Atlantic Performances.* New York: Columbia University Press, 1996.

Robbins, Bruce. *The Servant's Hand: English Fiction from Below.* New York: Columbia University Press, 1986.

Roberts, Sasha. "Reading in Early Modern England: Contexts and Problems." *Critical Survey* 12 (2000): 1–16.

Robertson, James. "The Adventures of Dick Whittington and the Social Construction of Elizabethan London." In Gadd and Wallis, *Guilds, Society and Economy in London 1450–1800,* 51–66.

Rowe, George E. *Distinguishing Jonson: Imitation, Rivalry, and the Direction of a Dramatic Career.* Lincoln: University of Nebraska Press, 1988.

Rutter, Carol Chillington. *Documents of the Rose Playhouse.* Manchester, UK: Manchester University Press, 1984.

Salzman, Paul, ed. *An Anthology of Elizabethan Prose Fiction.* Oxford: Oxford University Press, 1987.

Sanders, Eve. *Gender and Literacy on Stage in Early Modern England.* Cambridge: Cambridge University Press, 1998.

Schalkwyk, David. *Shakespeare, Love, and Service.* Cambridge: Cambridge University Press, 2008.

Schlueter, June, ed. *"Two Gentlemen of Verona": Critical Essays.* New York: Garland, 1996.

Schoone-Jongen, Terence G. *Shakespeare's Companies: William Shakespeare's Early Career and the Acting Companies, 1577–1594.* Farnham, UK: Ashgate, 2009.

Schwyzer, Philip. "Summer Fruit and Autumn Leaves: Thomas Nashe in 1593." *English Literary Renaissance* 24 (1994): 583–619.

Sessions, W. A. *Henry Howard, the Poet Earl of Surrey: A Life.* Oxford: Oxford University Press, 1999.

Shakespeare, William. *The Norton Shakespeare.* 2nd ed. Edited by Stephen Greenblatt et al. New York: W. W. Norton, 2008.

Shannon, Laurie. *Sovereign Amity: Figures of Friendship in Shakespearean Contexts.* Chicago: University of Chicago Press, 2002.

Sidney, Philip. *The Defence of Poesy.* In *Sir Philip Sidney: The Major Works,* edited by Katherine Duncan-Jones, 212–50. Oxford: Oxford University Press, 2002.

Siemon, James. "'But It Appears She Lives': Iteration in *The Winter's Tale.*" In *William Shakespeare's "The Winter's Tale,"* edited by Harold Bloom, 47–58. New York: Chelsea House, 1987. First published in *PMLA* 89 (1974): 10–16.

Simons, Louise. "Rerouting *The Unfortunate Traveller:* Strategies for Coherence and Direction." *Studies in English Literature* 28 (1988): 17–38.

Simpson, A. W. B. *A History of the Common Law of Contract: The Rise of the Action of Assumpsit.* Oxford: Clarendon, 1975.

Slights, Camille Wells. "Common Courtesy in *The Two Gentlemen of Verona.*" In *Shakespeare's Comic Commonwealths,* 57–73. Toronto: University of Toronto Press, 1993.

Smallwood, R. L., and Stanley Wells. Introduction to *The Shoemaker's Holiday*, by Thomas Dekker, edited by R. L. Smallwood and Stanley Wells, 1–70. Manchester, UK: Manchester University Press; Baltimore: Johns Hopkins University Press, 1979.

Smith, Bruce. *Homosexual Desire in Shakespeare's England: A Cultural Poetics*. Chicago: University of Chicago Press, 1991.

Sokol, B. J. *Art and Illusion in "The Winter's Tale."* Manchester: Manchester University Press, 1994.

Spufford, Margaret. *Small Books and Pleasant Histories: Popular Fiction and Its Readership in Seventeenth-Century England*. Athens: University of Georgia Press, 1981.

Stallybrass, Peter. "Footnotes." In *The Body in Parts: Fantasies of Corporeality in Early Modern Europe*, edited by David Hillman and Carla Mazzio, 313–25. New York: Routledge, 1997.

———. "Worn Worlds: Clothes and Identity on the Renaissance Stage." In *Subject and Object in Renaissance Culture*, edited by Margreta de Grazia, Maureen Quilligan, and Peter Stallybrass, 289–320. Cambridge: Cambridge University Press, 1996.

Stevenson, Laura Caroline. *Praise and Paradox: Merchants and Craftsmen in Elizabethan Popular Literature*. Cambridge: Cambridge University Press, 1984.

Stokes, James, ed. *Records for Early English Drama. Somerset*. Vols. 1–2. Toronto: University of Toronto Press, 1996.

Stow, John. *A Survey of London*. Vol. 1. Edited by Charles Lethbridge Kingsford. Oxford: Clarendon Press, 1908.

Straub, Kristina. *Domestic Affairs: Intimacy, Eroticism, and Violence Between Servants and Masters in Eighteenth-Century Britain*. Baltimore: Johns Hopkins University Press, 2009.

Strier, Richard. *Resistant Structures: Particularity, Radicalism, and Renaissance Texts*. Berkeley: University of California Press, 1995.

Suzuki, Mihoko. "'Signorie ouer the Pages': The Crisis of Authority in Nashe's *The Unfortunate Traveller*." *Studies in Philology* 81 (1984): 348–71.

———. *Subordinate Subjects: Gender, the Political Nation, and Literary Form in England, 1588–1688*. Burlington, Vt.: Ashgate, 2003.

Taussig, Michael. *Mimesis and Alterity*. New York: Routledge, 1993.

Thirsk, Joan. *Economic Policy and Projects: The Development of a Consumer Society in Early Modern England*. Oxford: Clarendon Press, 1978.

Timpane, John. "'I Am But a Foole, Looke You': Launce and the Social Functions of Humor." In Schlueter, *"Two Gentlemen of Verona": Critical Essays*, 189–211.

Tribble, Evelyn. "Marlowe's Boy Actors." *Shakespeare Bulletin* 27 (2009): 5–17.

Turner, Henry S. *The English Renaissance Stage: Geometry, Poetics, and the Practical Spatial Arts 1580–1630*. Oxford: Oxford University Press, 2006.

Turner, Robert Y. *Shakespeare's Apprenticeship*. Chicago: University of Chicago Press, 1974.

Vitkus, Daniel. Introduction to *Piracy, Slavery, and Redemption: Barbary Captivity Narratives from Early Modern England*, edited by Daniel Vitkus, 1–54. New York: Columbia University Press, 2001.

———. *Turning Turk: English Theater and the Multicultural Mediterranean, 1570–1630*. New York: Palgrave Macmillan, 2003.

Walsh, Brian. "Performing Historicity in Dekker's *The Shoemaker's Holiday*." *Studies in English Literature* 46 (2006): 323–48.

Watt, Tessa. *Cheap Print and Popular Piety, 1550–1640*. Cambridge: Cambridge University Press, 1991.

Weil, Judith. *Service and Dependency in Shakespeare's Plays*. Cambridge: Cambridge University Press, 2005.

Wells, Stanley. "The Failure of *The Two Gentlemen of Verona*." In Mason, *Shakespeare: Early Comedies*, 160–71. First published in *Shakespeare Jahrbuch* 99 (1963): 163–73.

West, William N. "'But this will be a mere confusion': Real and Represented Confusions on the Elizabethan Stage." *Theatre Journal* 60 (2008): 217–33.

Whigham, Frank. *Ambition and Privilege: The Social Tropes of Elizabethan Courtesy Theory*. Berkeley: University of California Press, 1984.

Williams, Raymond. *Marxism and Literature*. Oxford: Oxford University Press, 1977.

Wilson, Eric. "Abel Drugger's Sign and the Fetishes of Material Culture." In *Historicism, Psychoanalysis, and Early Modern Culture*, edited by Carla Mazzio and Douglas Trevor, 110–34. New York: Routledge, 2000.

Wolf, Janet. "'Like an Old Tale Still': Paulina, 'Triple Hecate,' and the Persephone Myth in *The Winter's Tale*." In *Images of Persephone: Feminist Readings in Western Literature*, edited by Elizabeth T. Hayes, 32–44. Gainesville: University Press of Florida, 1994.

Woodbridge, Linda. *Vagrancy, Homelessness, and English Renaissance Literature*. Urbana: University of Illinois Press, 2001.

———, ed. *Money and the Age of Shakespeare*. New York: Macmillan, 2003.

Worden, Thomas. "Idols in the Early Modern Material World (1599): Deloney's *The Gentle Craft*, Dekker's *The Shoemaker's Holiday*, and Shakespeare's *Henry V*." *Exemplaria* 11 (1999): 431–71.

Wright, Eugene P. *Thomas Deloney*. Boston: Twayne, 1981.

Wrightson, Keith. *Earthly Necessities: Economic Lives in Early Modern Britain*. New Haven, Conn.: Yale University Press, 2000.

Yachnin, Paul. *Stage-Wrights: Shakespeare, Jonson, Middleton, and the Making of Theatrical Value*. Philadelphia: University of Pennsylvania Press, 1997.

Yates, Julian. *Error Misuse Failure: Object Lessons from the English Renaissance*. Minneapolis: University of Minnesota Press, 2003.

INDEX

Admiral's Men, 91, 103, 105, 186n71
aesthetics, 4, 11, 24, 125; didactic
    literature and, 13, 16; social life and,
    38; subjectivity and, 63
aesthetic service, 3, 8, 62, 69, 108; agency
    through, 157; defined, 4; extremes
    of, 24; instability for patriarchal
    structures, 43, 55; patriarchal duty
    and, 54; as resistance, 161–62;
    service economy and, 102; social
    advancement and, 17; subjectivities
    formed by, 15, 16, 18, 162; women in
    vanguard of, 18
agency, 4, 44, 69, 74, 93, 163; patronage
    and, 108; of Shakespearean servants,
    136; socially mixed, 144; of women, 18
Alchemist, The (Jonson), 7, 12, 18, 107–9,
    131; criminal enterprise in, 110–11;
    dedication ("To the Reader"), 19,
    123–24, 125, 128, 130; performance
    of, 121; rhetoric of patronage in, 20;
    rogue servants in, 110–21; service as
    disreputable profession, 24
alchemy, 112–13, 118, 187n13
Alleyne, Richard, 103–4
Amphitruo (Plautus), 31, 172n12
Anabaptists, 60–62, 65, 115
Anatomie of Absurditie, The (Nashe), 73
Anderson, Linda, 10
Antigonus (Shakespeare character), 149,
    192n26
Antipholuses (Shakespeare characters),
    32–33, 155, 173n17, 174n29; bonds
    with servants, 33–35; as twinned
    masters, 30–31
Antony and Cleopatra (Shakespeare), 33
appendixes, 55–56
apprentices/apprenticeship, 11, 17, 20, 99,
    111, 154; gender and, 47, 175n50; in
    The Gentle Craft, 75, 79; importance
    in urban economy, 187n11; Jonson
    and, 132; marriage and, 85, 86, 88;
    Shakespeare and, 27, 136; soldiering
    and, 86–87
Arab, Ronda, 185n64

Ariel (Shakespeare character), 25, 162;
    representations of Prospero, 157–59; as
    slave and servant, 157, 193n37
aristocracy/aristocrats, 77, 83, 87, 118,
    154, 180n6; African slaves in service
    to, 156; capitalistic urban economy
    and, 23; cycle of inheritance and
    consumption, 95; disguised in humble
    form, 62, 94; downward mobility and,
    66, 183n44; exchanges of identity and,
    93, 97, 98; Inns of Court students,
    36; service as apprentices, 12; service
    institutions rooted in household, 10; in
    The Shoemaker's Holiday, 94; treated
    in low style, 8; values of, 75; writers
    and patronage of, 19, 20, 54, 56, 68
Aristotle, 5–6, 78, 127
Arte of English Poesie, The (Puttenham), 8
artisans and the artisanal, 6, 96, 122, 154,
    185n55; in audiences, 94; authors as,
    75; mythologizing of, 82; servants as,
    75, 86, 92, 95; theater and, 103
Ascham, Roger, 7, 8, 166n18
Astrophil and Stella (Sidney), 70, 71
audiences, 21, 74, 102; for The Comedy
    of Errors, 35–38; Jonson's address to,
    124; royal, 93; Shakespeare and, 135,
    137, 164; sympathetic identification
    and, 33
Auerbach, Erich, 166n20
authors/authorship, 21, 108, 125;
    authors as servants, 11, 12, 125, 134;
    authorship as service, 162; marginal
    position of, 109; between patronage
    and commerce, 129, 134; patrons of,
    19, 57; readership's anonymity and, 21
Autolycus (Shakespeare character), 8, 24,
    137, 138, 149, 162; artifice in service
    role of, 139; deceptions of, 151–52;
    illusion of emancipation from service,
    142, 152–53; as "merry beggar," 152;
    as rogue, 136

Bakhtin, Mikhail, 182n35
ballads, 73, 75, 78, 88, 101

Bartholomew Fair (Jonson), 135, 190n51
Becon, Thomas, 14, 156
Ben-Amos, Ilana Krausman, 167n34, 181n23
Benfield, Robert, 122
Bevis of Hampton, 78, 181n20
Bible, 14, 61, 177n14
Blackfriars playhouse, 112, 121, 137
Boehrer, Bruce, 109–10
bonds, rhetoric of, 33–35, 173nn15–16
bookbinders, 17, 20
Book of the Courtier (Castiglione), 139–41, 144, 150–51
Borne, William, 104
bourgeois subject/state, 5, 165n6
Brathwait, Richard, 15
Bristow, James, 103
Brome, Richard, 130–32
Brown, Paul, 160, 193n45
Bruster, Douglas, 21
Burbage brothers, 121
Burnett, Mark Thornton, 10, 183n44

Caliban (Shakespeare character), 9, 25; aesthetic service as resistance, 161–62; imitation and, 159–60; patriarchal service opposed by, 159; as "servant-monster," 135; as slave, 157, 159, 193n37; subjectivity of, 163
Camillo (Shakespeare character), 24, 137, 138, 139, 145–54
capitalism, 3, 12, 16, 25, 138; entrepreneurs, 107, 108; in London, 88; paternalistic service and, 169n59; self-deception of masters and, 125; servants' self-definition and, 82; service in contractual and occasional forms, 10, 11, 167n34; slavery and, 155; subjectivity and, 18; theater and, 102, 121–22; tragicomic genre and, 137, 190n6; ventures detached from labor, 116. *See also* economy, commercial/urban; service, capitalist forms of
Castiglione, Baldesar, 139, 146
cave, Plato's allegory of, 64
Caveat for Common Cursitors, A (Harman), 114, 139, 141–44
Caxton, William, 81, 82, 183n36
character, as verb, 41, 174n36
Charlton, H. B., 9–10
Christianity, 81, 82
Clark, Peter, 17

class, social, 10, 28, 75, 166n20, 189n32; class consciousness, 88; class struggle, 11; corporate class of London, 115; imitation and, 49; new alignments of, 23; "othered" servant class as proletariat, 13; upward mobility and, 55, 83
Cocke, John, 20
Colie, Rosalie, 166n21
colonialism, 160–61, 193n45, 194n45
Comedy of Errors, The (Shakespeare), 25, 27–28, 41, 49, 136; audience disorder in *Gesta Grayorum*, 35–38; bonds' significance in, 33–35; literate characters in, 30–33; Shakespeare's apprenticeship and, 22
Common, Dol (Jonson character), 19, 110, 111, 116–17, 122, 124; alchemy and, 112–13; as equal sharer in "venture tripartite," 115–16, 119; illusion of liberation from labor, 117; as prostitute, 114, 118–19; service as capitalist enterprise and, 120
Common, Subtle (Jonson character), 110, 111, 122, 124; alchemy and, 112–13, 118; illusion of liberation from labor, 117; poverty of, 114; service as capitalist enterprise and, 120
conduct books, 13
coney-catching pamphlets, 77, 114, 115
consumption/consumer society, 17, 169n56
Cordwainers' Guild, 75, 76, 180n12, 184n45
courtesy literature, 42
courtiers, 8, 42, 45, 150; in audiences, 154; entrepreneurial, 17; imitation of one another, 38; "old" service represented by, 25; pretensions of, 107; rogues intertwined with, 138–44, 153, 157; in *Two Gentlemen of Verona*, 39, 42, 43; in *The Winter's Tale*, 24, 144, 146
Crab (dog character), 43–44, 45
craftsmanship, 6, 77, 87
Crewe, Jonathan, 65
criminality, 110–11, 143
Crispin brothers (Deloney characters), 80, 81–82, 84–88, 183n36, 183n44; shoemaking as ennobled profession and, 87–88; soldiering and, 98
Cynthia's Revels (Jonson), 123

Dame Pliant (Jonson character), 119–20, 189n30
decorum, violations of, 8, 166n21
Defence of Poesy, The (Sidney), 5, 68, 69, 73; on pleasure subordinated to moral purpose, 70; principle of decorum and, 8; on skill of artifice, 77
Dekker, Thomas, 3, 12, 21, 136, 163, 184n50; audiences and, 91, 106; in debtor's prison, 105, 186n74; fiction–drama link and, 105–6; incipient capitalist economy and, 73–74; prolific output of, 105; public aesthetic of, 91, 102; representations of service, 23–24
Deloney, Thomas, 3, 12, 21, 136, 163; fiction–drama link and, 105–6; Nashe and, 73; representations of service, 23–24
Diamante (Nashe character), 60, 65, 66–67, 177n19
didactic literature, 13–16, 47, 53; "bad" servants warned against in, 59; catastrophic telos of, 81; divine basis for service and, 61; on eye-service, 98; servant's spiritual and affective condition, 64; Shakespeare's rebuttal of, 137, 149; *The Unfortunate Traveller* and, 63
Dionne, Craig, 115
Discoveries (Jonson), 24, 108, 125–29, 130, 131, 139, 190n49
divine, image of the, 6
Dowd, Michelle, 119, 169n63
downward mobility, 11, 18, 42, 44–45, 48, 66; servants turned rogue, 144; in *The Shoemaker's Holiday*, 76, 96
Dowton, Thomas, 104
drama, 4, 5, 8; absence of service as dystopia for, 164; artificial separation from prose, 21; as autonomous aesthetic form, 29; critics' concentration on, 12, 167n38; of Dekker, 105; didactic morality plays, 29; dispossession of servants in, 18; history and, 25; humanist reception of, 37; mimetic properties of service in, 9; prose fiction linked to, 105. *See also* theater
Dromios (Shakespeare characters), 22, 28, 32–33, 36, 155; bonds with masters, 34–35; errant messenger role and, 30–31; Plautus plays and, 31, 172n12

Duncan-Jones, Katherine, 30, 50

Eagleton, Terry, 5, 165n6
economy, commercial/urban, 23, 66, 91; book buyers' power in, 54; of London, 98; patronage and, 57; playwrights and, 123; prostitution and, 18; rogues' reinvention of self in, 110; servants benefited by, 104; service economy, 17, 75, 89; shadow economy, 18. *See also* capitalism
Elizabeth I, Queen, 43, 92–93, 120
Ellinghausen, Laurie, 107
England, early modern, 5, 9, 163; class mobility in, 42; material conditions of service in, 11; rural unemployment in, 142; slavery and, 156
English Gentleman, The (Brathwait), 15
Enlightenment, 5, 159
entrepreneurs, 107, 108, 111, 121
"Epistle to my Lady Covell" (Jonson), 133, 135
eroticism. *See* sexuality/eroticism
errant messengers, 31
ethnography, colonial, 9
Euphues, the Anatomy of Wit (Lyly), 21
Evett, David, 10, 167n33, 167n38
eye-service, 14, 15, 16, 53; in *The Alchemist*, 118; in *Discoveries*, 128; *The Shoemaker's Holiday* and, 98
Eyre, Margery (Dekker character), 99, 100
Eyre, Simon (Dekker character), 93, 105; "merry shoemaker" performance, 101–2; social mobility of, 96, 97, 99; transgressive costuming of, 97
Eyre, Simon (Deloney character), 75, 76, 80; social mobility of, 88, 89–90

Face (Jonson character), 110, 111, 114, 122, 124; actors playing role of, 122; alchemy and, 112–13; illusion of liberation from labor, 117, 118, 125; return to servitude, 120–21; service as capitalist enterprise and, 120
family, rhetorical ordering of the, 13
Famous History of the Valiant London Prentice, The, 86
Ferdinand (Shakespeare character), 156–57
fiction, prose, 4, 5, 8; absence of service as dystopia for, 164; appropriative nature of, 63; artificial separation from

fiction, prose (*continued*)
    drama, 21; of Deloney, 73, 76, 90, 105;
    dispossession of servants in, 18; drama
    linked to, 105; as emerging form, 54;
    formal self-awareness of, 23; history
    and, 25; idea of the public and, 21;
    mimetic properties of service in, 9; of
    Nashe, 53–54, 69, 72, 176n3
Field, Nathan, 122
Florizel (Shakespeare character), 147–48,
    152, 153
folk stories, 78
form, dramatic and literary, 164; changes
    in, 11, 12; matter and, 8; social and
    political arrangements shaped by, 9,
    166n26; tragicomic, 135
Forman, Valerie, 137
Fosset, Thomas, 15, 16
Four Prentices of London, The
    (Heywood), 87
Fumerton, Patricia, 114, 121

gaze, erotic, 47
Gebauer, Gunter, 9
gender, 13, 28
Gentle Craft, The (Deloney), 12, 132,
    180nn9–10; *The Alchemist* compared
    with, 107, 114–15; chivalric romances
    and, 78, 82; literary categories and,
    76–77; *The Shoemaker's Holiday*
    compared with, 73–76, 95; shoemaking
    as ennobled craft, 82–91; as source for
    The Shoemaker's Holiday, 23; sources
    for, 82–83; upward social mobility
    promoted in, 55
George a Green (anonymous play), 79, 80,
    182n30
Gesta Grayorum, 36–38, 173n25, 174n28
Girard, René, 43
Globe theater, 121, 122, 136
Goldberg, Jonathan, 41, 159, 190n49
Golden Legend, The (Caxton), 81, 82
Gouge, William, 15
Greenblatt, Stephen, 50
Greene, Robert, 148
Greene's Groats-worth of Wit, 49–51, 67
guild system, 27, 73, 96, 132, 183n43
Gurr, Andrew, 137, 189n34, 193n37
Guy-Bray, Stephen, 178n25
Guy of Warwick, 78, 181n20

Halasz, Alexandra, 75, 180nn7–8
Hallett, Charles, 40

Harman, Thomas, 114, 139, 142, 151
Harris, Jonathan Gil, 96
*Health to the Gentlemanly Profession of
    Servingmen, A* (service treatise), 18,
    146
Helgerson, Richard, 133, 186n2
Heminges, John, 103
Henry VI, Part 1 (Shakespeare), 30
Henry VI, Part 3 (Shakespeare), 50
Henry VIII, King, 68
Henslowe, Philip, 43, 103, 104, 105,
    186nn71–72
Hermione (Shakespeare character), 138,
    145, 146, 148–49, 150, 152, 155
heterosexuality, 47, 49
Heywood, Thomas, 87, 104
Hibbard, G. R., 59, 177n10
hierarchy: costuming transgression
    against, 97; destabilization and
    inversion of, 13; dismantled by
    prose fiction, 67; divine, 8, 173n17;
    patronage and, 19; slaves and, 155;
    undercut by performances, 39
Hobsbawm, E. J., 80, 185n65
Holcombe, Thomas, 103
homoerotic bonds, 39
homosexuality, 47
*honour of an Apprentice of London,
    The*, 86
Howard, Jean, 118, 119, 188n30
Hugh, Sir (Deloney character), 90, 94
humanism, 7, 37, 129, 159
Hutjens, Linda Ann, 86
Hutson, Lorna, 43, 175n41

identities, elite, 22, 28, 38, 69; aesthetic
    production of, 39; as function of
    actions versus birth, 42
identity, 5, 9, 13, 90; exchanges of,
    75, 96, 100, 164; high and low, 19;
    individual and collective forms of, 11;
    literacy and, 31; loss of social identity,
    16; misrepresentation and, 27–28;
    patriarchal, 53; servant–master bond
    and, 35
idleness, 110–11, 142
imitation (*imitatio*): authority challenged
    by, 166n19; in *Book of the Courtier*,
    139–40; of Christ, 14; decorum
    violated by, 8; didactic literature
    and, 13; in *Discoveries*, 125–29,
    139; performance of *The Comedy of
    Errors* and, 37–38; poetry as form of,

129; restrictions on use of, 7; social advancement and, 16; in *The Tempest*, 159–60
industry and diligence, moral convention of, 114, 116
Inns of Court, 22, 36, 38, 173n23
instrumentality, 4
intellectual property rights, 109

Jack of Newbury (Deloney), 77, 85, 179n2
James I, King, 162, 184n50
Jane (Dekker character), 99–100
Johannes fac totum (Jack of all trades), 49, 50
Johnson, Richard, 86
Jonnes, Richard, 104
Jonson, Ben, 7, 12, 163; author as servant, 108, 186n2; contradictory authorial persona of, 107; plagiarism in work of, 109–10; on the "servant-monster," 135–36, 157; servant-rogues of, 24; service in later writings of, 130–34; Shakespeare criticized by, 135; theatrical service of, 121–25
journeymen, 75, 80, 84, 185n60
Julia/Sebastian (Shakespeare character), 19, 22; as composite of servant and mistress, 28; cross-dressed as page boy, 39; in disguise as male servant boy, 30; as mistress to Lucetta, 40–42; performance of downward mobility, 44–45; restored to former position, 48–49; in servant and master roles, 45
Julius Caesar (Shakespeare), 33

Kathman, David, 103, 123, 186n67, 189n40
Kempe, Will, 43
King Henry the VIII and the Cobbler, 80
King Lear (Shakespeare), 45, 156
kings, treated in low style, 8
King's Men, 20, 24, 103; actors of, 122; at Blackfriars playhouse, 121; Globe theater and, 122; shareholders in, 112
knaves, 45, 102, 175n46
Korda, Natasha, 18, 188n29; on women's work in theater, 121–22

labor, 13, 115, 121, 123, 143; aesthetics of, 77; avoidance of, 113, 114, 141; capitalist control of, 112, 187n15;

courtiers and, 141; freedom from, 111, 117, 120; investment and, 109, 116, 122; labor markets, 114, 155; slavery and, 156–57; in theater, 104, 162, 186n72, 189n35; types of service and, 17; upward mobility and, 85
laborers, 107, 187n10
Lacy, Rowland (Dekker character), 92, 93, 102; downward mobility of, 96; as "Hans," 94–95, 96; layered persona of, 94, 96; soldiering and, 105
Lady Elizabeth's Men, 186n72
land enclosure, 11
Lanier, Douglas, 31
Launce (Shakespeare character), 9–10, 22, 41, 43–45, 175n47
Leinwand, Theodore, 187n15, 188n27
Leontes (Shakespeare character), 138, 139, 144–55
Levine, Caroline, 166n26
Life of Saint Winifred, The, 82
literacy, 21, 31–32, 80, 173n21
literature: aesthetic properties of service and, 4; coney-catching, 114, 115; courtier, 139; craftsman, 74–75, 179n4; pastoral, 78; popular forms of, 74; rogue, 114, 139, 154
Lodge, Thomas, 21
Loewenstein, Joseph, 109, 123
London, 75, 80, 100, 105; civic authorities in, 81; commercial economy in, 98; corporate class of, 115; plague in, 110; scarcity of commodities, 89; Shakespeare in, 29; theaters of, 38, 71, 102, 112, 121, 122, 133, 154; underworld of, 117; workers' wages in, 104
Lord Chamberlain's Men, 30, 36, 49, 121
love, courtly, 42, 46, 48, 69
Lovewit (Jonson character), 110, 112–13, 119; actor playing role of, 122; hierarchical privilege represented by, 120–21; house of, 131, 133
Lucentio (Shakespeare character), 3, 4–5
Lucetta (Shakespeare character), 22, 40–42
Lyly, John, 21, 77

Machiavelli, Niccolò, 128
Madden, John, 43
Madeline, Richard, 175n50
Mamillius (Shakespeare character), 145
Mammon, Sir Epicure (Jonson character), 113, 116–17, 118

Margolies, David, 21
Marotti, Arthur, 54
marriage, 85, 86, 88, 119, 149, 188n30
Marx, Karl, 187n15
Marxism, 10
masques/masquing, 94, 108, 123, 161
Masten, Jeffrey, 39, 43, 49, 175n41
masters: apprentices' marriage to
    widows of, 85; audiences as, 164;
    destabilized, 74; as examples to
    emulate, 16; as gulls, 125; husbands
    as, 18; imitation of servants, 4–5; as
    knaves, 45; replaced by servants, 16;
    servants as extensions of, 15; servants'
    impersonation of, 146, 150. See also
    servant–master relationship
matter, form and, 8
McNeill, Fiona, 100
Menaechmi (Plautus), 31, 37
Mentz, Steve, 177n7, 179n3
merchants, 36, 75, 89, 154
military service. See soldiering
mimesis, 4, 5–6, 8, 28; colonial, 161;
    courtly service and, 139; disorderly, 38;
    imitatio and, 37; interdictions against
    improper use of, 7; as "metaliterary
    anthropological concept," 9; Nashe's
    critique of, 69, 71
Mimesis and Alterity (Taussig), 9
Miranda (Shakespeare character), 156,
    159
mobility, social, 24, 27, 35, 163. See also
    downward mobility; upward mobility
monasteries, dissolution of, 168n44

Nashe, Thomas, 3, 8, 12, 53–55, 136;
    aristocratic patronage and, 56–58,
    177n7; banqueting house imagery,
    69–71, 178n33; Deloney compared
    with, 77; mechanical birds symbolism
    of, 71–72, 179n37; as possible author
    of Greene's Groats-worth of Wit, 51,
    53, 67; reading public/consumers and,
    58–59; Shakespeare's play cowritten
    with, 30
Neill, Michael, 10, 81
New Catechism (Becon), 14, 156
Newcomb, Lori Humphrey, 170n73
New Inn, The (Jonson), 130
Newman, Karen, 189n32
"Night of Errors," 37, 38
Nine Worthies, The (Johnson), 86–87
Northern Lasse, The (Jonson), 131

Oatley, Rose (Dekker character), 94, 95,
    100
"Ode to Himself" (Jonson), 130–31,
    132
Of Domesticall Duties (Gouge), 15
Orgel, Stephen, 47
Othello (Shakespeare), 40, 156

pages, courtly, 55, 176n4, 176n6
Pandosto (Greene), 148
patriarchy. See service, patriarchal and
    neofeudal
patronage, 19, 68, 134; authorship and,
    129; court, 93; Jonson's appeals to,
    123, 125; Nashe and, 55–58, 177n7;
    poetry and, 128
Paul, biblical Epistles of, 14, 33, 35, 61
Paulina (Shakespeare character), 19, 24,
    137, 138, 146–55; artifice in service
    role of, 139; deceptions of, 151–52
peasants, 141, 169n56
Pembroke's Men, 186n71
performance, 4–5, 30, 63, 69, 70;
    aesthetic self-consciousness and, 39; in
    capitalist context, 17; courtly service
    as, 42; of downward mobility, 44–45;
    economic changes and, 17; ethical
    judgments and, 137; fraudulent and
    unethical, 141, 143; insubordination
    behind convincing performance, 14,
    161; layered, 22, 47, 48; as mimetic
    activity, 4; mimetic exchange of
    identity and, 96, 97, 150; pastoral
    masquing, 94; patronage and, 19;
    servants as material for character
    and, 33; of social inclusion, 101;
    social mobility and, 120; theatrical
    aspect of service, 23, 40–41, 102, 108;
    tragicomedy and, 24
Perry, Curtis, 35
plagiarism, 109–10
Plato, 64
Plautus, 31, 33, 37
playing companies, theatrical, 20, 103
playwrights, 94, 104; apprenticeships of,
    30, 172n7; constraints on, 24; market
    economy and, 123; patronage and, 19,
    20; as servants, 11, 162
plot, 6
Plutarch, 184n45
Poetics (Aristotle), 5–6
poets/poetry: of Jonson, 108, 130–34;
    mimesis and, 5–6, 28, 68; patronage

and, 123; poets as servants, 6, 127, 128–29
Polixenes (Shakespeare character), 138, 139, 145, 146–48
Pope, Alexander, 171
print culture/medium, 23, 109, 138, 171n78
prodigal narrative, 76–77
production, new patterns of, 17, 169n56
Prospero (Shakespeare character), 9, 135, 157, 163; appeal to audience, 164; Ariel's representations of, 157–59; Caliban's insurrection and, 161; discourse of service and, 20; identification with servant, 162
prostitutes/prostitution, 18, 99, 114, 118; marriage economy and, 119, 188n30; poetry as female mistress and, 128
Proteus (Shakespeare character), 9, 39, 40, 46–49, 48–49; courtly ideals and, 42, 174n38; Proteus as Greek god compared with, 174n40
public, reading/theatergoing, 58–59, 74, 75; Dekker and, 91; Deloney and, 91, 181n16; economic power of, 106; Jonson and, 107–8; poet's relation to, 129
public sphere, 21, 180n7
Puritans, 15
Purpoole, Prince of, 36
Puttenham, George, 8

Queen's Men, 30, 50

Ralph (Dekker character), 24, 93, 97–101, 105
Rambuss, Richard, 41
Rappaport, Steve, 88, 99, 185n60
reason, aesthetics and, 5
reception, public, 108, 135, 154
representation, 21, 155; doubleness of, 31; identity and, 11; instability in, 27; intervention in history, 12; mimesis and, 9; misrepresentation, 23
Republic, The (Plato), 64
revenge tragedies, 63
Roach, Joseph, 4, 6
Robbins, Bruce, 12, 13
Robertson, James, 184n46
rogues, 24, 79, 107, 121; alchemical practice of, 112–13; in The Alchemist, 133, 135; in audiences, 154; authors in role of, 125; capitalism and, 109;

courtiers intertwined with, 138–44, 153, 157; female, 151; transformed into entrepreneurs, 108; in The Winter's Tale, 136, 146
romances, chivalric, 75, 77, 78, 82, 90
Rosalynde (Lodge), 21
Rose playhouse, 103, 104
Rowe, George, 127
Rutter, Carol Chillington, 104

saints' tales, 78
Sanders, Eve, 38
Schalkwyk, David, 10, 17n37, 147
Schoolmaster, The (Ascham), 7–8
Scott, Joan Wallach, 80
sempsters, 100
sermons, religious, 13
servant–master relationship: biblical warrant for, 14, 35; capitalism and, 74; changing of places, 3; duration of, 167n34; fraudulent enactment of, 24; intimacy of, 14; in Jonson's poetry, 130–34; mockery of, 143; retainer and lord, 10, 11; servant as mimetic reproduction of master, 138; slavery and, 159; subjectivity defined by, 10; theatricality of, 41
servants, 4, 11, 18, 187n10; as ahistorical appendages, 10; as children, 145, 192n20; clowning and commentary of, 43–44; contaminating influence of, 7; covenant, 30; dispossession of, 24; female, 18, 19; impersonation of masters, 146, 150; interiority/subjectivity of, 15, 53, 89; as literate agents, 31; loss of personhood, 66; masters replaced by, 16; mimetic skills of, 6–8; new forms of subjugation for, 135; as objects of exchange, 163; prototypical servant as male, 166n18; as rogues, 24; self-determination and slavery of, 25; social and political hierarchies disrupted by, 10; tragedy and, 166n20; unethical and self-serving, 107, 124, 128; in The Winter's Tale, 137; as witches, 151, 192n30
Servants Dutie, The (Fosset), 15
service: absence of, 152, 164; as aesthetic performance, 143; catastrophic narrative about, 11; courtly, 136; decay of, 13; erotic dimension of, 85–86, 95; margins of, 114, 120; marriage and, 149; mimetic properties of, 9;

service (*continued*)
  narratives of, 16; "out of service," 99,
    142; performance of, 5, 21, 25; refusal
    of, 113; as representational practice,
    3; slavery and, 155–56; social ordering
    in flux and, 9; as theater, 23, 102–6; as
    universal condition, 81, 111
service, capitalist forms of, 3, 10, 11;
    circulation and substitution associated
    with, 135; dispossession and, 109;
    emergence of, 22; patronage and,
    19–20, 108; performance of service
    role, 17; servants as literate agents, 31;
    Shakespeare and, 136, 154. *See also*
    capitalism
service, patriarchal and neofeudal, 3, 12,
    25, 115, 138, 169n59; deterioration/
    decline of, 11, 13, 28, 163, 168n44;
    economy detached from, 24; eye-
    service and, 14; failure to conform to
    ideology of, 65; marriage compared
    with, 149; "new" capitalist service
    pulled back toward, 107, 111; servant's
    internal disposition toward master,
    17; shoemakers as bridge to capitalist
    forms, 79; in *The Shoemaker's Holiday*,
    98; subjectivity unreliable to, 54;
    theological justifications for, 60, 61; in
    The Unfortunate Traveller, 59
service manuals, 13, 33, 89
Sessions, W. A., 68, 178n24
sexuality/eroticism, 85–86, 95, 100,
    128, 133, 152; boy actors and,
    47; homoerotic bonds, 39, 49;
    modern theories of identity and, 13;
    prostitution as commercial activity and,
    119; subjugation and, 128
shadows, metaphor of, 64, 177n17
Shakespeare, William, 3, 12;
    "apprenticeship" of, 22, 27, 29–30,
    50; authorial identity of, 162; in
    Chamberlain's Men, 49; criticized in
    Greene's Groats-worth of Wit, 49–51;
    Deloney compared with, 77; Jonson's
    criticism of, 135; Nashe compared
    with, 55; public nature of theater and,
    136; as servant, 29–30, 50
Shakespeare in Love (film, 1998), 43
shareholding principle, 19, 20, 24, 112,
    116, 121, 189n34
Shawe, Robart, 104
Shoemaker's Holiday, The (Dekker), 8,
    91–102; *The Alchemist* compared

with, 107, 112; dedication of, 91–92;
    dispossession of servant in, 24; *The
    Gentle Craft* compared with, 23,
    73–76; performance of, 91; theater of
    service and, 102–6
shoemakers/shoemaking, 17, 21, 73,
    179n5; as bridge to capitalist forms
    of service, 79; class identity and,
    180n6; as ennobled craft, 82–91,
    183n45; intellectualism of, 80;
    lameness associated with, 100,
    185n65; "merry shoemaker" motif, 80,
    101–2; mythological origins for, 82; as
    performers, 80–81; poverty of, 79, 80;
    social position of, 93, 184n53
shrew, as female character, 151, 152
Sidney, Philip, 8, 55, 128, 165n10, 178n28;
    Astrophil and Stella, 70, 71; Nashe's
    criticism of, 68–69; on poetic mimesis,
    5–6, 37; on theater, 28; on tragicomedy,
    136
Silvia (Shakespeare character), 42–43,
    45, 48
Simons, Louise, 71, 179n35
Simpson, A. W. B., 34, 173n21
Slack, Paul, 17
slaves/slavery, 22, 23, 33, 66; classical,
    155; inter-Atlantic (African), 155, 156,
    193n36, 193n40; as metaphor, 156–57;
    in Plautus, 31; racialized, 25; service
    as alternative to, 84; service as slavery,
    126; sexual, 60, 65; tricky slave, 79
Smallwood, R. L., 105
soldiering, 86–87, 98, 100, 105; avoidance
    of military duty, 16; rogues as former
    soldiers, 114
Southampton, Earl of, 19, 56, 57, 58, 68
Speed (Shakespeare character), 22, 39–40,
    41, 46, 172n11
Spencer, Gabrell, 104
spinsters, 100
Stallybrass, Peter, 97, 184n53
Stationers' Company, 75
Stefano (Shakespeare character), 160,
    194n45
Stevenson, Laura Caroline, 75, 179n4
stichomythia, 40
*Story of Saint Ursula and the Virgins,
    The*, 82
Stourton, Baron, 144
Stow, John, 90, 184n48
Straub, Kristina, 13
Strier, Richard, 10, 138, 192n26

subjectivity, 10, 63, 162; aesthetic agency
and, 136, 154; conferred by service,
24; conflicting ideas of elite subjectivity,
39; crisis in, 11, 16; intimate
relationship with service, 81; new
alignments of, 23; republican, 163;
subject formation, 3, 5
Surly (Jonson character), 116
Surrey, Earl of (historical), 68, 69, 178n33
Surrey, Earl of (Nashe character), 53,
59, 61, 150; dual genealogy of, 68,
178n24; Jack's assumption of identity
of, 62, 64–65, 71; as representative of
anachronistic ideals, 69, 178n25; as
stand-in for Earl of Southampton, 68
Survey of London (Stow), 90
Suzuki, Mihoko, 68, 85

Taming of the Shrew, The (Shakespeare), 3,
4–5, 21–22
Taussig, Michael, 9, 161
Taylor, Joseph, 122
Tempest, The (Shakespeare), 7, 9, 24;
aesthetic slavery in, 155–62; epilogue
of, 163–64; metamorphosis from
tragedy to comedy, 159; performance
history of, 136–37; racialized slave in,
25; rhetoric of patronage in, 20
textuality, 31
theater, 19, 23; apprenticeship in, 27,
29–30, 172n6; capitalist dispossession
of, 76; covenant servants in, 30;
ethical experience of playgoing, 137;
mixed social identity of, 28; playing
companies, 20, 103; professionalization
of, 122. *See also* drama
Thirsk, Joan, 17, 113, 169n56
Thomas of Reading (Deloney), 179n2
"To Fine Grand" (Jonson), 123
"To my old Faithfull Servant" (Jonson),
131–32
"To Penshurst" (Jonson), 108
tradesmen, 36, 75, 78, 87, 154
tragedy/tragicomedy, 135, 162, 166n20;
Jacobean revenge tragedy, 150; Sidney's
disapproval of, 70, 136; in *The
Tempest*, 159; theatergoing public and,
137; in *The Winter's Tale*, 24, 147, 154
Tranio (Shakespeare character), 3, 4
Trinculo (Shakespeare character), 160,
194n45
Turner, Henry, 6
Turner, Robert Y., 29

Two Gentlemen of Verona, The
(Shakespeare), 9–10, 19, 27–28,
38–49, 136, 154; as "apprentice"
work, 48; courtly ideal in, 42, 174n39;
homosociality in, 39, 175n41; mastery
critiqued in, 38–39; Shakespeare's
apprenticeship and, 22; *The
Shoemaker's Holiday* compared
with, 94

unemployment/underemployment, 11, 142,
169n58
Unfortunate Traveller, The (Nashe), 8,
12, 53, 73; as challenge to Sidney's
construction of poetic mimesis,
67–72; dedication of, 19; form in, 54;
patronage and, 55–57; reading public/
consumers and, 58–59; trading places
of master and servant in, 59–67; *The
Winter's Tale* compared with, 150
upward mobility, 12, 55; in *The Alchemist*,
119; in *The Gentle Craft*, 84, 88; in
The Shoemaker's Holiday, 76, 96, 99
Ursula (Deloney character), 85–86, 95

vagrancy/vagabonds, 16, 99, 143, 192n16
Valentine (Shakespeare character), 39–40,
42, 46, 48, 174n38

wage labor, 11
Walsh, Brian, 96
Watt, Tessa, 78, 80–81
Weil, Judith, 10, 167n37
Wells, Stanley, 105
West, Sir William, 21, 174n28
Whigham, Frank, 42
Whittington, Dick, 88, 184n46
Williams, Raymond, 179n5
Wilton, Jack (Nashe character), 53,
54, 59–60, 71–72, 150; Anabaptists
and, 60–62, 65; as appendix, 55;
commercial/commodified forms of
service and, 58; commercial economy
and, 67; enslavement of, 65–66;
identity exchanged for master's, 62–63;
upward and downward mobility of, 60
Winter's Tale, The (Shakespeare), 7, 8;
courtier and rogue intertwined in,
138–39, 141–42, 144; as courtly play,
24; performance history of, 136–37;
The Tempest compared with, 157, 161;
tragicomic space of service in, 144–55
witches/witchcraft, 151, 152, 192n30

women: English humanist program and, 175n41; forms of female service, 151; male apprentices linked to, 47, 175n50; in "Night of Errors" audience, 38; service forms available to, 119, 188n29; in theater, 121; in vanguard of aesthetic service, 18

writing, craft of, 91
Wroth, Lady Mary, 19, 124–25
Wulf, Christopher, 9

Yates, Julian, 67, 179n37
yeomen, 11, 16, 115, 169n56

ABOUT THE AUTHOR

Elizabeth Rivlin is an assistant professor of English at Clemson University.